CLASSICAL LIBERALISM AND INTERNATIONAL ECONOMIC ORDER

'Students and researchers who have an interest in issues of international economic order will welcome this text. . . . It will play a most important pioneering role.'

Viktor Vanberg, Freiburg

Classical liberalism has frequently been applied to 'domestic' political economy. This book is innovative inasmuch as it links classical liberalism to questions of international economic order.

Razeen Sally begins with an outline of classical liberalism as applied to domestic economic order. He then surveys the classical liberation tradition from the Scottish Enlightenment to modern thinkers like Knight, Hayek and Viner. Finally, he brings together the insights of thinkers in this tradition to provide a synthetic overview of classical liberalism and international economic order.

Sally's deployment of classical liberalism strikes a different note from other 'liberal' interpretations in economics and political science. In particular, classical liberalism points to the domestic preconditions of international order, and advocates unilateral liberalisation in the context of an institutional competition between states.

This unusual work of modern theory, intellectual history and international political economy offers new perspectives for economic theorists, political scientists and historians of economic and political thought.

Razeen Sally is Lecturer in International Political Economy at the London School of Economics and Political Science.

ROUTLEDGE ADVANCES IN INTERNATIONAL POLITICAL ECONOMY

CLASSICAL LIBERALISM AND INTERNATIONAL ECONOMIC ORDER

Studies in theory and intellectual history

Razeen Sally

London and New York

First published 1998
by Routledge
11 New Fetter Lane, London EC4P 4EE

Simultaneously published in the USA and Canada
by Routledge
29 West 35th Street, New York, NY 10001

Typeset in Baskerville by
Florencetype Ltd, Stoodleigh, Devon
Printed and bound in Great Britain by
Biddles Ltd., Guildford and King's Lynn

British Library Cataloguing in Publication Data
A catalogue record for this book is available
from the British Library

Library of Congress Cataloging in Publication Data
Sally, Razeen, 1965–
Classical liberalism and international economic order : studies in
theory and intellectual history / Razeen Sally.
p.   cm.
Includes bibliographical references and index.
1. Free enterprise—History. 2. Liberalism—History.
3. International economic relations—History. I. Title.
HB95.S25   1998
330.12′2′09—dc21   98–4867
CIP

ISBN 0–415–16493–1 (hbk)

CONTENTS

The cosmos scarce will compass nature's kind,
But man's creations need to be confined.
Goethe, *Faust II*, 2 (Laboratory)

Internationalism, like charity, begins at home.
Wilhelm Röpke

ACKNOWLEDGEMENTS

My primary acknowledgement is, of course, to the men, long dead-and-buried, whose thoughts are the inspiration for, and subjects of, this book. My attempt at a synthesis of classical liberalism and international economic order springs from a fascination with a handful of original texts penned by scholars from different countries and at different ages in human history, and yet with a common thread of thought that unites them – at least in my mind. Therefore, however corny it may sound, my original and enduring debt is to Smith's *Wealth of Nations,* Hume's *Political Essays,* Knight's *Ethics of Competition,* Viner's *Long View and the Short,* Eucken's *Grundsätze der Wirtschaftspolitik,* Röpke's *International Order and Economic Integration* and, not least, Hayek's *Constitution of Liberty.* These are my *livres d'orientation* and they form the working material for my shot at combining a 'book about books', that is, an exercise in intellectual history, with an over-arching theoretical presentation of what classical liberalism has to say that is *different* and *relevant* on the subject of international economic order.

The four years of research on the book took me from London to Freiburg and Cologne. My thanks are due to the Institut für Wirtschaftspolitik in Cologne and the Walter Eucken Institut in Freiburg for hosting me at various stages of research, and in particular to Professors Hans Willgerodt and Christian Watrin of Cologne University, and Dr Lüder Gerken of the Walter Eucken Institut. The Anglo-German Foundation, the German Academic Exchange Service, the Economic and Social Research Council (award R000221361) and the Alexander von Humboldt Foundation financed research stays in Germany to do work on the German neoliberal tradition. I should like to express my gratitude to these institutions for their generous financial support.

The London School of Economics was my intellectual home as a student, and so it remains as a teacher thirteen years after first setting eyes on the unassuming Old Building in Houghton Street. It is with enormous pride that I recall an LSE tradition of classical liberal political economy, begun by Edwin Cannan and continued through the twentieth century by Lionel Robbins and F.A. Hayek in the first instance, but one should also mention Arnold Plant, Ronald Coase, Peter Bauer and Hla Myint, among many others. Furthermore, it is with a definite sense of gratification and fulfilment that I have come across a new generation of bright and exciting graduate students here in our Aldwych abode who have shared my eccentric fascination with the 'wrong ideas of dead men' (the dismissive label for intellectual history these days, particularly in economics). The arduous preparation of lectures, and the cut-and-thrust of discussion with students in my seminar on Selected Thinkers in Political Economy, have indeed helped the drafting and redrafting of the chapters in this volume. My thanks go to these students and I dearly hope they enjoy – and cast a critical eye upon – the finished product.

Bits and pieces of the book have also been presented to the LSE interdepartmental seminar on Theorising Capitalism, inspired by Sir Arthur Knight and organised by Nancy Cartwright. I am grateful to colleagues in the seminar for their comments and, moreover, for the mental hygiene that comes with serious discussion that overcomes disciplinary and departmental barriers.

Finally, there are individuals who have kindly taken an interest in the studies of this book at various stages of its preparation. To their criticism and encouragement I am greatly indebted. I should particularly like to thank Arthur Knight, Meghnad Desai, Hans Willgerodt, Christian Watrin, Terence Hutchison and Viktor Vanberg.

Some of these chapters were published separately in article form. Chapter two is an enlarged version of 'УТО ТАКОЕ ЛИБЕРАЛИИЗМ?' ['What is liberalism?'], *Sapere Aude: Selected Works of the Moscow School of Political Studies*, no. 5 [Law and the State], 1996, pp. 76–108. I am indebted to my remarkable and intrepid friends Lena Nemirovskaya and Yuri Senokossov for publishing a talk originally delivered to a seminar of the Moscow School of Political Studies in the Altai Mountain Republic in July 1996. Lena and Yuri are in the energetic vanguard of introducing and inculcating a liberal spirit in their long-suffering Motherland, not least through their political seminars that continue to enthuse and surprise. Chapter six first saw the light of day as 'Ordoliberalism and the social market: classical political economy from Germany', *New Political Economy* 1, 2, 1996, pp. 233–257; chapter four as 'The political economy of Frank Knight: classical liberalism from Chicago', *Constitutional Political Economy* 8, 2, 1997, pp. 121–136; and chapter seven as 'The international political economy of Wilhelm Röpke: liberalism "from below"', *Millennium: Journal of International Studies* 26, 2, 1997, pp. 321–348. Many elements of chapters two and nine were combined in 'Classical liberalism and international economic order: an advance sketch', *Constitutional Political Economy* 9, 1, 1998, pp. 19–44. All the original articles were more-or-less modified to appear in this book as chapters that hang together with common themes in a coherent whole. The introduction and chapters three, six and eight have not been published before.

London School of Economics
October 1997

1

INTRODUCTION

A recurring theme in this book is the notion of a spontaneous order: the mutual interaction of multitudinous individual components that generates a regular, self-reproducing pattern (or order) of activities. Now the essential point about a spontaneous order is that it is definitely not a preconceived design; there is no single or group mind behind it – there is nobody 'minding the whole store', as Thomas Schelling fittingly expresses it. The individual elements of the order have their own action and motives, with little or no inkling of the macro-order that will eventuate from their action and inter-action. As Schelling goes on to say, 'micromotives' lead to 'macrobehaviour' that individual agents neither foresee nor intend; and yet the result – the macro-order – is a self-stabilising system, not a mere anarchic chaos of events.[1]

One of the pillars of the Scottish Enlightenment, Adam Ferguson, captures this translation from micromotives to macrobehaviour in a felicitous phrase that will crop up on a number of occasions in the following chapters: (social) orders are 'the result of human action, but not the execution of any human design'. These are orders that, to Adam Smith, spring to life through the operation of an Invisible Hand; to F.A. Hayek, they are spontaneous orders; and to Paul Krugman, they are self-organising systems.[2]

Of course, not all orders work this way. In the realm of social affairs, however, this process of spontaneous evolution is perhaps the best explanation available of the development of language and speech, the establishment and expansion of the English (and later US) common law, and, most importantly for our purposes, the operation of a decentralised market economy coordinated by a price mech-anism. Moreover, as I will argue in later chapters, the spontaneous order is a better characterisation of a liberal international economic order than any alter-native explanation.

Descending from the macro-order to micromotives, writing a book is rather different from the process outlined above. A book is usually a preconceived design, the intended product of its author's mind, rather like a machine designed and put into operation by an engineer. My Ph.D. thesis, for example, was such a premeditated affair, from the conception of the initial idea, the elaboration

1

of the theoretical model, the conduct of empirical research, through to the writing of successive chapters.

What I find initially intriguing about this book is that it is strangely different from the usual way books are authored. There was no preconceived design at the outset; the end-product became the unintended outgrowth of a series of separate studies in intellectual history begun just over four years previously.

When I launched myself into the study of the German neoliberal tradition of law and economics, I had absolutely no idea that this would lead to a much more encompassing and sweeping monograph on classical liberalism and international economic order. Initially, I thought that the work of Walter Eucken and Franz Böhm in Freiburg, and of their allies Wilhelm Röpke, Alexander Rüstow and Alfred Müller-Armack, formed part of a distinctive German tradition of historical and institutional economics that had veered away from the Anglo-Saxon mainstream from the first half of the nineteenth century. However, it gradually became apparent to me that German neoliberalism had much more in common with the classical liberalism of the Scottish Enlightenment than the historicism of List, Schmoller and Sombart. Its ethical concern for individual freedom secured by a framework of legal rules, as well as its advocacy of a significant but circumscribed agenda of public policy, led straight back to Adam Smith's *Wealth of Nations* and forward to Hayek's *Constitution of Liberty* (the most recent expression and update of what Smith had in mind).

Soon after studying German neoliberalism I began what I thought were wholly separate studies of two US economists, Frank Knight and Jacob Viner. Once again I detected clear and strong parallels with the early design and compass of Hume and Smith, which only made me want to delve deeper into the works of the Scots in the Glasgow and Edinburgh of the eighteenth century.

Only at this stage did it dawn upon me that my excursions into the life-work of individual thinkers were part of the larger whole of classical political economy, first mapped out by Hume and Smith, carried on, although perhaps in somewhat diluted form, by the nineteenth-century English economists, and resurrected by a number of thinkers in the twentieth century, ranging from Edwin Cannan, Arnold Plant, Lionel Robbins, Ronald Coase, Hla Myint and Peter Bauer at the LSE, Eucken, Böhm *et al.* in Germany, to Knight, Simons and Viner in Chicago (although Viner left Chicago for Princeton), and, last but far from least, Hayek, whose peripatetic *émigré* life led him from one centre of economic liberalism to another through the turbulence of the twentieth century (from Vienna to London to Chicago to Freiburg).[3]

While putting the pieces of the jigsaw puzzle together it occurred to me that all these thinkers, unwittingly or self-consciously, were essentially updating Adam Smith and, perhaps to a lesser extent, David Hume, for modern times. In the process what they had to say struck me as quite different, not only in comparison to nonliberal or antiliberal contemporary thought, but also to other varieties of modern liberalism, including the rational actor paradigm in neoclassical economics and the 'social' (or social democratic) liberalism that has insidiously worked its way into intellectual discourse and public chatter in North America and Europe.

Hence classical political economy came to be one connecting thread through the different thinkers covered in this book. Nevertheless, it is far from being the only connecting thread. Since graduate school days my academic specialisation has been the field of international political economy, especially that part of it that covers trade policy. A developing and increasingly consuming interest in the intellectual history of trade economics and political economy led me to the study of three thinkers, Wilhelm Röpke, Jacob Viner and Jan Tumlir, all of whom combined a theoretical bent with clear and controversial opinions on the increasingly interventionist and collectivist trend of international economic policy in the twentieth century. These were three contrasting personalities with many differences of intellectual approach, but I detected much common ground between them, and, following a closer reading of *The Wealth of Nations* (particularly Book IV) and some of Hume's *Political Essays*, I realised that this common ground was first ploughed by the Scots in their musing on the international economic order of their time.

This realisation soon became the second – and crucial – connecting thread of the book. By this stage, midway in the research span of these interrelated studies, it was transparent that I was writing a book on the theme of classical liberalism *and international economic order*. From then on everything else was a filling-in exercise, elaborating each tradition of thought and drawing the links between them, particularly as far as international economic order was concerned, as well as pointing to some differences within and between the various traditions covered.

The foregoing version sounds purely 'intellectual-historical' in motivation, but this is far from being the case in reality. I cut my teeth on modern policy analysis as a graduate student and retain a working interest in the international economic policies of my time. Hence one other motivating factor for this book: the keen desire to relate the ideas of the men I study – some, like Smith and Hume, long dead-and-buried, others, like Hayek and Tumlir, only recently departed – to the ideological battles, policy dilemmas, institutional constraints and exigencies of the end of the second millennium.

And so the following few hundred pages have been written with a definite theme in mind, but that theme was not cast in stone at the *point de départ* of research. The evolution of my own knowledge reminds me of Sir Karl Popper and Michael Polanyi in their separate accounts of how personal knowledge evolves and progresses – in a nonlinear, bit-by-bit fashion, by slow degrees fitting the pieces of the puzzle into something that has shape and form. The final product is seemingly architectonic but, unlike the work of an accomplished architect, it does not issue from a grand master-plan before the building work begins.[4]

So much for the genesis and gestation of this work. Now it is high time to justify its writing. Why classical liberalism and international economic order?

What is the 'beef' in the subject, to borrow the terminology of a recent US president?

There would not be anything astonishingly novel or path-breaking about a tome on classical liberalism in political economy and its renewal in the twentieth century. Some of the books I will draw upon, such as Henry Simons's *Economic Policy for a Free Society*, Walter Eucken's *Grundsätze*, Knight's collections of essays and, most notably, Hayek's *Constitution of Liberty* and his three volumes of *Law, Legislation and Liberty*, have already done that in one way or another. Finally, one should also mention those deeply engaging political philosophers of a conservative disposition, such as Michael Oakeshott and Bertrand de Jouvenel, whose propinquity to classical liberalism is quite striking. All these thinkers and many others have revivified Hume and Smith for our day and age.

Nevertheless, all the scholars mentioned above operate pretty much with a 'closed economy' model in mind, that is to say, they are thinking of political-economic processes that take place within nations. They pay little or no attention to relations *between* nations, let alone to a systemic view of the international economic order. This is exactly where there is a yawning gap in modern understanding. Through Hayek and others, a classical liberal view of individual freedom, the institutional-legal framework and the scope of public policy, has reappeared for *national order*, but there is no generally appreciated classical liberal view of *international order*. Inasmuch as there is a liberal defence of an open, market economy-based international order, it is left to neoclassical economists with their rational actor postulates and models of perfect competition, and political scientists who extol the virtues of intergovernmental policy coordination. An explicit recognition of how individual freedom is bound up with what happens beyond the nation-state is not really apparent. Moreover, there is little concrete awareness of the *order* that surrounds cross-border market-based transactions, especially in terms of the underlying legal and extralegal framework that protects property rights and contracts, and the public policies that make the international economic order oscillate between openness and closure.

This is rather odd. The classical liberal argument seems to stop at the national border, which appears particularly inadequate at a time when economic interdependence between nations is increasing and impinging ever more on 'domestic' activities. Surely the classical liberal case has to move from 'behind the border' and travel 'beyond the border' (to borrow terms from the trade policy lexicon).

It is not as if a classical liberal argument on international economic order has never been made. It had great prominence in both Hume's *Political Essays* and Smith's *Wealth of Nations*; indeed Adam Smith elaborated a comprehensive theory of international economic order in Book IV of his great work. Then the English economists of the following century took on board much of what was set out by the Scots, although some aspects of the Scottish *political economy* case for a liberal international economic order became gradually diluted as the nineteenth century progressed. In the twentieth century the baton has been picked up by the likes of Jacob Viner, Wilhelm Röpke and Jan Tumlir, although none of them matched Smith in developing an overarching system of international political economy. Unfortunately, the work of these moderns (which I hold in great esteem) has not had the panoramic survey and the resonance of, say, Hayek's *Constitution of Liberty* in 'domestic' political economy. The classical liberal argument on international economic order has either had insufficient sweep, force and verve, or it has simply fallen on deaf ears.

At a time when there is so much background noise, popular and otherwise, on the state of the international economic order, and at a time when global communications make most of us more aware of its opportunities and constraints than ever before, it is high time, with the aid of Hume, Smith, Viner, Röpke, Tumlir and others, to reconstruct and set out a classical liberal perspective on international economic order. To be worth the effort, the latter should have a distinctive message and strike a different note to the conventional 'liberal' treatments of the same subject.

My desire to help plug this gap, to draw the link between classical liberalism and international economic order with the support of past sages, is one justification for this book. There is another 'negative' justification that arises from a lingering discontent with the present state of academic international political economy, particularly in the liberal tradition.

The best practitioners in international political economy are the relatively small numbers of neoclassical international economists who have a nose for policy issues and institutional constraints. Jagdish Bhagwati and Paul Krugman are, perhaps, the outstanding examples. Even so, neoclassical economists, implicitly or explicitly, tend to apply what Krugman calls 'maximisation and equilibrium', that is, the combination of rational utility-maximisation and general equilibrium-based perfect competition, as the benchmark to analyse and evaluate the international economic order. At least implicitly, the case for a liberal international economic order is predicated upon such a perfect competition model.

This approach is in stark contrast to the classical liberal defence of a liberal international economic order that, from Smith and Hume onwards, has never relied on 'maximisation and equilibrium', rather assuming that human beings are fallible and that competition is imperfect. On the contrary, the classical liberal case centrally relies on an institutional foundation of law and appropriate public policy at different levels of governance, displaying much greater sensitivity to real-life institutional constraints and policy choice than the neoclassical tradition. The appalling ignorance of the history of economic thought on the part of most modern economists renders them largely insensible to these concerns.

The situation is somewhat different with respect to the increasing numbers of political scientists who have something to say on issues of international political economy. First, one should make the distinction between US and European practitioners.

The Americans, to their credit, are more careful and precise than the Europeans in making theoretical propositions and in applying them to policy issues. On the downside, however, there is a tendency among quite a large number of US political scientists to restrict the study of international political economy to a miniscule set of questions, usually revolving around the conditions that facilitate or hinder policy coordination between governments. Quite apart from anything else, this conformism of approach stymies truly individual thinking.

One gets the distinct impression that most European noneconomists who pronounce upon issues of international political economy are either old social democrats who hark back to the *Trentes Glorieuses*, the Golden Age (in the eyes of its neoKeynesian beholders) that collapsed in the mid-1970s, or come from the barely reconstructed socialist Left, filling old bottles of Marxism, structuralism and dependency with new vintage, *en vogue* critical theory, postmodernism, feminism, environmentalism and goodness knows how many other varieties of plonk. There seems to be an awful lot of reliance on sociological mumbo-jumbo – always eyebrow-raising, given sociology's well-earned credentials as the most dubious of the modern social sciences. Lastly, there are far too many European political scientists and sociologists who write about international political economy with an almost complete ignorance of the most basic propositions of economic science. Without a platform of economic understanding, it is impossible to say anything worthwhile about political economy. The result is a predictable and vacuous mix of do-it-yourself economics and what Krugman dismisses as Pop Internationalism.

Both US and European political scientists in international political economy have a rather skewed and reductionist view of liberalism, resulting from a near-total ignorance of the intellectual history of economic liberalism. Indeed I would hazard a guess that those political scientists in international political economy who have carefully read Hume and Smith, not to mention Ricardo, the two Mills, Senior, Torrens, Cairnes and Marshall, can be counted on the fingers of less than two hands (although that does not prevent many of them from quoting the usual well-known aphorisms from *The Wealth of Nations*). The product of this chronic deficiency is a straight equation of economic liberalism with the rational utility-maximising actor, perfect competition, an unqualified *laissez faire*, an extreme harmony of interests doctrine and a 'nightwatchman' state – all completely foreign to what Hume and Smith had in mind, and almost completely foreign to the nineteenth-century classical economists!

Furthermore, in political science circles, a brand of thinking that travels with the label of 'neoliberal institutionalism' almost monopolises the advocacy of a liberal international economic order. The latter has almost nothing in common with classical liberalism, but it has quite a lot in common with the turn-of-the-century 'new liberalism' and twentieth-century versions of social democracy. Neoliberal institutionalists, most of them occupying positions in US universities, have a strong, and often seemingly unconditional, attachment to international organisations and elaborate mechanisms of intergovernmental negotiation and policy coordination. They regard such mechanisms as essential to the maintenance of a relatively open and stable international economic order. At the same time most of them are at least implicit defenders of interventionist governments, generous welfare states, and corporatist arrangements uniting governments and well-organised interest groups within nation-states – all the hallmarks of a mixed economy, not a free market economy.

From a classical liberal standpoint, very few of these planks of neoliberal institutionalism correspond to a truly liberal international economic order, as I shall argue in subsequent chapters. However, because observers do not link classical liberalism to questions of international economic order, these reservations, not to mention an alternative liberal conception of international economic order, rarely rise to the surface.

Thus my dissatisfaction with the state of liberalism in international political economy, and my feeling that a full-blooded classical liberal advocacy of international economic order is hardly voiced and articulated, form the preamble to a statement of objectives for this book. The chief objective is, of course, to lay out a classical liberal view of international economic order. I have chosen to work towards this goal via an intellectual-historical method, examining an array of thinkers over a period of two centuries, all of them updating, adding to and renewing the tradition founded by Hume and Smith.

I find writing about these different thinkers, within the context of classical liberal political economy, interesting and valuable in its own right, that is, as an exercise in intellectual history. Equally, I find that their work and message shed a powerful and penetrating light on the challenges of the international economic order that we face today and, perhaps, that we will face for a long time to come. Put differently, the intellectual history in which I indulge in the following pages intends to be of relevance to modern institutions and policy realities.

A brief word on the intended audience for this book. It aims at those interested in international political economy in the broad sense of the term, bearing in mind that this is cross-disciplinary turf trampled on by economists, economic historians, political scientists and lawyers, not forgetting the policy practitioners and the intelligent lay public who should always prevent academics from monopolising any kind of turf. I suspect that it will appeal most to economists and lawyers of the 'constitutional' and 'institutional' varieties, some of whom are interested in international issues (alas, not all that many!). Hopefully, the book will engage some political scientists as well, although the adopted method and the subject matter might appear very different from what they usually have to deal with. Finally, I sincerely wish that there are some political philosophers and historians of economic thought out there who will cast a sympathetic eye upon my work, even if it elicits criticism for not being sufficiently rigorous as intellectual history and too eager to use past thought as a searchlight on modern policy.

Before I launch into a breakdown of the following chapters, there are two points that need to be cleared up. First, not all the chapters directly address the question of international economic order. Three chapters – on the domestic foundations of classical liberalism (chapter two), Knight (chapter four) and German neoliberalism (chapter six) – concentrate more on domestic than international political economy. The reason for this is that classical liberalism in political economy is a 'bottom-up' theory: one cannot grasp its perspective on international economic order without an extensive treatment of what classical liberalism has to say on the subject of domestic (or intranational) economic order. From a classical liberal standpoint, a liberal international economic order is, to a very large extent, the outgrowth or by-product of appropriate governance within the nation-state. Therefore the domestic or national *preconditions* of international order are at the very heart of classical liberalism, and this is why it is very necessary to rehearse the domestic theory of classical liberalism before proceeding to its international components. Chapter two tries to summarise a classical liberal view of domestic economic order, and other chapters supplement it with the thought of Knight and German neoliberalism. All three chapters aim to set the domestic context of classical liberalism and international economic order.

Second, there is no separate chapter on Hayek, which might strike some readers as somewhat surprising, given Hayek's shining star in the classical liberal firmament and the inestimably great importance attached to his work in all chapters of this book. Nevertheless, there has been so much written on Hayek since the late 1970s that I feel that I could not really add anything new, even at the margin, in a chapter devoted exclusively to him. I trust that readers will notice his great influence in my interpretation of classical liberalism in both its domestic and international incarnations.

Part I lays the foundations of classical liberalism, chapter two concentrating on domestic political economy and chapter three on its international counterpart. By going back to the source of classical liberalism, this part relies heavily on the Founding Fathers, Adam Smith and David Hume. Their thought is more important than any other individual thinker or group of thinkers in chapter two, and chapter three focuses exclusively on their international political economy.

Chapter two tries to carve out a special space for classical liberalism in political economy, pointing to its differences with other versions of liberalism that are popular in the 1990s, and particularly stressing its differences with the rational actor/perfect markets paradigm in neoclassical economics and rational choice. The chapter also seeks to counter the outrageous stereotyping of classical liberalism that is current in academic and nonacademic circles. Building on psychological assumptions of actor behaviour, notions of market order, and the framework of law and public policy that supports the economic order, this discussion sets the domestic context for the rest of the book.

Whereas chapter two is a broad overview of classical liberalism, chapter three is more specific in two senses, homing in on 'international' political economy, and doing so by recourse to the writings of Hume and Smith. This chapter has a definite 'intellectual-historical' flavour, although it does signal important lessons for modern international economic policy. The argument emphasises the neglect, or at least the misinterpretation, of the international side of the Scots' political economy. Scholars tend to overlook Hume and Smith's stress on the dynamic gains from trade and how commercial openness interacts with domestic institutional change. Then follows a long excursion into Adam Smith's political economy justifications for free trade, and unilateral free trade in particular, before concluding with Hume and Smith's rather 'realist' view of the interstate political system. This chapter thus sets the international political economy context for subsequent chapters devoted to questions of international economic order.

Part II crosses the Atlantic – at least from the perspective of a Londoner teaching at the LSE – and lands in the Chicago of the early and mid-twentieth century in order to study the work of Frank Knight and Jacob Viner. They have done more to stamp modern classical liberalism with an American imprint than anybody else who comes to mind.

Chapter four is on the founder of the Chicago School, Frank Knight. It has relatively little to say about his path-breaking technical economics, but quite a lot to say about his political economy, all the way from his working assumptions of actor behaviour and market order to his treatment of liberalism, the problematic nexus between individual freedom and social order, and the connection between democratic politics and a free market economy. In most respects Knight renews classical liberalism; and in his discussion of democratic politics he probably adds a very important new dimension to it. One conclusion of the chapter is that Knight's classical liberalism is remarkably different from the narrower neoclassical liberalism, based on rational choice, of the later generations of the Chicago School.

Chapter five turns to Jacob Viner, who taught at Chicago for a long period but does not really count as a *bona fide* member of the Chicago School. Two aspects of the chapter have to be singled out. First, Viner is widely acknowledged as one of the two outstanding historians of economic thought in the twentieth century (along with Joseph Schumpeter). His unsurpassed scholarship on Adam Smith's political economy figures prominently in the first half of the discussion. Second, Viner is one of the twentieth century's leading international (political) economists, both in his superlative coverage of nineteenth-century classical trade theory and in his insights into twentieth-century international economic policy. His combination of intellectual history, theory and policy represents one milestone in the renewal of a Smithian approach to international economic order in our day and age.

Part III homes in on the German neoliberal tradition, centred on the Freiburg Ordoliberal School, a fusion of law and economics, and the 'sociological neoliberalism' associated with Wilhelm Röpke, Alexander Rüstow and Alfred Müller-Armack. Quite exceptionally in the history of German economics, otherwise renowned for its antiliberal and anti-Anglo-Saxon stance through the nineteenth century and well into the twentieth century, this mid-twentieth-century tradition of thought takes its bearings – at least in large part – from the Scottish Enlightenment.

Chapter six surveys the wide range of thought in German neoliberalism, from the constitutional mix of law and economics in the works of Walter Eucken and Franz Böhm, to the sociological concerns of Röpke and Rüstow, and the rather ambivalent content of 'social market economy' in the thinking of Müller-Armack. The chapter argues that Freiburg-style ordoliberalism, despite some reservations, renews the institutional analysis of Hume and Smith in its concern for an appropriate political-legal framework that can sustain a market exchange system. It also anticipates breakthroughs in the recent New Political Economy and the New Institutional Economics. Like these newer strands of thought, ordoliberalism draws attention to the deleterious economic and legal effects of unconstrained public and private power, and emphasises the legal underpinning of a sustainable free market order, particularly in the effective enforcement of private law.

The sociological side of German neoliberalism has been subject to varying interpretations, and elicits much criticism in chapter six for its romantic wishful thinking and the latitude it gives to *ad hoc* state intervention. Nevertheless, Röpke and Rüstow seek to explore the moral, noneconomic foundations of a sustainable liberal order – what lies 'beyond supply and demand', to borrow one of Röpke's most famous phrases. Like Hayek and Knight, and Smith, Hume, Burke and Tocqueville before them, Röpke and Rüstow try to combine the liberal principle of freedom with the conservative requirement of social order that relies so much on traditions and grown institutions.

Chapter seven switches to the only German neoliberal who built up a wide-ranging corpus of writing on international political economy, Wilhelm Röpke, bearing in mind that nearly all the other German neoliberals concentrated on questions of national economic order. Röpke, from his vantage point in Geneva, was the only German neoliberal with a long line of books published in English and other non-German languages – indeed he was the only German neoliberal with an international reputation as a political economist. The chapter argues that Röpke's international political economy, with a distinct classical liberal derivation, strikes a markedly different note from other liberal explanations of the international economic order. First, unlike rational choice, he does not rely on rational utility-maximisation and perfect market models. And second, like Smith and Hume, he portrays a liberalism 'from below', emphasising the domestic preconditions of a liberal international economic order. This approach accords pride of place to unilateral policy action at the national (not the international) level. At the same time he is very sceptical of international organisations and policy coordination between governments. Röpke's 'liberalism from below' stands in striking contrast to the modern penchant for intergovernmental policy coordination – what I call liberalism 'from above' – propagated by neoliberal institutionalists, among others.

Part IV has just one chapter (chapter eight), devoted to the international political economy of Jan Tumlir, a Czech *émigré* who ended up as director of research at the GATT in Geneva. While not a paid-up member of any of the aforementioned traditions of thought, Tumlir is very much influenced by most of the classical liberals covered in this book. His theory of 'democratic constitutionalism' owes much to the guiding light of Knight (and later James Buchanan), his appreciation of the spontaneous order to Hayek, and his appreciation of the legal dimension of economic order to Böhm. All these scholars who inform Tumlir's own work write about domestic order, but Tumlir attempts to translate their legal-economic constitutionalism into something applicable to the international economic order. He came tantalisingly close to exposing a comprehensive view of international economic order through a classical liberal lens – more so than any other twentieth-century thinker – but his sudden death in 1985 robbed the world of the *magnum opus* it was eagerly awaiting.

In common with Röpke, Tumlir emphasises the domestic preconditions of international economic order and has much sympathy for unilateral free trade. He is also rather sceptical of the sort of intergovernmental policy cooperation that widens the discretionary power of politicians and bureaucrats, and remains well hidden from national legislatures and judiciaries. However, Tumlir differs from Röpke in pointing to the underlying constitutional foundations of both national and international liberal economic orders, and the rule-bound connections between the two. His clear preference for legal solutions, such as his recommendation to incorporate the freedom to trade across borders into national laws, is a reflection of his wish to take foreign economic policy out of the arena of discretionary, power-based diplomacy and put it under the rigid constraint of juridically enforced rules. His end-objective, like that of Knight, is to reverse the mercantilist and corporatist trend of modern democratic politics and restore the constitutional due process that limits both executive discretion and the political power of organised interests.

Part V (chapter nine) concludes the book with a detailed synthesis of classical liberalism and international economic order. It draws on all the thinkers and traditions of thought scrutinised in the previous chapters in order to expound a classical liberal perspective of international economic order that is relevant to modern times. The chapter begins by outlining the two versions of liberalism that enjoy most popularity in international political economy, rational choice and neoliberal institutionalism. Classical liberalism differs from both by eschewing rational utility-maximisation/perfect market models, and by remaining sceptical of intergovernmental policy coordination and international organisations. Borrowing from the Scots, Viner, Röpke and Tumlir, the argument puts great stress on the domestic or intranational preconditions of international economic order. It also has much to say about a 'Smithian' methodology (especially on the free trade versus protection issue), the notion of an 'international spontaneous order' and its 'public utility', and the supporting legal and public policy crutches of a liberal international economic order.

The 'liberalism from below' that is at the heart of classical liberal international political economy also entails a restatement of the eighteenth- and nineteenth-century advocacy of *unilateral* commercial liberalisation. Then follows a sympathetic consideration of a market-like process of 'institutional competition' that enables governments to emulate each others' policies and legal arrangements in search of better institutional practice. Finally, and in contradistinction to (pseudo) theories of globalisation that are *à la mode* in the late 1990s, the chapter strongly argues that increasing international economic interdependence is perfectly compatible with the continued existence of an international political system of sovereign nation-states. At the end of the day, a liberal international economic order is fundamentally dependent on appropriate governance, in both domestic and foreign economic policy, *at the national level* rather than in terms of intergovernmental policy coordination. This I consider to be the central message of David Hume, Adam Smith and their successors for the modern international economic order.

I shall permit myself to wind up this introduction with a couple of points culled from the conclusion of the final chapter. This book adopts an intellectual-historical method, but it also has a keenness to address issues of modern international economic policy. Given the broad canvas put on display in the following chapters, intended to present the general theoretical features of classical liberalism in international political economy, it has not been possible to branch out into detailed policy analysis. Nevertheless, I think it very necessary to apply classical political economy to the nitty-gritty of modern international economic policy in a way that differs from and improves upon rational choice and neoliberal institutionalism. As the conclusion of chapter nine explains, I aim to do just that in a subsequent project with an application of classical political economy to modern commercial policy reform in emerging markets.

Notes

1 Schelling (1978), pp. 20–22.
2 See, for example, Krugman (1995).
3 The Mont Pelérin Society, founded by Hayek and Röpke in 1947, has been a repository of classical liberalism from London, Vienna, Freiburg and Chicago for five decades. Some the thinkers studied in this volume were participants in its first gathering at Mont Pelérin-sur-Vevey and remained stalwarts of the Society.
4 See Polanyi (1997) and Popper (1966).

Part I

THE FOUNDATIONS OF
CLASSICAL LIBERALISM

2

WHAT IS CLASSICAL LIBERALISM?

It is no exaggeration to say that it is impossible to understand the evolution and the meaning of Western liberal civilisation without some understanding of classical political economy.

Lord Robbins

The main merit of the individualism which [Adam Smith] and his contemporaries advocated is that it is a system under which bad men can do least harm. It is a social system which does not depend for its functioning on our finding good men for running it, or on all men becoming better than they now are, but which makes use of men in all their given variety and complexity, sometimes good and sometimes bad, sometimes intelligent and more often stupid.

F.A. Hayek

This chapter presents an overview and synthesis of classical liberalism in political economy, drawing on a tradition spanning over two centuries of thought. It emphasises the differences between classical liberal political economy and other 'liberalisms', particularly the kind of liberal theory based on the rational actor/perfect markets paradigm in neoclassical economics. The aim of the chapter is to lay the groundwork for the studies to come in the book. An overview of classical liberalism is the entry point to, and context for, separate considerations of the Scots (Smith and Hume), Americans (Knight and Viner), Germans (Eucken, Böhm and Röpke) and others (such as Tumlir) in a common intellectual tradition.

Further, the reader should note that the presentation of classical liberalism here, in its general contours, is primarily relevant to domestic or national political economy, that is, what happens within the nation-state. *Prima facie*, this might seem inappropriate or not particularly relevant to a book on international political economy. However, it is indispensable if the end-objective is to present a classical liberal argument on international economic order, for, as we shall see in later chapters, the latter requires an investigation of the *domestic or national preconditions of international order*. Thus, from a classical liberal standpoint, any notion of international order has to begin with an examination of national

15

order. The task of this chapter is to set the domestic context of classical liberalism and international economic order.

The discussion begins with a potted survey of liberal theories before going on to explore classical liberalism as a distinctive system of political economy. An overview of classical liberalism starts with an inquiry into its psychological assumptions of the individual and working assumptions of market order; proceeds to the distinction between a 'spontaneous' order and a 'constructed' one; examines the link between individual freedom and social order; identifies and explains classical liberalism's normative criterion of public utility; and, finally, lays out its presumptions for law and policy.

Different approaches to liberalism

Liberalism is not one simple, undifferentiated doctrine. As with other doctrines or ideologies, there are varieties of liberalism. All liberals agree on the primacy of the freedom of the individual and, relatedly, individual choice, which distinguishes liberalism from, for example, socialism and nationalism. But some liberals argue in favour of these core values by means of highly abstract reasoning.

One line of thinkers holds that individual freedom is 'God-given' or corresponds to an original principle, a 'law of human nature', from which the theorist can derive concrete action by purely logical reasoning. Natural law doctrine is central to the *oeuvre* of John Locke, Thomas Hobbes and the *philosophes* of the French Enlightenment. Another set of writers contends that liberalism is the wave of the present and the future, conforming to the inexorable 'laws of history and progress'. This is one strand of John Stuart Mill's thinking. Then there are those who argue that liberal principles of government and society are founded on an original social contract. This is integral to the thought of Locke and, more recently, John Rawls. Finally, a certain breed of liberals cleaves to the doctrine of utility, undertaking a cost-benefit calculation of individual utilities geared to 'maximising' social welfare. This way of thinking, inspired by Jeremy Bentham, is at the heart of neoclassical welfare economics and the work of Robert Nozick.[1]

Anyone passionately concerned with policy in the real world would be just a little bit sceptical of some or all these approaches to liberalism on the grounds that they are rather too abstract and perhaps oversimplified to be of direct relevance to concrete practice. In their desperate search for simple, universal principles applicable everywhere and in all ages, they neglect the complexities of history and circumstance, overlooking differences of time and place. Further, the assumption of extreme individualism – the isolated Crusoe who acts egoistically and rationally, integral to the *homo oeconomicus* of neoclassical economics – is bloodless and unrealistic, unable to account for the social conventions that surround individuals in families and wider communities.[2]

There is one further objection to hyperabstract theories of liberalism, or of any other doctrine for that matter. Overambitious theoretical devices, flying in the face of reality, are not exclusive to liberalism; they are *sine qua non* to the overwhelming bulk of socialist and totalitarian doctrine. Rousseau, Marx, Comte and others have deployed laws of history, natural law and the social contract to erect their theories of collectivism. Surely this must be a salutary warning: hyperabstraction, far removed from reality, beguiles the intellectual mind; its theoretical products can easily serve as nostrums for all sorts of social ills; and its consequences can be catastrophic for mankind, as is abundantly evident from the attempt to implement the thought of Rousseau and Marx in the past two centuries.[3]

Classical liberalism as a realistic alternative

Having expressed reservations on the foregoing approaches to liberalism, I now propose to expound a theory of classical liberalism that aims to be more 'realistic' and policy-relevant. The classical liberalism employed in this chapter, from Smith and Hume to Viner, Knight, Eucken and Hayek, is particularly germane to political economy. To reiterate, the domestic political economy of these thinkers is the stepping-stone to a consideration of classical liberalism and international economic order.

Assumptions of individual freedom and market order

Let us revisit the core value of liberalism, individual freedom. In the first instance, classical liberalism defines individual liberty *negatively* and seeks to secure it in rules of law: binding rules proscribe certain actions that interfere with individuals' delimited private sphere, particularly their property, in order to protect them from arbitrary coercion; but this still leaves them free to act in any way not specifically forbidden.[4] As long as someone stays within the limits of the law, he is perfectly free to 'pursue his own interest his own way', according to Adam Smith. Moreover, this latitude of action encompasses a *positive* aspect of individual freedom, for, acting in his own interest, or that of his family, friends or acquaintances, man discovers an inestimably vast range of present and future actions, allowing for the powerful expression of his individuality in all departments of life.[5]

Thus, classical liberalism defines individual freedom negatively, but it is also positive in that individuals use their freedom to do many different things in different ways, out of which social progress occurs. In the sphere of economic transactions, this translates into the freedom to produce and consume goods and services – the basis of a social order comprising an extensive division of labour and market exchange. Hence the normative core of classical liberalism is the approbation of economic freedom or *laissez faire* – Adam Smith's 'obvious and simple system of natural liberty' – out of which spontaneously emerges a vast and intricate system of cooperation in exchanging goods and services and catering for a plenitude of wants.[6] As Smith says:

> All systems either of preference or of restraint, therefore, being thus completely taken away, the obvious and simple system of natural liberty establishes itself of its own accord. Every man, as long as he does not violate the laws of justice, is left perfectly free to pursue his own interest his own way, and to bring forth his industry and capital into competition with those of any other man, or order of men.[7]

Most neoclassical economists would not cavil at this conception of economic freedom. Nevertheless, the classical liberal case for individual liberty is much more subtle and sophisticated, and, as Ronald Coase argues, ultimately more compelling, than the more restricted efficiency argument that follows from the rational actor paradigm in neoclassical economics and rational choice.[8] Unlike neoclassical economics, classical liberalism does not implicitly assume that the economic order is freestanding or that it operates autonomously under its own laws; rather it is highly attentive to what the German economist Walter Eucken calls the 'interdependence of orders': the interpenetration and mutual reinforcement of the economic, political and legal orders of society.[9] When distilled to bare essentials, the difference between classical liberalism, on the one hand, and neoclassical economics and its political economy complement, rational choice, on the other hand, is the difference between what Terence Hutchison calls a historical-institutionalist 'Smithian' methodology and an abstract-deductive 'Ricardian' methodology. The former relates technical economics to wider intellectual currents and their 'fit' with political and legal institutions; the latter strictly divorces economic analysis from entanglements with institutional analysis in other social sciences. As Hutchison remarks:

> This 'Smithian' model, starting from a realistic view of man and his psychology, and recognising the all-pervasiveness of ignorance in human affairs, gives as important a place in its objectives to freedom and the Rule of Law as it does to the attainment of some ideal, optimal economic efficiency. [Its] kind of case for the competitive market economy is [by contrast with the neoclassical Ricardian case] formulated in much broader terms, comprehending the political and social order, and especially the legal foundations of the economic order.[10]

For a start, the classical liberal tradition has a complex and realistic model of man in mind, emphatically not the fantastically unreal postulates of *homo oeconomicus*. Adam Smith and David Hume do not think of man as a rational utility-maximiser with perfect knowledge,[11] nor does the leading exponent of classical liberalism in recent times, F.A. Hayek. Turning the rationality assumption on its head, classical liberalism takes man to be largely irrational, governed by his 'passions', not his 'reason', according to David Hume; he is fickle, not singlemindedly purposive; and far from being free of error, he has erroneous expectations and makes mistakes all the time.[12] The Scots and their successors do not presuppose an *ex ante* rationality actuating competitive markets; rather the institutions of a competitive market goad men into *gradually* becoming more rational in matching means to ends – rationality improves *ex post* by degrees and by *force of circumstance*.[13]

The central insight of Adam Smith is that the freedom of production and consumption engenders a division of labour with increasing occupational and geographical specialisation. This brings about a much improved employment and allocation of resources and, ultimately, greater national wealth.[14] However, the division of labour is only one aspect of the case for a free market economy; the existence of a *division of knowledge* is the other.

Far from assuming perfect knowledge, the classical liberal tradition, most explicitly and elaborately in the work of F.A. Hayek, holds that *constitutional ignorance* permeates the order of economic activities. Knowledge of relevant facts for market exchange is highly fragmented and widely dispersed among millions of individuals in complex societies. It is preponderantly knowledge of the 'tacit' variety, embodied in localised skills and traditions; only a tiny proportion of 'useful' knowledge is of the 'scientific', articulated kind. Men cannot possibly have a survey and control of relevant facts at their fingertips to make 'correct' (or optimal) decisions in markets: they are partially and perpetually ignorant, and all the more so in complex (as opposed to primitive) social orders with widely dispersed tacit knowledge.[15]

Hayek bases his advocacy of economic freedom not on the existence of full knowledge but on constitutional ignorance. The genius of the market economy is that it allows individuals to use freely what partial knowledge they have in everyday activities of production and consumption. The competitive market is by a long shot the best available device to coordinate existing (fragmented, dispersed and tacit) knowledge, as well as to create new knowledge, in order to cater for material wants. Prices, the heart and soul of a competitive market, impersonally coordinate knowledge in complex societies. General rules of conduct that govern property and contract also aid such knowledge-coordination. They act as symbols or signposts for individuals to cope with their ignorance, anticipate trends and adapt their behaviour. Both prices and general rules enable individuals to make better, although by no means perfect, choices through trial-and-error.

The above depiction of competition based on pervasive ignorance and the impersonal coordination of partial knowledge is really rather similar to the Smithian characterisation of the Invisible Hand. The latter is a metaphor for a coordinating mechanism of the activities of individuals who, apart from their own production and consumption, know very little of the wider economy. In contrast, a standard neoclassical framework, particularly in general equilibrium and rational expectations theories, expects each individual to have a comprehensive model of the economy in mind in the present *and the future*.[16]

Compared to these merits of competitive markets, central planning, and even *ad hoc* measures of government intervention, are much inferior in allocating goods and services. Governments lack access to and control of requisite information in order to plan or guide markets, and what little information they marshal is coordinated in a centralised and cumbersome, not to say ham-fisted, manner.[17]

The basic neoclassical model states 'given' conditions in terms of static equilibria in which markets clear when price equals marginal cost. Hayek, following the Scots, does not consider the market to be a static and precise equilibrium device operating under given conditions; rather it is a dynamic *process* of endogenous change and growth in which means, wants and technology are constantly transformed and in which individual activity is exploratory and experimental. To Hayek, competition is less about equilibrium and more about a 'discovery procedure', an ongoing, open-ended process that coordinates and generates knowledge in a decentralised manner to adapt to uncertainty and environmental flux.[18] As Lord Robbins opines on the subject of the classical economists:

> But it is clear that the claims of the classical economists for competition and the market do not rest upon any very precise mathematical or semi-mathematical conception of statical equilibrium. Indeed, I cannot help suspecting that if they had been confronted with the systems of this sort which have been developed since their day, they would have some hesitation in acknowledging a near family relationship. Their conception of the mechanism of the System of Economic Freedom was surely something more rough-and-ready, something much more dynamic and real than these exquisite laboratory models. Their claim, in essence, was not so much that the system of markets was always tending to some refined equilibrium adjustment, but rather that it provided a rough pointer and a rough discipline whereby the tumultuous forces of self-interest were guided and held in check.[19]

It should be clear by now that classical liberalism, from the Scottish Enlightenment to Hayek, distinguishes itself from neoclassical economics and (extreme varieties of) rational choice by eschewing unrealistic, hyperabstract assumptions of Economic Man and market order, favouring instead realistic assumptions and an evolutionary analysis of market process.[20] The institutional analysis of the two traditions could not be further apart. Neoclassical economics, particularly in its welfare economics incarnation, compares idealised or fictional conditions (e.g. Pareto-optimal equilibria in perfectly competitive markets) to real-life 'imperfections'. This 'Nirvana' treatment classical liberalism rejects as utterly irrelevant to the needs of practical policy, preferring in its place a concrete and historical comparative method: real-life competition with its myriad institutional arrangements is evaluated in relation to *realistic* alternative institutional arrangements to coordinate knowledge and allocate resources. This follows Adam Smith's method of comparing a pre-existing mercantilist system to incipient 'natural liberty' in *The Wealth of Nations*. The key objective of 'realistic' economic modelling is to be *relevant* to policy, helping it to improve or become less unsuccessful.[21] It is Smith, after all, who describes political economy as 'a branch of the science of the statesman or legislator' with the objectives of providing

> a plentiful revenue or subsistence for the people, or more properly to enable them to provide such a revenue or subsistence for themselves; and secondly, to supply the state or commonwealth with a revenue sufficient for the public services. It proposes to enrich both the people and the sovereign.[22]

Thus, classical political economy fundamentally preoccupies itself with evaluating the working properties of alternative sets of rules and institutions that guide real human behaviour in the *dynamic long run*. This involves the science of *catallactics* – the study of real-world market exchange – not the neoclassical method of abstracting from rules and institutions and concentrating on a purely formal, short-term and static 'logic of choice' or 'maximisation under constraints'.[23]

This ties in with perhaps *the* distinguishing institutional feature of classical liberalism, and the central political economy insight of David Hume, that men, far from optimising case-by-case, from one moment to the next, *follow rules* over a long time span in order to overcome their inescapable ignorance and uncertainty in complex social orders. As Hume argues:

> Human intelligence is quite insufficient to comprehend all the details of the complex human society, and ... it is this inadequacy of our reason ... which forces us to be content with abstract rules; and further that no single human intelligence is capable of inventing the most appropriate abstract rules because those rules which have evolved in the process of growth of society embody the experience of many more trials and errors than any individual mind could acquire.[24]

Rationalist constructivism, critical rationalism and the spontaneous order

The Smithian methodology of classical liberalism also strives to account for the emergence and maintenance of order (political, economic and legal) in the coordination of individuals in complex societies. Hayek avers that mainstream modern economics, in conjunction with most social thought in the past two centuries, is plagued by a 'rationalist constructivism': there is a heroic optimism in the perfectibility of men and their ability to master and control their environment. Men construct or design their social institutions of law, money, markets and property. These are free inventions of human reason that men can reconstruct at will, as if on a *tabula rasa*. There is a concomitant contempt for all orders that men do not rationally construct or that spontaneously 'grow', such as traditions and conventions of social behaviour. These should be effaced if they get in the way of political blueprints. The logical deduction of such rational Cartesian action is the *constructed* (or designed) order of society, likened to a machine with relatively simple cause–effect relations and operated by the simplistic rationality of Engineering Man.[25]

Hayek contrasts the above approach to order generation, indelibly marked by the French Enlightenment and its successor traditions, with a classical, historical-institutional and evolutionary approach, more characteristic of the Scottish Enlightenment. Scottish 'critical rationalism' (a term coined by Sir Karl Popper) considers men too unintelligent, and social processes too complex, for 'extended' orders of millions of individuals to be 'constructed' in the Cartesian sense. Institutions and morals (e.g. private law, money, private property, exchange, the variability of price, competition within and between trades, technical knowledge) are, in the famous words of Smith and Hume's Edinburgh contemporary, Adam Ferguson, 'the result of human action, but not the execution of any human design'. Far from social institutions and morals being the result of comprehensive human design, they are *unintended by-products*, or epiphenomena, of human action.[26] This is precisely the connotation of the Invisible Hand in *The Wealth of Nations*: man's self-interested activity, free of artificial restraints and within the framework of the law, conduces to the public good as an unintended by-product of human action – 'an end which was no part of his intention'.[27]

To David Hume, social institutions are not deliberate inventions of human reason; rather they are *artefacts* of selective cultural evolution arising from the practical experience of mankind. A few individuals try out something new; their innovations, if perceived to be successful, are gradually but progressively imitated by larger numbers, out of which emerge regularities of conduct and norms of social behaviour. These are tried, tested, discarded and adapted slowly over time – 'sifting and winnowing', as Hayek characterises it – surviving a long-run historical process of cultural evolution if they prove *useful* to the social group, that is, if they enable it to survive and flourish. This is what Hume means by (long-run) *public utility* or social usefulness. Thus, institutions develop via a nonlinear process of social evolution; human reason could not have designed such extremely complicated institutions.[28]

The psychological premises and evolutionary epistemology of 'critical rationalism' lead to the theorisation not of a mechanical and simplistic constructed order, but of a highly differentiated *spontaneous order* or *cosmos* of social activities. It is spontaneous because it relies on self-generating and self-organising properties. Far from having simple cause–effect relations between a limited number of stable elements (as in a constructed order), it has a wide variety of elements – individuals, households, organisations, etc. – in constant mutation, too complex for the human mind to master. Whereas human deliberation can consciously shape a constructed order, a more complex spontaneous order is only very partially amenable to collective direction. The most important spontaneous order is the *catallaxy* (or 'exchange order') of the market, brought about by the (spontaneous, not designed) mutual adjustment of multitudinous individual components in which people act within the rules of the law of property, tort and contract.[29]

A *cosmos* comprises rules with a spontaneous, 'invisible hand' origin (i.e. undesigned and evolved practices spread by imitation and adaptation, not requiring any deliberate coordinating effort) and deliberately made or designed rules, particularly in the form of general rules of conduct. The evolutionary theory expounded here by no means discounts wilful human action, whether in the guise of action within organisations (e.g. enterprises, clubs, trade unions) or the design of general rules of conduct in the legal framework. However, it does signal that a plethora of *ad hoc* interventions by governments in the process of resource allocation, for example, regulating prices, controlling production and interfering with private property, abrades and even destroys the self-generating and self-organising properties of the spontaneous market order.[30]

Freedom and order

This evolutionary theory, unlike rationalist constructivism, places great importance on the order-maintaining devices of grown habits, customs and traditions. The latter, in conjunction with the formal rules of law, prevent a degeneration into anarchy and license. Classical liberalism has always been concerned about the nexus and tension between freedom and order. It has never conceived freedom on a *tabula rasa*, believing that this sort of conception, when practically implemented, is destructive of 'grown' order in civil society and disintegrates into anarchy, which in turn sows the seeds of a totalitarianism that obliterates any semblance of freedom. In this respect, Smith and Hume are opposed outright to revolutionary change and rather wary of what we would now call 'social engineering'. This kind of 'blueprint' rarely succeeds in achieving stated objectives; it destroys the soundness of public opinion and inflames public passions, breeding fanaticism; and it endangers the regularity of government and the laws.[31]

Thus, in contrast to rationalist constructivism, which subsumes an extreme version of rational choice and many modern liberal theories, classical liberalism does not assume that society is composed solely of anomic Crusoes interacting exclusively and impersonally on the basis of exchange and contract; rather it assumes that individuals are born into families and conditioned by wider social groups – the *corps intermédiaires* sandwiched between the individual and the state – from which evolve (informal) norms of mutual cooperation. To a classical liberal, the orders that make up society consist of exchange and contract 'thickened' by traditions and voluntary associations. In the evolutionary scheme, progress occurs, that is, greater individual liberty extends the variety and complexity of the order, on the basis of the existing order and by means of gradual, piecemeal change. Evolutionary social theory rejects the rational-constructivist predilection for destroying traditions and redesigning the order *de novo*.[32]

Public utility and individual choice

It is apposite at this juncture to interpose an explicit normative premise that undergirds this discussion on classical liberalism. The tradition from Smith to Hayek openly combines positive with normative analysis, generalised *description* with *prescription*. A positive treatment of how different real-world economic orders work and how they interact with political, social and legal orders is clearly in evidence, but there is an admixture of a subjective criterion, a value preference, to *compare* alternative sets of rules and institutions and to *select for* the order deemed to be 'appropriate', 'desirable' or 'good'.[33] And, following Hume, it is the normative touchstone of *public utility* that leads classical liberals to prefer the spontaneous order of the market to the command economy or even the mixed economy. They prefer the market order because it is more 'useful' to human beings *en masse*, and particularly the poorer or disadvantaged sections of society, than any alternative mode of cooperation to provide material benefit. In the spirit of Hume, Hayek argues that the market order, more than any viable alternative, enables the species to survive and flourish. It has stood the test of rigorous cultural selection or competition between rival social practices over a long period of time, and it has done so better than other coordinating mechanisms of human activity.[34]

Such utility cannot be separated from *individual choice*. The market order, more than any competing economic order or any realistically conceivable political order, facilitates and vastly expands the individual's choice of means and ends by recourse to 'exit' – in economic terms, the consumer rejecting the products of one supplier in favour of those of another. As argued before, such individual choice allows for the powerful expression of individuality and diversity – 'pursuing his own interest his own way', as Adam Smith puts it, or 'using own knowledge for own purposes', according to Hayek. It is important to stress here that the freedom of the individual not only is concerned with the creation of material wealth, but also is more generally concerned with the freedom of expression in all aspects of life, political, economic, social and cultural, which is the essence of an 'open' society.

Individual choice in decision-making on *all* matters, not only on material goods and services, first and foremost serves the interest or benefits the individuals involved, and *thereby*, as an unintended by-product of human action, or by means of an Invisible Hand, is of utility to society at large. It is on this basis of a seamless whole of self-interest and public interest that Hume defends the institution and legal foundation of private property, serving the interests of the property owner, but also benefiting society through the stability of ownership, the reciprocal recognition of ownership rights, and the exchange of property rights that animates wealth-creation.

Note that this conception of utility has virtually nothing in common with the narrower utilitarian efficiency argument of welfare economics, a 'rational' and static cost-benefit calculation by which the market is supposed to maximise aggregate economic welfare. Classical liberalism not only rejects an exclusive efficiency argument, which does not account for individual choice in all its variety, but also rejects the definition of efficiency by means of perfect markets and an interpersonal measurement, comparison and aggregation of (subjective, unquantifiable and incomparable) utilities.[35]

One further point on the subject of utility deserves mention. As argued earlier on in this chapter, some liberal theories, past and present, derive their normative criteria from metaphysical conceptions of the 'good' or, in more secular fashion, from abstract, simple and universal principles of 'natural rights' – the product of 'pure' reason. The classical liberal tradition, however, plants itself in the *terra firma* of sceptical and empirical argumentation based on the observation of practical experience. Hence the classical liberal advocacy of individual freedom is neither reliant on divine revelation nor on abstract natural rights,[36] but on the practical inference that a higher level of economic welfare materialises from individual choice than the choice of a collective authority. Furthermore, even fallible individuals are better at making their own decisions than having decisions made for them by stupid, ignorant and profligate governments.[37] The following passages from Adam Smith capture such pragmatic considerations:

> It is the highest impertinence and presumption, therefore, in kings and ministers, to pretend to watch over the oeconomy of private people, and to restrain their expense, either by sumptuary laws, or by prohibiting the importation of foreign luxuries. They are themselves always, and without any exception, the greatest spendthrifts in the society. Let them look well after their own expense, and they may safely trust private people with theirs. If their own extravagance does not ruin the state, that of their subjects never will.[38]

And further, in reference to the system of 'natural liberty':

> The sovereign is completely discharged from a duty, in the attempting to perform which he must always be exposed to innumerable delusions, and for the proper performance of which no human wisdom or knowledge could ever be sufficient; the duty of superintending the industry of private people, and of directing it towards the employments most suitable to the interest of society.[39]

And finally:

> What is the species of domestic industry which his capital can employ, and of which the produce is likely to be of the greatest value, every

individual, it is evident, can, in his local situation, judge much better than any statesman or lawgiver can do for him. The statesman, who should attempt to direct private people in what manner they ought to employ their capitals, would not only load himself with a most unnecessary attention, but assume an authority which could safely be trusted, not only to no single person, but to no council or senate whatever, and which would nowhere be so dangerous as in the hands of a man who had the folly and presumption enough to fancy himself fit to exercise it.[40]

The economic framework: law and policy

Adam Smith and David Hume have three components of an integrated theory: ethics or moral philosophy, political economy and jurisprudence. After considering normative criteria, it is now time to outline how the classical conception of political economy reposes on a *legal* foundation.

Many commentators, including some in international political economy with at best a superficial acquaintance with classical liberalism, lump the latter together with other liberal theories that, in addition to assuming utility-maximising rational action, cleave to a 'harmony of interests' doctrine, a minimalist 'nightwatchman' state and an absolutist *laissez faire*.[41] This may apply to the nineteenth-century Manchester School and some versions of twentieth-century liberalism, but it is foreign, intellectually and temperamentally, to classical liberalism. Although the latter tradition accords pride of place to the workings of spontaneous, 'invisible hand' forces, it does not take this line of reasoning to ridiculous or doctrinaire extremes. It readily acknowledges that there is a very imperfect harmony between self-interest and the public good, with plenty of potential for conflict between groups, and between individual and general interests. Hence the supreme importance of an appropriate legal framework to mediate between clashing interests and reconcile individual self-interest with the public good. Classical liberals strongly believe in 'liberty under the law' and therefore a *qualified*, not an absolutist, *laissez faire*.[42]

The maxim of 'liberty under the law' flows directly into the classical liberal notion of procedural justice. To Adam Smith, justice is 'but a negative virtue, and merely hinders us from hurting our neighbour'.[43] It consists of general rules of conduct applied equally to all people, regardless of particular circumstances of time or place. It is negative in so far as it *proscribes*, instructing people what not to do so that individuals' delimited private sphere, including their property, is protected from arbitrary coercion. This still leaves individuals free to do anything not specifically forbidden.[44] To Smith and Hume, it is (procedural) justice that maintains order in a complex society. Self-interest animates economic freedom and eventuates in social utility, but its predatory extremes (e.g. invading the property of another, not upholding contractual obligations) are kept in check by the rules of justice.

Moreover, it is frankly Utopian to rely on benevolence or the Christian 'love of thy neighbour', whose strong influence is in any case very largely restricted to family, friends and close acquaintances. In a large, complex society, most of whose members are strangers to each other, it is chimerical to depend on benevolence as a principle of social cohesion. Self-interest predominates, and only common agreement on and adherence to procedural rules of justice can hold it within reasonable bounds. This explains Smith's insistence that justice is 'the only principle by which the bulk of mankind are capable of directing their actions'.[45]

It should be added that procedural justice differs radically from popular modern notions of 'equality of opportunity', 'social justice' and 'distributive justice'. The latter are concerned with redistribution from one group (or set of groups) to another group (or set of groups). This requires government to interfere with private property and the freedom of individual choice in order to make discriminatory interventions in favour of some groups and at the expense of others. This classical liberalism rejects, for, by privileging some over others in an arbitrary political game of redistribution, it offends against the Rule of Law, whose general rules of conduct are supposed to uphold equal, that is, nondiscriminatory, treatment.[46]

To reiterate, justice is a 'negative' virtue intended to protect individual liberties. Classical liberals, following the Scots, eschew 'positive' interpretations of justice, especially of the distributive sort, for that would simply expect too much from an imperfect human nature and inadequate human capacities. Social or distributive justice is contingent on a proper evaluation of merit and on 'good' men to run the system. A more pessimistic classical liberalism, arguably equipped with a more realistic, hard-boiled appreciation of man, holds that the evaluation of merit is highly uncertain and inevitably subjective, and that no system of public affairs should be dependent on good men to run it; rather, as Hayek puts it, the classical liberal system, especially in its reliance on the legal framework, is one 'under which bad men can do least harm'.[47]

General rules of conduct represent a meta-legal or political doctrine, binding and limiting legislative power and executive discretion. This is the core of the classical liberal conception of the Rule of Law and limited government, and it links the discussion on justice and law with public policy in the classical liberal scheme.

Within the confines of the Rule of Law, the office of government in conducting public policy is analogous to that of the umpire or referee, enforcing the 'rules of the game' but not interfering or 'playing' in the 'game' itself, let alone preprogramming or doctoring the results of the game.[48] In other words, the task of government is to regulate the 'order' of economic activities while refraining from becoming a participant in the market process. To Walter Eucken, the legitimate role or 'order policy' (*Ordnungspolitik*) of the state is to supply and enforce the regulatory framework of a competitive order, guaranteeing price stability, open markets, private property, liability and the freedoms of trade, association and contract. However, the state should not intervene in market processes of resource allocation through, for example, price and production controls (see chapter six).[49]

To Eucken's legal colleague in the Freiburg School of Law and Economics, Franz Böhm, the concentration of the state's functions on the formulation and enforcement of general rules of conduct secures a 'private law society': rules of private law legally protect the freedom of individuals in the use of their property and in the exchange of goods and services according to (private law) contracts. Following the Scots and anticipating the New Institutional Economics of Coase and others, Böhm insists it is the private law society, subsuming a system of comprehensive and enforceable property rights, which is the bedrock of a functioning market economy (also see chapter six).[50]

The classical liberal follows Adam Smith in allotting three functions to government: first, defence in external affairs; second, 'the exact administration of justice' or the enforcement of general rules of property and contract to prevent force and fraud; third, a public goods function, providing macroeconomic stability and services ranging from street lighting and sanitation facilities to health, education, public transport and a basic safety net for the indigent (although this does not mean that public authorities should manage, let alone monopolise, the services they fully or partly finance).[51] This ensemble of government activities goes well beyond the miniscule range of the 'nightwatchman' state propagated by the Manchester School and other absolutist advocates of *laissez faire* who envisage a simple, minimal and cut-and-dried role for the state, as if 'written on half a sheet of notepaper', as Lord Robbins sardonically puts it. On the contrary, the central economic policy function of government, the formulation, maintenance and constant refinement of general rules of conduct, especially pertaining to property and contract, is an immensely complicated, extensive and ongoing task, with very necessary experimentation and adaptation to deal with changing circumstances.[52] The New Institutional Economics pioneered by Ronald Coase underlines this insight in no uncertain terms.

In the classical liberal scheme there is a complex amalgam of positive and negative functions of government,[53] irreducible to the nightwatchman state. Nevertheless, contrary to social democratic or socialist doctrines, classical liberalism draws a dividing line between the 'legitimate' and 'illegitimate' activities of government, or, as Jeremy Bentham puts it, between the *agenda* and the *nonagenda* of government. The litmus test of what separates *agenda* from *nonagenda* is political 'negativism': the government should not interfere in individuals' delimited private sphere, including their property, and *ipso facto* it should refrain from intervening in the market process, leaving producers and consumers free to make their own choices according to freely forming prices.[54] Lord Robbins conveys the same point thus:

> The classical liberal proposes, as it were, a division of labour: the state should prescribe what an individual shall not do, if they are not to get in each other's way, while the citizen should be left free to do anything

that is not forbidden. To the one is assigned the task of establishing formal rules, to the other the responsibility for the substance of specific action.[55]

A welfare economics orientation provides a rationale for 'functional' government intervention in the market process, that is, controls on prices, production and consumption, to 'correct market failure'. A classical liberal orientation shifts the focus of attention from market failure to 'government failure'. Governments are chronically unable to intervene efficiently in the market process, and government intervention in property rights and resource allocation usually ends up by exacerbating market failure. Unlike welfare economics, classical liberalism eschews direct process-level government intervention. Rather it indirectly seeks to improve the functioning of the market by refurbishing the *order of rules* (constitutional political rules and the rules or regulatory framework of market order) that influences market behaviour.[56]

Conclusion

Commentators tend to caricature and peremptorily dismiss classical liberalism as antediluvian, usually out of ignorance of the tradition, not least on the part of students of international political economy. It continues in various guises to be a living and breathing tradition of ethics, political economy and law that, contrary to the received wisdom, steers clear of *homo oeconomicus*, perfect markets, a harmony of interests doctrine and a nightwatchman state. It has a realistic appraisal of human action and market order; a coherent theory of the spontaneous order; a sensitivity to the link between individual freedom and social order; a clear normative criterion of public utility to select for a preferred economic order; and a wide-ranging coverage of the legal and governmental dimensions of economic order that sustain the 'natural liberty' of free market exchange. Now the scene is set for the studies to come on the intellectual history of classical liberalism in both domestic and international political economy.

Notes

1 See John Gray, 'Contractarian method, private property and the market economy', pp. 161–198, 'Mill's and other liberalisms', pp. 217–238, and 'Postscript: after liberalism', pp. 239–266, all in Gray (1989); Robbins (1952), pp. 23, 40–41, 46, 57.
2 John Gray, 'Mill's and other liberalisms', in Gray (1989), pp. 217, 224–230.
3 On the subject of Rousseau, Benjamin Constant could not be more cutting:

> On verra, je le pense, que la métaphysique subtile du Contrat social n'est propre, de nos jours, qu'à fournir des armes et des prétextes à tous les genres de tyrannie, à celle d'un seul, à celle de plusieurs, à celle de tous, à l'oppression constituée sous des formes légales, ou exercée par des fureurs populaires.
>
> (Constant (1992 [1814]), p. 131)

(I think one will see, in our day, that the subtle metaphysics of the social contract furnish only artillery and pretexts to all sorts of tyranny – to the tyranny of a single person, to that of many, and to that of all. It serves the purpose of oppression constituted under legal forms, and the kind of oppression stoked by popular fury.)

Alexis de Tocqueville similarly decries the use of overabstract general theories that attribute causation to one or two general factors, conveniently brushing aside the particularities of history. See Tocqueville (1986 [1840]), Book II, p. 486.

4 Hayek (1960), pp. 14–20.

5 John Gray, 'Limited government', in Gray (1993), pp. 14–15.

6 Frank H. Knight, 'Economics', in Knight (1956), p. 9.

7 Smith (1976 [1776]), Book IV, ch. IX, p. 208.

8 R.H. Coase, 'Adam Smith's view of man', in Coase (1994), p. 116.

9 Eucken (1990 [1952]), p. 332 f.

10 Terence Hutchison, 'Walter Eucken and the German Social Market Economy', in Hutchison (1979), pp. 167–168.

11 Coase, op. cit., p. 116.

12 As Hume says, 'Reason is, and ought only to be the slave of the passions, and can never pretend to any other office than to serve and obey them'. Also note his reference to the 'imperfections and narrow limits of human understanding'. See Hume (1978 [1740]), 'Abstract', p. 657, and Part III, Section III, p. 415. In his *Political Essays* he speculates whether 'all men [were] possessed of so perfect an understanding, as always to know their own interest', and concludes that 'this state of perfection is likewise much superior to human nature'. See 'Of the original contract', in Hume (1994 [1752]), p. 192.

Smith shares Hume's rather pessimistic view of human nature in equal measure. He refers to 'so weak and imperfect a creature as man', 'the weak eye of human reason', 'the narrowness of his comprehension', 'the slow and uncertain determinations of our reason', and, not least, 'the coarse clay of which the bulk of mankind is formed'. See Smith (1982 [1759]), Part II, Section I, p. 77, Part III, Section II, p. 128, Section V, pp. 162–163, Part VI, Section II, p. 237.

13 Hume (1978 [1740]), Book II, Part III, pp. 413–415; Hayek (1982), vol. 3; Terence Hutchison, 'From William Petty to Adam Smith', in Hutchison (1994), p. 18.

Kenneth Arrow argues that rationality in classical liberalism is a case of preferring 'more' or 'less' in a rough-and-ready sense; it is not a matter of rational utility-maximisation. See his contribution 'Economic theory and the hypothesis of rationality', in Eatwell, *et al.* (1987a), p. 200.

14 Robbins (1958), p. 234.

15 Hayek (1960), pp. 22, 25–27, 33.

16 Arrow, op. cit., pp. 203–205.

17 On constitutional ignorance, see Hayek (1982), vol. 2, pp. 115–118, 121; Hayek (1944), pp. 36–37.

18 Hayek (1982) vol.2, p. 117.

Competition as a 'discovery procedure' is in some respects similar to what Douglass North terms 'adaptive efficiency': the evolution of the economy through time by means of decentralised decision-making, exploring many alternative solutions to changing problems. See North (1990), pp. 80–81.

19 Robbins (1952), p. 16.

20 As Terence Hutchison remarks:

Adam Smith's 'vision' has *not* been 'translated': it has been fundamentally distorted and eviscerated into a piece of 'rigorous' and vacuous hyperabstracted, static analysis, based on a range of fantastically unrealistic assumptions, and on a highly questionable concept of a 'Pareto-optimum' [which we would say has no strong claim to be considered optimal] ... this hyperabstracted mathematical analysis – would, quite justifiably, have bored the pants off Adam Smith as almost totally irrelevant to what he was interested in.

See Terence Hutchison, 'The uses and abuses of academic economics', in Hutchison (1994), p. 289.

21 Hayek (1982), vol. 3, pp. 65–71; Jacob Viner, 'International trade theory and its present-day relevance', in Smithies *et al.* (1955), p. 105; Smith (1976 [1776]), Book IV, ch. IX, p. 208; Hume, *An Enquiry Concerning the Principles of Morals*, in Hume (1975 [1777]), Section I, p. 174.

22 Smith (1976 [1776]), Book IV, p. 449.

23 Vanberg (1994), pp. 2–3, 13; Buchanan (1992), pp. 134–135.

24 Quoted in Vanberg (1994), p. 120.

25 Hayek (1982), vol.1, pp. 9–14.
Note Smith's incisive critique of rationalist philosophy in the following passage:

> The man of system, on the contrary, is apt to be very wise in his own conceit; and is often so enamoured with the supposed beauty of his own ideal plan of government, that he cannot suffer the smallest deviation from any part of it. He goes on to establish it completely and in all its parts, without any regard either to the great interests, or to the strong prejudices which may oppose it. He seems to imagine that he can arrange the different members of a great society with as much ease as the hand arranges the different pieces upon a chess-board. He does not consider that the pieces upon the chess-board have no other principle of motion besides that which the hand impresses upon them; but that, in the great chess-board of human society, every single piece has a principle of motion of its own, altogether different from that which the legislature might choose to impress upon it.
>
> (Smith (1982 [1759]), Part VI, pp. 233–234)

26 Hayek (1960), pp. 55–56.
To quote Ferguson at greater length:

> Like the winds that come we know not whence, and blow whithersoever they list, the forms of society are derived from an obscure and distant origin; they arise, long before the date of philosophy, from the instincts, not from the speculations, of men. The croud of mankind, are directed in their establishments and measures, by the circumstances in which they are placed; and seldom are turned from their way, to follow the plan of any single projector ... Every step and every movement of the multitude, even in what are termed enlightened ages, are made with equal blindness to the future; and nations stumble upon establishments, which are indeed the result of human action, but not the execution of any human design.
>
> (Ferguson (1995 [1767]), p. 119)

27

> As every individual, therefore, endeavours as much as he can both to employ his capital in the support of domestic industry. ... He generally, indeed, neither intends to promote the public interest, nor knows how much he is promoting it. By preferring the support of domestic to that of foreign industry, he intends only his own security; and by directing that industry in such a manner as its produce may be of the greatest value, he intends only his own

gain, and he is in this, as in many other cases, led by an invisible hand to promote an end which was no part of his intention. Nor is it always the worse for the society that it was no part of it. By pursuing his own interest he frequently promotes that of society more effectually than when he really intends to promote it. I have never known much good done by those who affected to trade for the public good. It is an affectation, indeed, not very common among merchants, and very few words need be employed in dissuading them from it.

(Smith (1976 [1776]), Book IV, ch. II, pp. 477–478)

Compare the above passage on the Invisible Hand to the following passage in *The Theory of Moral Sentiments*:

They [the rich] are led by an invisible hand to make nearly the same distribution of the necessaries of life, which would have been made, had the earth been divided into equal portions among all its inhabitants, and thus without intending it, without knowing it, advance the interest of the society, and afford means to the multiplication of the species.

(Smith (1982 [1759]), Part IV, pp. 184–185)

For further allusions to the unintended effects of self-interested behaviour: 'Though those different plans were, perhaps, first introduced by the private interests and prejudices of particular orders of men, without any regard to, or foresight of, their consequences upon the general welfare of society'. Smith (1976 [1776]), 'Introduction and plan of the work', p. 3. And later:

The division of labour, from which so many advantages are derived, is not originally the effect of any human wisdom, which foresees and intends that general opulence to which it gives occasion. It is the necessary, though very slow and gradual, consequence of a certain propensity in human nature which has in view no such extensive utility; the propensity to truck, barter, and exchange one thing for another.

(Book I, ch. II, p. 17)

28 F.A. Hayek, 'The legal and political philosophy of David Hume', in Hayek (1991), pp. 107–108; Hume (1978 [1740]), Book III, Part II, pp. 489–491, 497, 529; David Hume, *An Enquiry Concerning the Principles of Morals*, in Hume (1975 [1777]), Sections III and V.
29 Hayek (1982), vol. 1, pp. 37–39, 41–42; vol. 2, pp. 108–109.
Michael Polanyi characterises the spontaneous order in the following manner:

When order is achieved among human beings by allowing them to interact with each other on their own initiative subject only to laws which uniformly apply to all of them . . . we have a system of spontaneous order in society . . . . The most massive example of a spontaneous order in society – the prototype of order established by an 'invisible hand' – is that of economic life based on an aggregation of competing individuals.

(Quoted in Vanberg (1994), pp. 252–253)

Jan Tumlir writes in a similar vein: 'Order is a system, the regularity of which is largely spontaneous, the result of general rules within which self-conscious choosing units – governments, firms, households, individuals carrying out their functions – act independently, but also interdependently'. Quoted in Hauser *et al.* (1988), p. 223.

30 Hayek (1982), vol. 1, pp. 45–46, 51.
31 Smith (1982 (1759)), Part VI, pp. 232–234; David Hume, 'Idea of a perfect common-wealth', in Hume (1994 [1752]), pp. 221–222.
32 Knight (1960), pp. 14, 34–35, 117, 139; Hayek (1960), p. 61 f.; (1982), vol. 3, p. 168 f.

This conservative streak in the Scottish Enlightenment, followed by twentieth-century classical liberals like Hayek and Knight, has a great deal of affinity with the conservatism of Edmund Burke, Alexis de Tocqueville and, more recently, Bertrand de Jouvenel and Michael Oakeshott. The sociological side of Wilhelm Röpke's *oeuvre* clearly expresses a 'liberal-conservatism'. See, for example, Wilhelm Röpke, *Gesellschaftskrisis der Gegenwart* and *Jenseits von Angebot und Nachfrage*, both in Röpke (1980).

33 Vanberg (1994), p. 6; Robbins (1981), pp. 7–8.
34 Hayek (1982), vol. 1, p. 18, vol. 2, pp. 17 f., 131, vol. 3, pp. 74–75; Robbins (1981), p. 8.
35 See Gray (1993), p. 79; Gray (1990), pp. 149, 156–158; Vanberg (1994), pp. 80, 210.
36

[The system of economic freedom] is not a closed system laid up in heaven, so to speak, deducible from a few simple concepts and capable of being transcribed on a couple of tablets of stone, but an evolving system, part natural growth, part artefact, continually adapting itself or being adapted to new conditions and new knowledge, whose only main general criterion is that it tends towards freedom rather than away from it.

(Lord Robbins, 'Freedom and order', in Robbins (1963), pp. 44–45)

37 Robbins (1952), pp. 23, 46, 52–53, 174, 176 f.; Frank H. Knight, 'Freedom as fact and criterion', in Knight (1947), p. 2.
38 Smith (1976 [1776]), Book II, ch. III, p. 367.
39 Ibid., Book IV, ch. IX, p. 208.
40 Ibid., Book IV, ch. II, p. 478.
41 See, for example, Gilpin (1986), pp. 28–31, 45, 82; Keohane (1984), pp. 51, 89; Polanyi (1944), pp. 68–69, 73, 141.
42 Jacob Viner, 'Adam Smith and *laissez faire*', in Viner (1958), pp. 216, 220–222, 228; Robbins (1952), pp. 22–26.
43 Smith (1982 [1759]), Part II, p. 82.
44 See Hume (1978 [1740]), Part II, chs I–VI.
45 On justice, see Smith (1982 [1759]), Part III, Section V, pp. 161–162. Smith also refers to justice as 'the main pillar that upholds the whole edifice. If it is removed, the great, the immense fabric of human society . . . must in a moment crumble into atoms'. Part II, Section II, p. 86.
46 Hayek (1982), vol. 2, pp. 2, 38, 62 f.
47 Hayek (1960), p. 529; 'The legal and political philosophy of David Hume', in Hayek (1991), p. 117.
48 Hayek (1960), p. 162 f.; Oakeshott (1993), p. 49.

Michael Oakeshott characterises the office of government in the following terms:

Governing is a specific and limited activity, namely the provision and custody of general rules of conduct, which are understood, not as plans for imposing substantive activities, but as instruments enabling people to pursue the activities of their own choice with the minimum of frustration.

(Quoted in Gray (1993), pp. 46–47)

And further:

> The office of government is not to impose other beliefs and activities upon its subjects, not to tutor or to educate them, not to make them better or happier in a way other than that which they have chosen for themselves, not to direct them, lead them or manage them; the office of government is merely to rule. And ruling is recognised as a specific and limited activity. The role of the ruler is not that of the manager but that of the umpire whose business it is to administer the rules of a game in which he does not himself participate.
>
> (Oakeshott (1993), p. 49)

49 Eucken (1990 [1952]), pp. 242, 254 f.
    Compare Eucken's *Ordnungspolitik* to Henry Simons's not too dissimilar formulation, in which the 'positive programme of the state', the legal and institutional framework for effective competition, is maintained *in order to avoid* the regulation of 'the heart of the contract' – the mechanism of relative prices and the division of labour. Simons (1948), p. 42.
50 Böhm (1966), pp. 75–76, 80–81, 85, 99–100. On the focus of Smith and Hume on laws of property and contract, see Hume (1978 [1740]), Book III, Part II; Smith (1982 [1759]), Part II, p. 84.
51

> According to the system of natural liberty, the sovereign has only three duties to attend to; three duties of great importance, indeed, but plain and intelligible to common understandings: first, the duty of protecting the society from the violence and invasion of other independent societies; secondly, the duty of protecting, as far as possible, every member of the society from the injustice or oppression of every other member of it, or the duty of establishing an exact administration of justice; and, thirdly, the duty of erecting and maintaining certain public works and certain public institutions, which it can never be for the interest of any individual, or small number of individuals, to erect and maintain; because the profit could never repay the expense to any individual or small number of individuals, though it may frequently do much more than repay it to a great society.
>
> (Smith (1976 [1776]), Book IV, ch. IX, pp. 208–209.)

52 Smith (1976 [1776]), Book IV, ch. IX, pp. 208–209; Robbins (1952), pp. 3, 22 f., 34 f., 57, 169 f.
53 Positive in the sense of *active engagement*, such as providing public goods and modifying and improving the framework of general rules; negative in the sense of *refraining* from doing certain things, such as interfering with private property and prices.
54 Hayek (1960), p. 220 f.; Frank H. Knight, 'Economic theory and nationalism', in Knight (1935), p. 289.
55 Robbins (1952), p. 196.
56 Vanberg (1988), pp. 23–24; Vanberg (1994), pp. 77, 122.

3

THE INTERNATIONAL POLITICAL ECONOMY OF DAVID HUME AND ADAM SMITH

Commercial openness, institutional change and unilateral free trade

Beginning with David Hume and Adam Smith, the emphasis on free trade has been not just one of the postulates, but the very heart or essence, of economic liberalism.

Jan Tumlir

Classical liberalism in political economy has waxed and waned since Adam Smith and David Hume laid its foundations. Arguably, the 'domestic' side of classical liberal political economy, covered in the previous chapter, has been kept alive and revitalised by the likes of Hayek, Knight and Eucken, to name but a few, in the twentieth century. Through their work, the legacy of the Scots has not been lost to modern generations.

However, the 'international' side of Hume and Smith's political economy has fared less well. Commentators tend to concentrate on the Scots' static, allocative efficiency argument in favour of free trade. It is then usual to pick holes in Smith's international economic analysis, pointing out that he failed to discover the theory of comparative advantage, rather basing his framework on the erroneous propositions of absolute advantage and the international exchange of surplus produce.[1]

These criticisms miss the point. They almost entirely overlook the centrality of the international political economy of Hume and Smith, which, as the subtitle of this chapter intimates, is fundamentally concerned with the nexus between commercial openness, the evolution of institutions within the nation-state, and economic growth. Put more explicitly, the Scottish case for free trade and the mobility of international capital rests on *dynamic* arguments; static analysis is a secondary and relatively minor part of the overall scheme. It is not altogether surprising that following generations soon forgot the dynamic treatment of economic growth and institutional change in Hume and Smith's international political economy. Nineteenth-century English economics concentrated at an early stage on a static model of the efficient allocation of given resources through specialisation according to comparative advantages, which gradually became subsumed in the general equilibrium analysis of twentieth-century neoclassical economics. The link between trade, growth and institutions – the very stuff of long-range policy and *political* economy – predictably receded into the distant and faintly visible background.[2]

In chapter two I underlined the fact that classical liberalism's economic model is one of dynamic, open-ended competition etched on a canvas of institutional evolution. This is how Smith conceives a changing division of labour, and how Hayek, later on, conceives competition as a 'discovery procedure'. In a seminal article, Nathan Rosenberg puts great stress on Smith's dynamic view of how appropriate institutions for the coordination of economic activities change incentives to favour hard work, thrift and enterprise – all the ingredients of a long-run increase in productivity and growth. Smith's model (and Hume's, as I shall argue later) is therefore some way off the ahistorical and institutionally empty perfect competition model. The latter considers the optimal allocation of a given quantity of resources among competing uses only with a given stock of technology.[3]

This chapter develops the argument that Hume and Smith apply a dynamic analysis to the international sphere of political economy just as much as to the domestic (intranational) sphere; indeed the two spheres tightly interlock in their institutional treatment. Both Hume and Smith advocate institutional arrangements to facilitate dynamic competition in international transactions as a natural extension of dynamic competition within the nation-state. This is a point of overwhelming importance that almost completely escapes the secondary literature in our times. It identifies one defining feature of classical liberalism's perspective on international economic order, and how it differs from a neoclassical perspective.

The following discussion begins with an outline of the main economic and moral-philosophical planks of Hume and Smith's international political economy in response to the mercantilist conventional wisdom of their day and age. It then proceeds to delve into their treatment of the gains from trade, both static and dynamic, with special emphasis on their dynamic analysis. Then follows a section on explicit 'political economy' arguments, especially in Smith, that buttress the economic arguments on the gains from trade. This section dwells on Smith's consideration of the relative merits of unilateral free trade and reciprocity, which he discusses primarily on political economy-cum-policy grounds. The chapter concludes with an evaluation of Smith and Hume's view of the interstate political system, again an oft-neglected aspect of their work in the modern literature.

General contours of the international political economy of Hume and Smith in response to mercantilist thought

The classical theory of commercial policy in Hume and Smith is a complex amalgam of theoretical and practical arguments that, in the words of Alfred Marshall, 'mixes up' politics and economics.[4] Equally, it is a combination of moral philosophy and economic analysis. Drawing on previous English and Scottish moral philosophy, Smith argues that 'natural liberty', that is, self-interested economic activity unshackled from government restraints, conduces to the public good, providing that it is indirectly influenced and moderated by an appropriate institutional framework (of good government and justice). The latter furnishes and enforces the 'rules of the game' without directing or controlling the private activities of individuals (see chapter two).

Smith breaks new ground, however, by extending this conception of natural liberty or *laissez faire*, suitably bounded by appropriate institutions, from internal (intranational) trade to encompass external (international) trade. He ventures even further by exposing, for the first time, a coherent economic analysis of free trade in the shape of a mutually interconnecting *system* of economic phenomena. Albeit in a far less comprehensive and certainly more fragmentary manner, David Hume combines a (moral-philosophical) cosmopolitan outlook with an economic analysis that was, in many respects, path-breaking for its time.[5]

It is now time to highlight some of the broad differences of method and emphasis between Hume and Smith in their approach to international political economy, although their common classical outlook on free trade and other international issues manifestly outweighs any divergences between them. Smith develops a comprehensive international political economy in *The Wealth of Nations*, especially in Book IV on 'Systems of Political Economy', with moral-philosophical backup sprinkled among his other writings, notably in *The Theory of Moral Sentiments*. In contrast, Hume's (domestic and international) political economy appears in a small number of short, pithy essays, usually known as his *Political Essays*, although his political economy has to be placed in the context of the philosophy, psychology and history of his three great works, *A Treatise of Human Nature*, *Enquiries Concerning Human Understanding and Concerning the Principles of Morals*, and his multi-volume *History of England*.[6] Unlike Smith, Hume never elaborated a 'system' of political economy.

Both Hume and Smith use a full-frontal assault on the prevailing mercantilist thinking of their day and age as the *point de départ* of their case for free trade. Hume launches his attack by contesting the mercantilist predilection for the accumulation of specie by means of an artificially engendered surplus in the trade balance (i.e. import protection and export promotion). This exercise is self-defeating, for, through the operation of automatically adjusting trade and specie flows (Hume's famous price-specie flow mechanism), money, like water, 'finds its own level', neither rising above nor sinking below the proportion of labour and commodities within the country.[7]

Smith has hardly anything to say on the monetary or balance of payments effects of trade, concentrating instead on mercantilism's 'two great engines', import protection and export promotion. He sets up the specific criterion of national wealth-maximisation – the increase of national real income (the market price valuation of the annual produce of goods and services) or, alternatively, the increase of income per capita – to evaluate the effects of various commercial policies in a consistent way. The bulk of Book IV of *The Wealth of Nations* concentrates on a detailed and closely argued analysis of the diminution of national wealth by the 'mercantile system', and, conversely, the increase of national wealth through the removal of artificial impediments to the exchange of goods and services across borders.[8]

Both Hume and Smith assail the mercantilist *Weltanschauung* of a zero-sum international marketplace with rigidly limited opportunities, inevitably leading to the presumption that one nation's gain is another's loss. Both forcefully expound the opposing contention that international trade is mutually beneficial or positive-sum in nature: home employment and national wealth are fostered, not endangered, by free trade. Hume expresses this bond of national economic self-interest and a cosmopolitian outlook thus:

> Nothing is more usual, among states which have made some advances in commerce, than to look on the progress of their neighbours with a suspicious eye, to consider all trading states as their rivals, and to suppose that it is impossible for any of them to flourish, but at their expense. In opposition to this narrow and malignant opinion, I will venture to assert, that the increase of riches and commerce in any one nation, instead of hurting, commonly promotes the riches and commerce of all its neighbours . . . . I shall therefore venture to acknowledge, that, not only as a man, but as a British subject, I pray for the flourishing commerce of Germany, Spain, Italy and even France itself.[9]

Smith speaks in similar tones:

> By such maxims as these [of mercantilism], however, nations have been taught that their interest consisted in beggaring all their neighbours. Each nation has been made to look with an invidious eye upon the prosperity of all the other nations with which it trades, and to consider their gain as its own loss. Commerce, which ought naturally to be, among nations, as among individuals, a bond of union and friendship, has become the most fertile source of discord and animosity.[10]

One qualification is apposite at this stage. Although Hume and Smith emphasise the benefits of free trade, they do make exceptions. In one of his essays Hume seems to defend the *ad hoc* imposition of tariffs to protect and nurture home industries, which does not square at all well with his other pronouncements on international trade (as we shall see later). Adam Smith admits to two legitimate departures from the presumption in favour of free trade: first, restricting imports on the grounds of national defence, though that impairs economic efficiency ('as defence, however, is of much more importance than opulence'); second, taxing imports in order to level the playing field with pre-existing taxes on domestic production.[11] The two less clear-cut departures from free trade discussed by Smith – imposing retaliatory duties and refraining from the unilateral removal of import barriers – will be examined further on in this chapter.

Commercial openness and the gains from trade

Moral philosophy, an emerging economic analysis and a critique of mercantilism are the points of entry to a deeper and wider investigation of Humean and Smithian international political economy. Now it is possible to survey their case for commercial openness, the economic rationale for which revolves around the static and dynamic gains from trade.

Static gains

Typically drawing on an array of previous writings, Adam Smith presents one 'static' argument in favour of free trade: a system unencumbered by artificial restraints engenders a *one-off* improvement in the allocation of domestic resources – cheaper imports replace more costly domestic production and divert labour and capital to more productive uses, resulting in greater national wealth. The following passage drives the point home:

> What is prudence in the conduct of every private family, can scarce be folly in that of a great kingdom. If a foreign country can supply us with a commodity cheaper than we ourselves can make it, better buy it of them with some part of the produce of our own industry, employed in a way in which we have some advantage. ... [If cheaper foreign imports are restricted] the industry of the country, therefore, is thus turned away from a more, to a less advantageous employment, and the exchangeable value of its annual produce, instead of being increased, ... must necessarily be diminished by every such regulation'.[12]

Smith does give detailed consideration to two major deviations from free trade: the support of infant industries and preferential trading arrangements (in his day, with the colonies). He rejects both policy preferences, for the promotion of infant industries or preferential trading arrangements diverts capital from other productive uses. Moreover, he is of the general opinion that the market is better at allocating capital to productive uses than having capital allocated in an arbitrary and discriminatory manner by government, favouring a few industries but potentially damaging the rest of the economy.[13]

Essentially, this is a static argument that points to the deleterious effects of resource and trade diversion from more to less productive uses, given a fixed supply of labour and capital at any one moment in time. Nevertheless, Smith is also attentive to the potentially negative dynamic effects of resource diversion: protection, by artificially inducing resources to flow in certain directions, diminishes the pool of investible savings, reduces capital accumulation and thereby retards growth.[14]

Hume has far less to say on most static, allocative efficiency effects of trade, but, like Smith, he is attentive to national differences in factor endowments and the mutual gain that eventuates from specialisation. Both recognise that capital-abundant developed countries should specialise in the export of capital- and skill-intensive production, and capital-scarce developing countries should specialise in the export of labour- and natural resource-intensive production.[15]

Credit should go to Adam Smith for firmly establishing, if not pioneering, the concept of opportunity costs or tradeoffs between alternative activities under resource constraints. Of course, he operates on the basis of absolute cost differences between nations, which leads him astray and causes him to miss some of the most important static gains from trade. He neglects differences of comparative costs between nations, apparently not realising that national gains can result even if a country does not have an absolute advantage in anything (or, put another way, that a good can be gainfully imported even if the home country enjoys an absolute cost advantage in producing that good). Nor does he quite grasp the insight that exports are not of national benefit in and of themselves; rather they are an indirect way of paying for imports, from which the gains from trade accrue (due to imports beneficially substituting for domestic production in which there is no comparative advantage). These essential elements of the static case for free trade stem from Ricardo, Torrens and the younger Mill, not Adam Smith, who is some way off the mark.[16]

Dynamic gains

As mentioned earlier, it is quite common to zero in on Smith and Hume's static analysis, proceed to comment on its defects (especially in Smith), and then gloss over their portrayal of the dynamic gains from trade. The latter, however, are the heart and soul of Smith and Hume's international political economy and of central importance to a classical liberal perspective on international economic order.

It is a mistake to assume that Hume and Smith take snapshots of the international economy only at a particular moment; rather their camera captures a moving picture of economic change and growth from premodern times to the advent and expansion of commercial society, with its transformation from barter to a money economy and the specialisation that comes with an increasing division of labour.

40

David Hume's comprehensive evaluation of commercial society takes in the psychology of an increasingly active human disposition – a 'spirit of industry' – that surges forward in tandem with the rise of commerce and manufactures, the cultivation of the arts and sciences, the institutional refinement of politics, increasingly influenced by an emergent middle class, and the establishment of stable, regular and equal laws of justice to protect property and contract. International trade plays an integral, perhaps even the most important, role in this scheme of commercial evolution. The exposure to foreign commerce raises the demand for a variety of new products, incites emulation by domestic industry and contributes to the diversification of the economic base.[17]

Adam Smith devotes an entire book of *The Wealth of Nations* (Book III: 'Of the Rise and Progress of Cities and Towns, After the Fall of the Roman Empire') to the development of towns and agriculture in successive stages of economic history. Foreign commerce plays a catalysing role, first in encouraging merchant trade in towns, which subsequently encourages agriculture in the countryside. Hume welcomes this leading role of foreign commerce in economic development with open arms. Smith is more sceptical, believing that a reverse process of agricultural development, leading to the growth of towns and then the increase of international trade, would have produced a higher rate of overall growth.[18]

This Humean and Smithian emphasis on international trade in a dynamic context, highly innovative for its time, is a far cry from the trend of international trade theory from the early nineteenth century. Instead of looking forward to the expansive opportunities for growth in a 'progressive state', nineteenth-century classical economics signalled the limits to growth in the form of diminishing returns to agriculture, population growth and the advent of a 'stationary state'. Foreign trade theory became increasingly formalised in a static, allocative efficiency framework with unrealistic assumptions such as a one factor model of the economy, the immobility of capital across borders and zero transportation costs. Successive models of comparative advantage assumed given and fully employed resources and a given stock of technology; free international trade merely reallocated existing resources more efficiently between domestic and export production, implying a movement along a preset production possibility frontier.[19]

Hla Myint, one of the outstanding interpreters of Adam Smith's theory of trade and development, argues that Smith's model of international trade is much richer and more realistic than the comparative advantage-based perfect competition models of nineteenth-century classical economics and twentieth-century neoclassical economics. Smith employs all three factors of production, compared to one in Ricardo and two in Hecksher-Ohlin. With an open-ended model of the domestic economy, he links international trade to longer-run changes in domestic factor supplies and their productivity. Capital accumulation and the extension of the division of labour form the vital bridge that connects international trade to domestic economic development.[20] These features of Smith's model of international trade, particularly the extension of the division of labour, will be taken up later.

While trade theory from the early nineteenth century increasingly abstracted from the political and legal contexts, this was not so with Smith (or Hume). Both nineteenth-century static analysis and twentieth-century neoclassical analysis based on the Hecksher–Ohlin model have advocated 'negative' policies of domestic and external market liberalisation to remove distortions to the effective allocation of resources. However, due to underlying assumptions of perfect competition, these analyses assume the full development of the domestic institutional framework – product and factor markets, government fiscal and administrative systems, legal systems of property and contract enforcement – as well as the full development of the social infrastructure of transport and communications. This is palpably not true anywhere in the world, and an institutional deficit is particularly evident in developing and transition countries. The neoclassical paradigm has nothing to say about this institutional deficit and how it can be righted; it is empty of institutional content.

The classical political economy of Smith and Hume favours the removal of government-induced distortions in the market. However, it goes beyond a simple, cut-and-dried neoclassical prescription to emphasise the cardinal importance of developing the institutional framework, especially in terms of improving the governmental and legal systems over time. This ongoing, long-term task requires strong, 'positive' functions of the state to formulate and enforce the 'rules of the game', particularly to ensure stable property rights, and to supply other public goods like transport and communications infrastructure (see chapter two). It is this emphasis on institutional development that is the basis of lowering the transaction costs of doing business and providing an environment conducive to saving, investment and entrepreneurship – the preconditions of productivity gains and growth.

How does commercial openness (i.e. free trade and capital mobility) fit into this scheme? The removal of government-induced distortions (e.g. quantitative import restrictions, high tariffs, exchange controls, foreign investment restrictions) certainly facilitates trade and foreign investment, as neoclassical theory would predict. However, neither trade nor foreign investment, even without the encumbrance of government restrictions, can flourish in an institutional vacuum. The expansion of a healthy export capacity and the provision of incentives for inward investment both presuppose the development of the governmental, legal and social infrastructure systems of the domestic economy. Of particular importance are stable and secure property rights for foreign and domestic investors.[21]

Both neoclassical economics and classical political economy emphasise that differing government policies do make a difference to economic development and explain differences in economic performance between countries; both agree that an 'outward orientation', that is, openness to trade and foreign investment, is more conducive to development and superior economic performance than 'inward-oriented' policies of *dirigiste* intervention and protection, especially by helping to keep domestic prices and costs in line with world prices and costs. But the classical liberal view extends further by looking at the way in which commercial openness combines with the domestic institutional infrastructure to deliver sustainable growth (as the following subsections will elaborate upon).[22]

These Smithian insights seem to be gradually gaining more currency in modern economic research, with more focus on the mutual interaction of sound policies (macroeconomic stability, currency convertibility, openness to trade and foreign investment, public investment in education, health and infrastructure) and sound institutions (enforcement of property rights and contracts, efficient public administration, proper regulation of financial markets). The combination of the two ultimately feeds into superior economic performance. Recent empirical work has shown that wide disparities in economic development, for example, East Asian success compared to relative failure in sub-Saharan Africa, largely result from different approaches by governments to institutions and policies, and the mix between them. The wave of economic policy reform in developing and transition countries during the last two decades has mostly concentrated on liberalisation, including trade and foreign investment liberalisation. Nevertheless, institutional reform attracts increasing attention in the 1990s.[23] This indicates at least some convergence to the paradigm set out long ago by Adam Smith.

Let us dwell on the Smithian view of economic development for a little bit longer. As Hla Myint points out, Adam Smith views the role of developing countries through the prism of commercial openness bound up with domestic institutional change. Given that the discipline of economics has overlooked this dynamic institutional treatment in Smith, it is not surprising that some development economists have misinterpreted him. They regard his advice to poor countries to specialise in agricultural and raw material production as a recipe for perpetuating a static trading relationship between developed and developing countries. Supposedly, this natural resource-based specialisation harms developing countries because of declining commodity terms of trade and diminishing returns.

Such a Cassandra-like scenario of perennial dependency (of developing countries on developed countries) is quite foreign to Smith's analysis. Far from defending an unchanging division of labour and a static trading relationship between developed and developing countries, he regards specialisation according to cost advantages and factor abundance as a two-stage process of economic mutation and improvement. First, it is a means of making the best of a given situation by allocating existing resources as efficiently as possible. Scarce capital should go to sectors that yield the highest revenues rather than squandering it in many different directions. Second, specialisation is a necessary preparation for, or a *prelude* to, long-run economic growth through the accumulation of savings, investment in the physical and human capital stock, and the gradual diversification of the economic base. To Smith, such a development trajectory depends crucially on appropriate institutions of government and the law to

43

furnish a welcome environment for the gains from specialisation to flow into investible savings and entrepreneurial opportunities.[24]

This is the kind of progressive state Smith envisaged for the land-abundant but labour- and capital-scarce North American colonies in his day: agricultural specialisation would lead to capital accumulation; investment could then flow gradually into manufactures. Once again he emphasised the vital importance of good governance – a combination of *laissez faire* or nonintervention in private economic activity, with the strong enforcement of property rights and the supply of public goods – to enable and ease the transition to a wealthier and more diversified economy.[25]

Without anywhere near as much elaboration and system as Smith, David Hume also sees commerce as a means of promoting the diversification of the economic base in the long-run through population growth, capital accumulation and technological advancement (discussed in the following subsection).[26]

So far, this section has outlined Hume and Smith's general orientation on commercial openness and the dynamic gains from trade. The following subsections break down their analysis into two kinds of dynamic gains that link commercial openness to domestic institutional change. One is based on international technology transfer and competitive emulation among nations; the other on increasing returns to scale that are associated with a widening market and an extended division of labour.[27] The former strand of reasoning stems from Hume, the latter from Smith. Both forms of dynamic gains are the prototypes of recent dynamic models in the New Growth Theory and the New Trade Theory, emphasising imperfect competition, increasing returns, the strategic behaviour of governments and firms, and changing comparative advantage. Proponents of these models argue that they improve upon the unrealistic assumptions of the perfect competition models of Ricardian and Hecksher–Ohlin comparative advantage theory.[28] As Paul Romer, a leading light of the New Growth Theory, comments:

> I am convinced that both markets and free trade are good, but the traditional answer that we give to students to explain why they are good, the one based on perfect competition and Pareto-optimality, is becoming untenable. Something more interesting and more complicated is going on here.[29]

As intimated earlier, Hume and Smith's dynamic institutional analysis never relies on a perfect competition model to argue that free trade is 'good', and realises full well that 'something more interesting and more complicated is going on here'.

Following the upcoming discussion on technology transfer and increasing returns, this section on dynamic gains will conclude with a brief overview of Hume and Smith's thoughts on the role of mobile capital and the distribution of the gains from trade between rich and poor countries.

Dynamic gains in Hume: technology transfer and competitive emulation

Neoclassical theory has traditionally treated technological change as exogenous – something 'outside' the economic system. The New Growth Theory attempts to *endogenise* technological change, making it a variable 'inside' the economic system and treating it as an explanatory factor of how the system itself changes.[30] Although the inventors of highly formal models of endogenous growth may not realise it, this view of technological change goes back to David Hume.

To Hume, wealth-creation is inherently a matter of 'ideas' or technology derived from the marketplace. Hume thinks of technology in the broadest sense of ideas embodied in products, laws and customs. Commerce flourishes with the wide dissemination of 'useful' ideas. The wider the market, the better are the chances for disseminating ideas.[31] This ties in with the case for free trade. In Hume's scheme, relatively open channels of cross-border trade become vehicles for the transmission of technology. As mentioned before, Hume holds that foreign commerce plays a strategic role in fostering a 'spirit of industry' at home; it does this through the diffusion of (foreign) product and process innovations in the local economy, enabling domestic producers to incorporate and imitate foreign technology. To Hume, 'this is perhaps the chief advantage that arises from commerce with strangers'.[32] Moreover, it is through such international technology transfer that nations accumulate physical and human capital, diversify the economic base and expand wealth over time. Indeed, Hume largely attributes Great Britain's long-run manufacturing progress to such local emulation of technological developments abroad.[33]

Hume puts technology transfer in the context of an open competition of learning and imitation among nations. As part of his broad, encompassing notion of technology, this 'imitation of foreigners' is concerned not only with the emulation of product and process innovations coming from abroad, but also with borrowing from foreign experience in the realm of the arts,[34] and in legal and political innovation. As he remarks, 'a noble emulation is the source of every excellence'.[35]

Hume sees the political, economic, legal and cultural progress of Europe in modern times as a direct product of an open-ended competition of neighbouring states. Indeed, he regards this 'European miracle' (to borrow the fitting words of Eric Jones) as a larger reflection of the astonishing progress of ancient Greece, built on the foundations of competitive emulation in learning and commerce among its republics.[36]

Thus, Hume's dynamic argument for commercial openness revolves around the flow of ideas across borders, inciting a mutually beneficial competitive emulation among nations in the production of goods and services, the institutional refinement of politics and the law, and the cultivation of the arts and sciences. This stream of thinking culminates in his last political-economic essay, 'Of the jealousy of trade':

It is obvious, that the domestic industry of a people cannot be hurt by the greatest prosperity of their neighbours. . . . But I go farther, and observe, that where an open communication is preserved among nations, it is impossible but the domestic industry of every one must receive an increase from the improvements of the others. . . . Every improvement, which we have since made, has arisen from our imitation of foreigners; and we ought so far to esteem it happy, that they had previously made advances in arts and ingenuity. But this intercourse is still upheld to our great advantage: notwithstanding the advanced state of our manufactures, we daily adopt, in every art, the inventions and improvements of our neighbours. The commodity is first imported from abroad, to our great discontent, while we imagine that it drains us of our money: Afterwards, the art itself is gradually imported, to our visible advantage: Yet we continue still to repine, that our neighbours should possess any art, industry, and invention; forgetting that, had they not first instructed us, we should have been at present barbarians; and did they not still continue their instructions, the arts must fall into a state of languor, and lose that emulation and novelty, which contribute so much to their advancement. . . . The emulation of rival nations serves rather to keep industry alive in all of them.[37]

Adam Smith is also aware of this link between technology transfer, open commerce and growth, possibly as a result of conversing with and reading Hume:[38]

But nothing seems more likely to establish this equality of force than that mutual communication of knowledge and of all sorts of improvements which an extensive commerce from all countries to all countries naturally, or rather necessarily, carries along with it.[39]

Nevertheless, this is a minor part of Smith's analysis, whereas it is centre stage in Hume's international political economy.

To repeat an earlier point, Hume's political economy is expressed in brief, compact essays, not an extensive treatise. Bearing this in mind, it is not altogether surprising that his treatment of technology transfer remains incomplete. He does not, for example, elaborate on what institutional arrangements in the home economy are most propitious to receive and diffuse foreign technology. Hume provides an intimation, a sketch, of the connection between commercial openness and institutional development, whereas Smith, in a political economy treatise *par excellence*, is more detailed and systematic in his coverage.

Dynamic gains in Smith: extending the division of labour, widening the market and increasing returns

Technology transfer and competitive emulation represent one kind of dynamic gain from trade; the other kind centres in Adam Smith's famous dictum that 'the division of labour is limited by the extent of the market'. The argument commences in the very first pages of *The Wealth of Nations*:

> The greatest improvement in the productive powers of labour, and the greater part of the skill, dexterity, and judgement with which it is anywhere directed, or applied, seem to have been the effects of the division of labour. . . . As it is the power of exchanging that gives occasion to the division of labour, so the extent of this division must always be limited by the extent of that power, or, in other words, by the extent of the market.[40]

Here, neatly expressed, is the kernel of a twofold contention. First, a greater division of labour improves productivity (or increases returns to scale): with a given level of input of capital and labour, there is a greater level of output. Second, a 'wider' or more extended market increases the possibilities for improving the division of labour and reaping productivity gains (or increasing returns).

The argument is then linked in Book IV to free international trade, for the latter serves to widen the extent of the market and bring about a more refined division of labour:

> By means of [foreign trade], the narrowness of the home market does not hinder the division of labour in any particular branch of art or manufacture from being carried to the highest perfection. By opening a more extensive market for whatever part of the produce of their labour may exceed the home consumption, it encourages them to improve its productive powers, and to augment its annual produce to the utmost, and thereby to increase the real revenue and wealth of the society.[41]

As Allyn Young comments, this is 'one of the most illuminating and fruitful generalisations which can be found anywhere in the whole literature of economics'.[42] Hla Myint interprets this nugget of Smithian insight thus:

> Free trade is a method of expanding the economic system horizontally. . . . Perhaps one may say that the difference between the modern concept of free competition and Smith's is that the former is a method of 'tightening up' the allocative efficiency within a given productive framework while the latter is a method of 'widening' the area of the economy.[43]

Mancur Olson, who attaches the utmost importance to this kind of dynamic gain from trade, expresses the same point in the following way: 'I believe the greatest reductions of trade restrictions in history have come from reducing the mileage rather than the height of trade restrictions'.[44]

International trade liberalisation is not the only way of widening the market. Intranational and international markets have historically widened through improvements in transport and communications (which is why Smith, unlike the nineteenth-century economists, does not assume that there are zero transportation costs). Geographical discoveries have also opened up new markets and presented new possibilities for a greater division of labour, as was the case with the North American colonies in Smith's time. Furthermore, as Olson argues, the greater competition from many foreign enterprises that issues from a widening market is a powerful external instrument to break up hitherto protected monopolies and oligopolies (or what Olson calls 'distributional cartels') in local markets.[45] This is what Gottfried Haberler is getting at when he says that free trade is the best antimonopoly policy ever devised (an argument picked up in the following section).

A widening international market and domestic economic development go hand-in-hand. Clearly Smith, unlike many postwar development economists, considers domestic agricultural improvement as the prior condition for economic development. Expanded agricultural output in land-abundant but labour- and capital-scarce countries leads to surplus produce that can be exported. Widening international markets provide an outlet for such an exportable surplus. This is the core of Smith's 'vent-for-surplus' theory of international trade.[46]

However, this is only the beginning of the development process. Agricultural exports, following on from expanded agricultural output at home, are the prelude and stepping-stone to capital accumulation and the subsequent diversification into labour-intensive manufactures, and then capital-intensive manufactures and services. This was the successful development path of Western Europe, the US and Germany in the eighteenth and nineteenth centuries, and of follower nations like Japan, South Korea and Taiwan in the twentieth century. All these factors are contingent, of course, on an envelope of improving transport and communications infrastructures, and appropriate institutions of government and the law. The latter bring out private investment opportunities implied by different factor proportions at different stages of economic development.

Widening the international market through openness to trade and investment mutually interacts with the development of the domestic institutional infrastructure. A wider market provides incentives for private actors to invest in entrepreneurial opportunities, which in turn helps improve the domestic organisational framework of markets. Greater national wealth also provides more leeway for public investment in governmental and legal systems as well as other public goods (e.g. health, education, transport and communications). Obversely, the improvement of the domestic institutional infrastructure, including governmental and legal systems, provides a more solid platform from which to exploit the opportunities of a wider international market. Therefore, commercial openness is conducive to climbing up the ladder of comparative advantage; it is the 'handmaiden' of domestic growth.[47]

Internationally mobile capital

Unlike his treatment of international trade, Adam Smith does not devote a great deal of attention to internationally mobile capital. Nevertheless, in isolated passages in *The Wealth of Nations*, he does display an awareness of the potential importance of capital moving from one nation to another in response to differences in costs and government regulations, especially on taxation. He refers, for instance, to 'the capital of a wholesale merchant, . . . seems to have no fixed or necessary residence anywhere, but may wander from place to place, according as it can buy cheap or sell dear'.[48] And further:

> The proprietor of stock is properly a citizen of the world, and is not necessarily attached to any particular country. He would be apt to abandon the country in which he was exposed to a vexatious inquisition, in order to be assessed to a burdensome tax, and would remove his stock to some other country where he could either carry on his business, or enjoy his fortune more at his ease.[49]

Quite in contrast with nineteenth-century classical economics and much of twentieth-century neoclassical economics, Smith does not resort to the unrealistic assumption of international capital immobility.[50]

Rich and poor countries

The thrust of Hume and Smith's international political economy is that commercial openness is in the national interest in the context of all-round gains for rich and poor countries alike. Nevertheless, there are differences of emphasis, and indeed of opinion, between the two Scotsmen on the distribution of the gains from trade.

While emphasising the mutually beneficial nature of international commerce, and that even poor countries with appropriate institutions and policies have the potential to grow fast – at any rate, faster than countries with inappropriate institutions and policies – Adam Smith seems to indicate that rich countries retain an inbuilt advantage over poorer followers. Richer countries with a more developed institutional framework and a plentiful stock of accumulated capital are in an intrinsically superior position to take advantage of technology transfer and further refine the division of labour.[51]

David Hume not only pays more attention to the distribution of the gain between rich and poor countries than Adam Smith, but also is much more optimistic about the prospects of 'catchup' by poor countries. In 'Of Money', Hume contends that poorer countries with cheaper costs of production, particularly in the use of labour, act as magnets for capital and are able to undersell richer countries in a number of areas, despite the 'first-mover' advantages of the latter in having a bigger endowment of financial, physical and human capital.

There seems to be a happy concurrence of causes in human affairs, which checks the growth of trade and riches, and hinders them from being confined entirely to one people; as might naturally at first be dreaded from the advantages of an established commerce. Where one nation has gotten the start of another in trade, it is very difficult for the latter to regain the ground it has lost; because of the superior industry and skill of the former. . . . But these advantages are compensated, in some measure, by the low price of labour in every nation which has not an extensive commerce, and does not much abound in gold and silver. Manufactures, therefore gradually shift their places, leaving those countries and provinces which they have already enriched, and flying to others, whither they are allured by the cheapness of provisions and labour; till they have enriched these also, and are again banished by the same causes. And, in general, we may observe, that the dearness of everything, from plenty of money, is a disadvantage, which attends an established commerce, and sets bounds to it in every country, by enabling the poorer states to undersell the richer in all foreign markets.[52]

In the context of free trade, this catchup by poorer countries eventually forces richer countries to give up producing goods in which their costs and prices have become too high.[53] Some of Hume's contemporaries interpreted this line of thought as indicating the inevitable onset of stasis or even decay in richer countries when prices and costs reach a certain level.[54] However, Hume is not thinking along these lines; rather he foresees richer countries continuing to grow in spite of losing their cost advantage. They do so by climbing up the ladder of development, concentrating on taking advantage of cross-border technology flows and emulating the technological innovations of neighbouring (rich) countries. Essentially, Hume envisages an all-round positive sum scenario in which poor countries begin catchup development by specialising in labour-intensive (or cheap labour) production; richer countries then specialise in higher value, capital- and skill-intensive production. The argument culminates in Hume's last – and best – essay in political economy, 'Of the jealousy of trade'.[55]

As ever the pragmatic Scottish empiricist, Hume applied his theory to trade between Scotland and England in the aftermath of the Act of Union. Unlike Josiah Tucker, for example, Hume believed that Scotland would not suffer from England's head-start in development and its more advanced condition; rather free trade would present Scotland with new opportunities for development, beginning with specialisation in goods in which the costs of production were cheaper than in England. This argument relates to the modern North–South relationship: following Hume, there is a complementarity of interest between developed and developing countries united in a bond of free trade. This is, of course, diametrically opposed to the thesis that developing countries remain stuck in a rut of dependency and underdevelopment compared to developed countries.[56]

Political economy arguments in Smith: rent-seeking, government failure and information costs

Having covered the link between domestic institutions and the dynamic gains from trade in Smith and Hume, it is now time to go on to more explicitly political arguments on the free trade versus protection issue.

Neoclassical economists habitually defend free trade based on a perfect competition model, while admitting that protection can improve national welfare under certain exceptional circumstances. Relying on the models of politics developed by the New Political Economy, many economists then go on to argue that governments are highly unlikely to adopt and administer protectionist policies in line with economic-theoretical recommendations, given that, among other reasons, the 'rent-seeking' preferences of a relatively small number of well-organised and politically powerful interest groups dominate policy processes (see chapter nine). Protectionism in practice almost always favours a small number of organised interests at the expense of the public good. Thus the last line of defence for free trade against protection is a *political economy* argument that real-life protectionism is economically irrational because it is riddled with politics. Ultimately, it is probably better to stick to a relatively depoliticised free trade regime.[57]

These insights of the rational choice-based New Political Economy are not particularly new; they have an impeccable pedigree in the history of economic thought over the past two centuries.[58] However, Adam Smith has a strikingly different and distinctly 'classical-liberal' way of setting out the case for free trade. First, like David Hume, he defends free trade on static and dynamic grounds *without recourse to the unrealistic assumptions of a perfect competition model*, as the previous sections have, I trust, made abundantly clear. Then he introduces and develops explicit political economy arguments to *fortify* the presumption in favour of free trade. Smith's central political economy argument revolves around what we would now call 'government failure'.

Old and new mercantilists present external trade in terms of interstate conflict, with one state gaining at another's expense. Smith is one of the first to dramatically shift the focus from the international arena to lay bare the differences of interest and the struggles of politics *within* the nation-state. He thinks of protection not as a means whereby one state defends itself against, or gets the upper hand over, other states; rather protectionist policies are the inevitable outcome of the political and economic power of producer interests at home.[59] David Hume has no mention of these intranational political processes in his *Political Essays*, although he does display an awareness of the problem in his *History of England*.[60]

Smith is intensely suspicious of 'merchants' who, in his day, actively and successfully lobbied political authorities for monopoly privileges, including protection from foreigners . This warded off unwelcome competition and kept prices artificially high.[61] Some of the most piquant and biting passages of *The Wealth of Nations* are reserved for a withering attack on the monopolistic power of the merchant interest, and how it is hugely destructive of the public interest of national wealth-maximisation.

> People of the same trade seldom meet together, even for merriment and diversion, but the conversation ends in a conspiracy against the public, or in some contrivance to raise prices. . . . To widen the market and narrow the competition is always the interest of the dealers. To widen the market may frequently be agreeable enough to the interests of the public; but to narrow the competition must always be against it, and can only serve to enable the dealers, by raising their profits above what they naturally would be, to levy, for their own benefit, an absurd tax upon the rest of their fellow citizens.[62]

And further on:

> Consumption is the sole end and purpose of all production; and the interest of the producer ought to be attended to, only so far as it may be necessary for promoting that of the consumer. . . . [However, due to restrictions on imports in the mercantilist system] the interest of the home consumer is evidently sacrificed to that of the producer. It is altogether for the benefit of the latter, that the former is obliged to pay that enhancement of price which this monopoly almost always occasions.[63]

In the final analysis, 'to promote the little interest of one little order of men in one country, [protection] hurts the interest of all other orders of men in that country, and of all men in all other countries'.[64]

Not only are 'merchants and manufacturers' extremely skilled in sophistical argumentation, persuading a gullible public that their (the merchants') private interest to screen out foreign competition is fully correspondent to the national interest; they are also overwhelmingly successful in persuading governments to adopt protectionist policies. Once these policies are in place, there is hardly any limit to 'the clamorous importunity of partial interests'. 'This monopoly [through protection against imports] has so much increased the number of some particular tribes of them, that, like an overgrown standing army, they have become formidable to the government, and upon many occasions intimidate the legislature'. In this way the 'partial interest' of producers captures political processes, with the government almost completely losing sight of 'an extensive view of the general good'. 'The sneaking arts of underling tradesmen are thus erected into political maxims for the conduct of a great empire'.[65]

Quite aside from (what we would now call) the rent-seeking argument outlined above, policies of protection face a 'knowledge problem' (as Hayek would call it): governments require superior information, relative to private actors, of the market in the present and the future if selective policies of promotion and protection are to lead to improved economy-wide performance. These informational requirements are a tall order, perhaps even an impossibility, in most conceivably realistic circumstances in complex economies, as Adam Smith is well aware:

> What is the species of domestic industry which his capital can employ, and of which the produce is likely to be of the greatest value, every individual, it is evident, can, in his local situation, judge much better than any statesman or lawgiver can do for him. ... To give the monopoly of the home market to the produce of domestic industry, in any particular art or manufacture, is in some measure to direct private people in what manner they ought to employ their capitals, and must, in almost all cases, be either a useless or a hurtful regulation.[66]

Given the power of the producer interest, Smith remains rather pessimistic about the prospects for full-blown free trade, which is 'as absurd as to expect that an Oceania or Utopia should ever be established'. Nevertheless, he cautiously entertains hopes of a gradual move in the direction of free trade that would be compatible with political realities. As a proximate step, legislatures should be

> particularly careful neither to establish any new monopolies of this kind, nor to extend further those which are already established. Every such regulation introduces some degree of real disorder into the constitution of the state, which it will be difficult afterwards to cure without occasioning another disorder'.[67]

Thus, Smith's plentifully stocked arsenal of political economy arguments illuminates the deleterious effects of protectionism in practice, fully cognisant of the institutional and political realities within which trade policy is made and managed. Free trade, on the other hand, is a means of pulverising entrenched domestic monopolies by forcing them to compete with domestic and foreign rivals, thus tilting the scales of power back in the direction of the home consumer.

For Smith, the goal of free trade does not stop at the 'economic' ambition to increase efficiency and national wealth. It is of the utmost importance to bear in mind that Smith assails protectionism not only or merely because it is economically inefficient, but also because it privileges a number of powerful interests over other persons and groups in opaque political processes. This makes a mockery of 'justice' or the Rule of Law, whose cardinal tenet is nondiscrimination or the equality of treatment between individuals (see chapter two). As Smith remarks:

> To hurt in any degree the interest of any one order of citizens, for no other purpose but to promote that of some other, is evidently contrary

to that justice and equality of treatment which the sovereign owes to all the different orders of his subjects.[68]

Therefore free trade, by removing the interpersonal and intergroup discrimination that issues from protection, is an instrument of domestic constitutional refurbishment (in addition to producing a higher degree of efficiency); it helps to bring about greater transparency and justice in national governance. This classical liberal idea of free trade as a means of rectifying government and constitutional failure is elaborated upon by Jan Tumlir in his work on 'democratic constitutionalism' (see chapter eight).[69]

Thus far, I have given consideration to Smith's general political economy arguments on the free trade versus protectionism issue. Now it is appropriate to see how he applies his approach to particular aspects of international commercial policy. The following subsection will home in on his characteristically political-economic and policy-oriented treatment of the vexed question of reciprocity and unilateralism in international trade.

Reciprocity versus unilateral free trade

One of the most controversial debates on trade policy in the nineteenth century concerned the pros and contras of unilateral free trade, that is, a national policy of free trade independent of the trade policies of other nations. Nearly all the classical economists defended unilateral free trade. Robert Torrens, however, was the significant exception, strongly advocating the opposing policy of reciprocity: the home country should reduce import barriers only if other countries reduced their barriers to the home country's exports in an equivalent fashion.[70]

Adam Smith prefigures many of these arguments, although he is unaware of the terms of trade argument that Torrens uses as the foundation of his case against unilateral free trade (see chapter five). Unilateralism has an economic-theoretical justification in the sense that free trade, *regardless of other nations' policies*, allows imports to spark a reallocation of domestic resources and bring about gains from trade.[71] However, it is striking that Smith seems not to rely heavily on abstract economic theory in evaluating the merits of unilateral free trade; rather he conducts his argument overwhelmingly in terms of the political economy of prevailing and probable policy realities.[72]

First, Smith considers the case of departing from a free trade regime by imposing retaliatory duties when foreign nations restrict the home country's manufactured exports. 'Revenge in this case naturally dictates retaliation, and that we should impose the like duties and prohibitions upon the importation of some or all of their manufactures into ours. Nations accordingly seldom fail to retaliate in this manner.'[73]

Such a policy of retaliation (or reciprocity) is justified when there is a 'probability' that foreign nations will repeal protectionist barriers, which 'will generally more than compensate the transitory inconveniency of paying dearer during a short time for some sorts of goods'. However, a policy judgement of this nature cannot be deduced from 'general principles' of economic theory, but has to be left as a matter of practical deliberation to 'that insidious and crafty animal, vulgarly called a statesman or politician, whose councils are directed by the momentary fluctuations of affairs'.[74]

Nevertheless, Smith is rather sceptical that reciprocity will have the desired effect, that is to say, there is little 'probability' of foreign markets being prised open in such a manner. In this case retaliation is damaging, for it shelters import-competing industries at home from foreign competition, while harming foreigners as well as everybody else at home through the higher prices that result from protection. 'Every such law, therefore, imposes a real tax upon the whole country'.[75]

Therefore, on the grounds of practical expediency, Smith, on balance, seems to favour the maintenance of a pre-existing regime of unilateral free trade rather than a politically risky policy of reciprocity whose costs are known but whose benefits are far from certain.

Smith then goes on to inquire whether there should be a (unilateral) repeal of longstanding barriers to imports. The risk of such a policy is that, if implemented suddenly, it would lead to a rush of imports that would cause significant dislocation to, and unemployment in, previously protected sectors. However, Smith thinks that the damage 'would in all probability, be much less than is commonly imagined', for, providing domestic markets – and labour markets in particular – were flexible, workers in previously protected, inefficient sectors could quickly move to more efficient sectors. The short-term costs of trade liberalisation would be greater, of course, if domestic markets remained riddled with government-protected monopoly privileges (e.g. the exclusive privileges of corporations and the statute of apprenticeships in Smith's day). Smith's policy preference then becomes clear: trade liberalisation should be coupled with wide-ranging domestic deregulation to establish the individual's freedoms of trade, contract and employment; this would engender a quick reallocation of domestic resources that would ensure that the short-term distress caused by trade liberalisation would be minimal.[76]

This still does not resolve the question of whether trade liberalisation should be swift or gradual. Smith, like Ricardo after him, seems to veer in the direction of gradualism in order to give adequate breathing space for domestic adjustment to occur. 'Humanity may in this case require that the freedom of trade should be restored only by slow gradations, and with a good deal of reserve and circumspection'.[77]

Hence, on political economy or policy-related grounds, Smith adopts a qualified and by no means clear-cut stance in favour of unilateral free trade. This sets the tone for the classical liberal tradition's approach to international commercial policy for the next century-and-a-half. As Lord Robbins comments:

From Adam Smith onwards, the classical tradition in regard to retaliation had been quite definitely that it was seldom worth the candle; and while the matter had not been talked about at length, the general tone of the literature certainly favoured a unilateral progress to free trade.[78]

Thus, Smith's hedged defence of unilateral free trade shows how much he places political economy at the forefront of his considerations of international commercial policy, complementing his treatment of the static and dynamic gains from trade. Furthermore, the Smithian outlook on unilateralism versus reciprocity is not a mere *curiosum* of intellectual history. As I shall argue later, particularly in chapter nine, the preference for unilateral free trade is highly indicative of a classical liberal approach to international economic order and is of great relevance to current policy realities, in spite of the predominance, until recently, of reciprocity in international commercial policy. Reaching back to Smith's political economy is, in my opinion, very relevant to a modern defence of unilateral free trade, even if it combines with an element of international policy cooperation (as in the World Trade Organisation) to take account of present institutional conditions and policy realities.

Hume and Smith on the interstate political system: economic liberalism and political realism

After covering both the economic and political-economic aspects of Hume and Smith's writings on international commerce, it is fitting to wind up this chapter with a look at their views on the international political system. Neither of them has an awful lot to say about the role of the state in relation to other states in the international system, quite in contrast with their extensive treatment of the role of government within the nation-state. Therefore it is not altogether surprising that this side of their work has not attracted a great deal of attention in the secondary literature. Nevertheless, it should become clear as this section unfolds that both Hume and Smith have a distinctive and rather 'realist' perspective of the role of the state in international affairs. Furthermore, they believe, at least implicitly, that this realism is reasonably compatible with expanding networks of commerce and a cosmopolitan outlook. This background classical liberal perception of the international political system is of considerable importance to this discussion, for it has a material bearing on the institutional framework and governance of commercial policy.

In the moral-philosophical and psychological sides of their work, both Hume and Smith strongly believe that human fellow-feeling (or approbation of others) – the famous 'sympathy' principle in eighteenth-century moral philosophy – might apply within a nation, but hardly at all between nations. Sympathy subsumes a sentiment of patriotism or 'love of country', but it does not extend to a 'love of mankind'. The latter is too abstract a concept for the generality of mankind, which is why not very many of us stoically consider ourselves as 'citizens of the world'. Both Hume and Smith opine that this is right and proper, for the public interest is secured when one fixes one's attention on something limited and proximate, stretching to patriotism or love of country, rather than something vague and uncertain like the love of humanity.[79] As David Hume remarks:

> And as nature has implanted in every one a superior affection to his own country, we never expect any regard to distant nations, where a competition arises. Not to mention, that, while every man consults the good of his own community, we are sensible, that the general interest of mankind is better promoted, than by any loose indeterminate views to the good of a species, whence no beneficial action could ever result, for want of a duly limited object, on which they could exert them-selves.[80]

And Adam Smith seems to concur wholeheartedly:

> We do not love our country merely as part of the great society of mankind: we love it for its own sake, and independently of any such consideration. . . . the interest of the great society of mankind would be best promoted by directing the principal attention of each individual to that particular portion of it, which was most within the sphere both of his abilities and of his understanding.[81]

Some commentators assume that the classical economists, while not holding to a harmony of interests doctrine within nations (see chapter two), implicitly believe in a harmony of interests between nations. In the more extreme *laissez faire* tradition of the Manchester School, there is supposed to be a harmony of inter-ests within and between nations. In Richard Cobden's view, open commerce between nations inexorably leads to a peaceful and harmonious international order.[82]

While some nineteenth-century classical economists adhere to a rather naive harmony of interests view of the interstate system, this is not true of Smith. As my colleague Andrew Walter cogently argues, Smith is more of a political realist.[83] Far from believing in free trade automatically leading to international peace, he is attentive to the permanent danger of interstate conflict. Open commerce does bring about greater contact and understanding between states, thereby mitigating interstate rivalries, but it is not strong enough a force to permanently overcome the inescapable problem of international political anarchy, that is, a system of nation-states without a superior and unifying polit-ical authority to enforce order in international relations. International order, therefore, must rely on a pragmatic combination of open commerce and a network of alliances and treaties to maintain a balance of political power between states; international order cannot rely on a harmony of interests. Furthermore, David Hume's views on the subject are very similar.[84]

Given such political realism, it defies belief that Hume and Smith, if alive today, would lurch to the Utopian extreme of advocating, even as a long-term objective, 'world government' or 'international authorities' to solve the problem of international political anarchy (as Lord Robbins and others did – see chapters five and seven).[85] This kind of thinking is entirely foreign to the cautious, pragmatic empiricism of the Scottish Enlightenment. To Hume and Smith, it would appear as French-style *tabula rasa* speculation, far too abstract and far too removed from grown or evolved social morals and traditions to be of relevance to political and economic realities.

Rather than indulging in chimerical speculations on world government, Hume and Smith stick to considerations of the nation and the national interest as practical objects of analysis. This is a point of absolutely vital importance. Note that Smith does not expatiate on the wealth of 'the world'; rather he focuses on the wealth *of nations*. First and foremost, the interrelation of economic phenomena is examined according to the criterion of *national*, not global, wealth-maximisation.

Similarly, Smith evaluates the static and dynamic gains from trade, as well as the political economy factors outlined in the previous section, in terms of the national interest.[86] In contradistinction to the mercantilists, however, he holds that, under free trade, the national interest corresponds to the global interest. In the first instance, free trade benefits the nation that sticks to a regime of commercial openness. However, *as a by-product*, such a regime benefits the rest of the world through a better allocation of world resources, not to mention the dynamic gains of technology transfer, competitive emulation and a widening market that spread across the globe. These worldwide gains increase when other nations follow the example of free trading nations by adopting a free trade regime themselves. This is the context for Smith's advocacy of unilateral free trade which the nineteenth-century classical economists believe in as well: one or a number of nations adopt free trade independently *in their own interest*; others, also acting in their self-interest, are likely to follow the example of pioneering free trading nations once the benefits of such a policy become readily apparent.

Given this mind-set, it is therefore not surprising that Smith and later classical economists are highly suspicious of a policy of trade liberalisation through interstate bargaining or reciprocity with its cumbersome, time-consuming procedures of negotiation, its risks of makeshift political compromises, and, not least, the prospect of mutually damaging, 'tit-for-tat' retaliation. Extrapolating into the second half of the twentieth century, Adam Smith and the rest of the classical liberal tradition would, therefore, be rather sceptical of too much reciprotarian management of the world economy through complex intergovernmental negotiations and international organisations; unilateral free trade, perhaps with limited backup in multilateral agreements (as in the World

Trade Organisation), would continue to be their preference. Given the return of unilateral trade liberalisation in emerging markets since the 1970s, this Smithian, classical liberal argument is hardly out of date; its time has come (see chapters seven and nine).

Thus, Smithian classical liberalism would have no truck with world government and would look askance at a heavy emphasis on intergovernmental policy coordination (or reciprocity). Nor would it have any time for the recurring contention that the nation-state is obsolescent in the face of 'globalisation' (the term that encapsulates transnational phenomena such as globally integrated financial markets, revolutionary changes in transport and communications technologies, and globally integrated production by multinational enterprises).[87] Some commentators go so far as to argue that these forces of globalisation have weakened and even overwhelmed the authority of national governments, giving way to the rising power of nongovernmental actors, particularly multinational enterprises.[88]

It is *de rigeur* among noneconomist observers and policy-makers to parrot the globalisation thesis. Going back to the Scots, and Adam Smith in particular, is a highly useful antidote to the Pop Internationalism (Paul Krugman) and Do-It-Yourself-Economics (David Henderson) that lie at the heart of popular notions of globalisation. First, despite intensifying international economic linkages in the past few decades, the extent of globalisation, at least in popular writings, is vastly overestimated, especially compared to the high point of international economic integration on the eve of the First World War.[89] Second, the state retains enduring importance in fulfilling its three core functions set out by Adam Smith (see chapter two). Domestically, it continues to be indispensable to the administration of justice and the provision of public goods. Externally, no other actors, including multinational enterprises and international organisations, are willing or able to replace the state's traditional foreign policy function of organising defence to avoid war and maintain peace. Nor are they capable of replacing the state's foreign economic policy function of deciding whether there should be a regime of openness or closure to trade and foreign investment. Put differently, no other actors are likely to substitute for the state in organising and executing *political* functions. Thus, states remain the most important political units in both domestic *and* international affairs – one reason why Adam Smith includes the latter as one of his three main functions of government.

The zenith of international economic integration in the last quarter of the nineteenth century and the first decade of the twentieth century coexisted with an international political system of sovereign nation-states, without world government, strong regimes of intergovernmental policy coordination or the replacement of government authority by nongovernmental actors. The classical liberals of the time, following Adam Smith, were perfectly happy with a combination of economic liberalism, in the form of increasing international economic interdependence, and a political realism that recognised and accepted the sovereignty of nation-states in the international realm. From a classical liberal perspective, this congress of economic liberalism and political realism applies to the end of the twentieth century as well. Greater trade, factor mobility and technology transfer do impose more onerous constraints on national political discretion, but this does not seriously diminish the governance functions of the individual state.[90] In its core domestic and foreign economic policy areas of activity, the state continues to exercise a wide range of choice that has a huge impact on domestic economic performance and development as well as on other states in the international system. The message of Adam Smith and, perhaps, of David Hume, is that it is still fundamentally a matter of appropriate domestic institutions and appropriate national-level policy as to whether an open international economy continues to exist and prosper.

Conclusion

This chapter has covered a wide expanse of territory in the international political economy of Hume and Smith. The history of economic thought has documented and interpreted their attack on mercantilism and their coverage of the static gains from trade. However, the core of their international economic analysis on the dynamic gains from trade has been mostly underemphasised or overlooked. Both Hume and Smith relate the dynamic gains from trade – mainly from technology transfer and competitive emulation in Hume, and mainly from a widening market and increasing returns in Smith – to the development of domestic institutions and the promotion of sustainable economic growth. Therefore a policy of commercial openness not only is concerned with the removal of distortions (as it is in a rudimentary neoclassical model), but also is intimately bound up with domestic institutional development. This is a Smithian message of acute relevance to the increasing number of states presently embarking on, or seeking to sustain and deepen, packages of comprehensive policy reform in both developing and transition countries.

Adam Smith then goes on to strengthen his treatment of the gains from trade with several political economy arguments that show up, in rather gory detail, the harmful effects of an inevitably politicised protectionist regime. He conducts his defence of unilateral free trade, with a lot of ifs and buts, on such political economy lines. The combination of (mainly dynamic) economic analysis and political economy argumentation in Smith represents just about the most complete case ever made in favour of free trade, as yet unsurpassed over two hundred years since the publication of *The Wealth of Nations*.

With an admixture of political realism in both Hume and Smith, emphasising the enduring importance of the individual nation-state in a world of increasing economic interdependence, the parameters and guidelines are now in place for a classical liberal perspective on international economic order. Twentieth century political economists like Viner (chapter five), Röpke (chapter seven) and Tumlir (chapter eight), fill out and update this model set up by Hume and, above all, Smith.

Notes

1 Robbins (1958), pp. 21–22.
2 West (1990), pp. 24–27; Bloomfield (1978), pp. 608–609.
3 Nathan Rosenberg, 'Some institutional aspects of *The Wealth of Nations*', in Cunningham Wood (1983), p. 108. Also see Rosenberg (1965), p. 128; Lal and Myint (1996), p. 324.
4 Lord Robbins, 'The classical theory of commercial policy', in Robbins (1971), p. 189; Phyllis Deane, 'Marshall on free trade', in McWilliams Tullberg (1990), pp. 128–129.
5 See Irwin (1996), pp. 64, 72, 75.
6 Eugene Rotwein, 'David Hume', in Eatwell *et al.* (1989), p. 134.
7 David Hume, 'Of the Balance of Trade', in Hume (1970 [1752 and 1758]), pp. 60–65. Also see Hume's letter to Montesquieu, 10 April 1749, in Hume (1970 [1752 and 1758]), pp. 188–189.
8 Smith (1976 [1776]), Book II, ch. V, p. 394, Book IV, ch. III, pp. 491, 514, 522–523; Irwin (1996), pp. 5, 76, 180.
9 David Hume, 'Of the Jealousy of Trade', in Hume (1970 [1752 and 1758]), pp. 78, 82.
10 Smith (1976 [1776]), Book IV, ch. III, p. 519.
   David Ricardo comments that Smith 'has attempted also to show that the freedom of commerce, which undoubtedly promotes the interest of the whole, promotes also the interest of each particular country'. Ricardo (1973 [1817]), ch. XXV, p. 227.
11 David Hume, 'Of the Balance of Trade', in Hume (1970 [1752 and 1758]), p. 76; Smith (1976 [1776]), Book IV, ch. II, pp. 484–487.
12 Smith (1976 [1776]), Book IV, ch. II, p. 479.
13 Ibid., Book IV, ch. II, pp. 474 f., 479–480, ch. VI, pp. 33–35, ch. VII, pp. 94–95, 110, 119.
14 Ibid., Book IV, ch. II, p. 479.
15 David Hume, 'Of the Jealousy of Trade', p. 79, and 'Of the Balance of Trade', p. 75, both in Hume (1970 [1752 and 1758]); Smith (1976 [1776]), Book II, ch. V, p. 388.
16 Irwin (1996), pp. 76, 90–92; Lord Robbins, 'The classical theory of commercial policy', in Robbins (1971), p. 192.
17 Eugene Rotwein, 'Introduction', in Hume (1970 [1752 and 1758]), pp. lxi, lxxii, lxxv–lxxvi, ci; David Hume, 'Of the Refinement of the Arts', pp. 22–24, and 'Of Commerce', pp. 10–11, 14, both in Hume (1970 [1752 and 1758]).
18 Eugene Rotwein, 'Introduction', in Hume (1970 [1752 and 1758]), p. cvii; Smith (1976 [1776]), Book III, ch. III, p. 429.
19 Hla Myint (1946), p. 124; Myint (1958), pp. 318, 321; Myint (1977), p. 234.
20 Myint (1977), pp. 231–232.
21 Lal and Myint (1996), pp. 16, 18, 83, 189–190.
22 Deepak Lal and Sarath Rajapatirana, 'Foreign trade regimes and economic growth in developing countries', in Lal (1993), pp. 185–186, 188–189, 191.
23 See, for example, World Bank (1996) and (1997); Sachs (1997); Lal and Myint (1996).
24 Myint (1977), pp. 246–247; Irwin (1996), pp. 84–86.
25 Myint (1977), pp. 235–236; Smith (1976 [1776]), Book II, ch. V, p. 388.
26 Eugene Rotwein, 'Introduction', in Hume (1970 [1752 and 1758]), p. lxxvi.
27 John Stuart Mill instances both these types of dynamic gain in a brief paragraph in his chapter on international trade. He calls them 'indirect effects, which must be counted as benefits of a high order'. Mill (1987 [1871]), Book III, ch. XVII, p. 581.
28 Bhagwati (1988), p. 31.
29 Romer (1994), p. 19.

30 Ibid., p. 3.
31 This insight is remarkably similar to the Hayekian explanation of knowledge-creation and dissemination (see chapter two).
32 David Hume, 'Of Commerce,' in Hume (1970 [1752 and 1758]), p. 14; Knud Haakonssen, 'Introduction', in Hume (1994 [1752]), pp. xxiii–xxiv; Berdell (1996), pp. 108–110, 113–114.
33 David Hume, 'Of the Jealousy of Trade', in Hume (1970 [1752 and 1758]), p. 78; Eugene Rotwein, 'Introduction', in Hume (1970 [1752 and 1758]), p. lxxiv.
34 'That nothing is more favourable to the rise of politeness and learning, than a number of neighbouring and industrious states, connected together by commerce and policy'. David Hume, 'Of the Rise and Progress of the Arts and Sciences', in Hume (1994 [1752]), p. 64.
35 Ibid., p. 76.
36 Ibid., p. 65. Also see Jones (1981) for a similar account of European progress.
37 David Hume, 'Of the Jealousy of Trade', in Hume (1970 [1752 and 1758]), pp. 78–80.
38 Myint (1946), pp. 128, 142.
39 Smith (1976 [1776]), Book IV, ch. VII, p. 141. Also see Book III, ch. III, p. 429.
40 Ibid., Book I, ch. I, p. 7, ch. III, p. 21.
41 Ibid., Book IV, ch. I, p. 469.
42 Quoted in Arthur Bloomfield, 'Adam Smith and the theory of international trade', in Bloomfield (1994), p. 125. Also see Young (1928).
43 Myint (1946), p. 121.
44 Olson (1982), p. 127.
45 Smith (1976 [1776]), Book IV, ch. I, p. 470; Myint (1977), p. 237; Olson (1982), p. 124.
46 Smith (1976 [1776]), Book II, ch. V, p. 394; Myint (1958), p. 323.
47 Myint (1977), pp. 239–242, 246; Hla Myint, 'Comment', in Skinner and Wilson (1976), pp. 157–159.
48 Smith (1976 [1776]), Book II, ch. V, p. 385.
49 Ibid., Book IV, ch. II, pp. 375–376.
50 Arthur Bloomfield, 'Adam Smith and the theory of international trade', in Bloomfield (1994), pp. 114, 116, 128.
51 Smith (1976 [1776]), Book IV, ch. III, p. 520; Elmslie (1994), pp. 656–658; Istvan Hont, 'The "rich country-poor country" debate in Scottish classical political economy', in Hont and Ignatieff (1983), pp. 298–299, 302.
52 David Hume, 'Of Money', in Hume (1970 [1752 and 1758]), pp. 34–35.
53 David Hume, 'Of Commerce', in Hume (1970 [1752 and 1758]), p. 14.
54 Hont, op. cit., pp. 275, 279, 295; Elmslie (1995), pp. 208, 211.
   Hume had a lively exchange of views with James Oswald and Josiah Tucker about the differential growth prospects of rich and poor countries. This became known as the 'rich country–poor country' debate. See Hont, op. cit.; Elmslie (1995); Irwin (1996), pp. 155–159.
55 David Hume, 'Of the Jealousy of Trade', in Hume (1970 [1752 and 1758]), p. 81. Also see Hume's letter to Oswald, 1 November 1750, p. 198 ('The rich country would acquire and retain all the manufactures, that require great stock or great skill; but the poor country would gain from it all the simpler and more laborious.'); Hume's letter to Lord Kames, 4 March 1758, pp. 200–201 ('The finest arts will flourish best in the capital: those of next value in the more opulent provinces: the coarser in the remote countries.'); both in Hume (1970 [1752 and 1758]).
56 Elmslie (1995), pp. 213, 215.
57 Lal and Myint (1996), p. 324; Wagner (1996), p. 5; Irwin (1996), p. 229.

58 Irwin (1996), pp. 227–229.
59 Lord Robbins, 'The classical theory of commercial policy', in Robbins (1971), p. 200.
60 Eugene Rotwein, 'Introduction', in Hume (1970 [1752 and 1758]), p. lxxix.
61 Smith (1976 [1776]), Book I, ch. X, pp. 132–133, 139.
62 Ibid., Book I, ch. X, pp. 144, ch. XI, p. 278.
63. Ibid., Book IV, ch. VIII, p. 179.
64. Ibid., Book IV, ch. VII, p. 126.
65. Ibid., Book IV, ch. II, p. 494, ch. III, p. 518.
66 Ibid., Book IV, ch. II, p. 478.
67 Ibid., Book IV, ch. II, pp. 493–495, ch. V, p. 52.
68 Ibid., Book IV, ch. VIII, p. 171.
69 Deepak Lal and Sarath Rajapatirana, 'Foreign trade regimes and economic growth in developing countries', in Lal (1993), p. 191.
70 Irwin (1996), pp. 105, 115; Nassau W. Senior, 'Free trade and retaliation', in Schonhardt-Bailey (1996); Robert Torrens, 'Letter to Nassau William Senior Esq., in reply to the article Free Trade and Retaliation', in Schonhardt-Bailey (1996).
71 Myint (1967), p. 128.
72 Irwin (1996), p. 82; Robbins (1958), p. 256.
73 Smith (1976 [1776]), Book IV, ch. II, p. 489.
74 Ibid., Book IV, ch. II, p. 490.
75 Ibid., Book IV, ch. II, pp. 490–491.
76 Ibid., Book IV, ch. II, pp. 491–493.
77 Ibid., Book IV, ch. II, p. 491. Also see Ricardo (1973 [1817]), ch. XIX, pp. 177–178.
78 Robbins (1958), p. 255. Also see Bhagwati (1988), pp. 26–27.
79 Smith (1982 [1759]), Part III, ch. III, pp. 154–155; Hume (1978 [1740]), Book III, Section XI, pp. 567–568.
80 David Hume, *Enquiry Concerning the Principles of Morals*, in Hume (1975 [1777]), Section V, p. 225.
81 Smith (1982 [1759]), Part VI, ch. II, p. 229.
82 Lord Robbins, 'A general view', in Robbins (1971), p. 35; Lord Robbins, 'Liberalism and the international problem', in Robbins (1963), p. 136.
83 Wyatt-Walter (1996).
84 Smith (1982 [1759]), Part IV, ch. II, p. 228, 230; Knud Haakonssen, 'Introduction', in Hume (1994 [1752]), p. xxii.
85 On Robbins and world government, see Lord Robbins, 'Liberalism and the international problem', in Robbins (1963), p. 36 f.
86 Robbins (1958), p. 254; Irwin (1996), p. 76.
87 On globalisation, see Reich (1992); Ohmae (1990) and (1995).
88 See Strange (1996).
89 Hirst and Thompson (1996), pp. 1–18.
90 Henderson (1986), p. 100.

Part II

AMERICAN EXCURSIONS: KNIGHT AND VINER

4

THE POLITICAL ECONOMY
OF FRANK KNIGHT

Classical liberalism from Chicago

*[Democracy] means cooperation in thinking and acting to promote progress,
moral, intellectual and aesthetic, with material and technical progress as the
basis of all, and all under the limitation of gradualism and 'seasoned' with
humour and play. The combination is the meaning of liberalism.*

Frank H. Knight

Frank H. Knight's main claim to fame is his undisputed position as the founder
of the Chicago School of economics, serving as teacher and mentor to a string
of Nobel Laureates at the University of Chicago.[1] He was also a path-breaking
economist, especially with his early, precocious work *Risk, Uncertainty and Profit*,
paving the way for future investigations into the economics of knowledge. Indeed,
F.A. Hayek, inspired by Knight, placed the economics of knowledge at the core
of his political economy and social philosophy.[2]

Knight's fame goes beyond his accomplishments as a technical economist.
He was also, like his contemporary Ludwig von Mises, and the following generation of F.A. Hayek, Lionel Robbins, Wilhelm Röpke and Walter Eucken, an
économiste-philosophe, whose cultivated, widely read scholarship ranged indeed well
beyond the narrow bounds of economic analysis. In fact the bulk of his scholarship dwelt on the nature of a liberal economic order and its social underpinning
in modern, fast-changing and democratic times. It is precisely this aspect that
marks him out as a classical political economist in the tradition of Adam Smith
and David Hume. Furthermore, no adequate survey and interpretation of the
renewal of classical political economy in the twentieth century can omit
the Knightian *oeuvre*. The latter, together with the tradition it founded at the
University of Chicago, stand alongside corresponding traditions in Vienna (the
Austrian School), London (at the LSE) and Freiburg (the Ordoliberal School of
Walter Eucken and Franz Böhm, covered in chapter six), as a lodestar for
economic liberals, first in facing the onslaught from increasingly popular collectivist schools of thought for most of the twentieth century, and more recently
in the revival of economic liberalism. Knight's students, Milton Friedman,
George Stigler and James Buchanan, have been in the vanguard of this liberal
revival.[3]

Knight's technical economics is undoubtedly of great importance to historians of economic analysis, but this is not the focus here. Rather I propose to concentrate on his wider political economy and place it in the context of the classical liberal tradition. It is useful, however, to begin with Knight's overall conception of economics and its limitations before proceeding to a more detailed treatment of his political economy. The discussion of his political economy revolves around the nature of liberalism, the nexus between freedom and order, and the appropriate role of modern democratic politics. As I will argue, there is a noticeable dichotomy, bordering on the schizophrenic, between the 'economics' and the 'political economy' of Frank Knight.

Economics and its limitations

To Knight, theoretical economics is an abstract, deductive science based on a few general principles, positing an 'economic man' (the infamous *homo oeconomicus*) whose deliberative, problem-solving behaviour under given circumstances is completely rational. Individuals attain given, desired goods and services (or 'provisional wants' used as means to achieve final wants) in the best possible manner, that is, through maximisation, by the correct apportioning of given means or resources among various modes of use under given constraints such as the available stock of technology. The economist states all conditions in terms of stable equilibrium at any one moment in time. In other words, economic science explains 'static' conditions, not the 'dynamic' movement from one state to another. The actors involved resemble anomic Crusoes, interacting impersonally and exclusively through markets.

Such assumptions of actor behaviour are the building-blocks of a theory of economic organisation in perfect markets, bringing together actors in a system of cooperation that unites production and distribution. Perfect markets are akin to frictionless conditions in theoretical mechanics: no monopoly power exists; exchange takes place instantaneously and costlessly, involving error-free competition as well as complete knowledge of relevant facts about wants, means and constraints, *in the present and the future*; and resources are fully employed. Knight defends this construct as a necessary, purely logical device that describes ideal, unrealistic conditions; it cannot say anything about concrete or actual behaviour.[4]

Knight is uncompromising in his attachment to this formal apparatus of economic science but, wearing his political economy hat, he is equally uncompromising and forthright in delimiting the sphere of economics and identifying what it *cannot* and *should not* explain. This is the point of departure for Knight's conception of the real-world economic order embedded in its changing political, legal and social contexts.

Knight's political economy begins with his comprehensive, frank and trenchant statements on the motivations and conduct of 'real' men as opposed to ideal-typical 'economic' men. Here his psychological assumptions differ radically from those he would argue are *sine qua non* to economic analysis. Indeed, he goes out of his way not to confuse or conflate *homo oeconomicus* with 'real man'. Knight is one of the rare neoclassical economists who can baldly assert that 'the notion that economics is a science explanatory of actual behaviour is the single most important confusion in the methodology of the science'.[5]

This confusion – the merging of separate categories, the abstract and the concrete – merges with the fallacy of 'scientism' – the application, the straight, crude translation, of natural science categories to social science. Social problems, emerging from human interests and motivations, are of a different order of subtlety and complexity compared to the problem sets of inert objects: human beings are active agents; inert objects are passive, merely 'acted upon'. 'Social problems begin where those of the natural sciences leave off': this applies in particular to the moral and legal framework where social problems take their rise and which are not amenable to formal economic analysis.[6]

Knight embarks on a voyage of psychological realism by dissecting the very assumptions precious to formal economics. 'All activity is economic [in terms of the rational matching of means to ends], but none is purely or merely economic'. The crux of the matter is that the three elements of economic behaviour – means, ends and technological constraints – are not 'given' in dynamic situations. For a start, ends or wants are not fixed; they are not scientific 'data'.

> We generally do not know at all accurately what we want and act in considerable measure to find out. And our interests are to a considerable extent explorative in a more intrinsic sense. . . . It is undoubtedly a firm principle that ends are more-or-less defined in the process of realisation.

Action is not therefore a straightforward, mechanical procedure of utility-maximisation; rather it is primarily exploratory and experimental, indicating an imprecise sense of direction in a world of error and lack of knowledge. In the process wants grow and change; they do not 'stay put' and therefore do not succumb to strictly economic scrutiny.[7]

Furthermore, goods and services do not correspond to real or final wants. The latter are not strictly 'individual' but inhere in social relations: they are 'conventional' wants such as 'getting ahead', 'keeping up with the Joneses', the play interest to make action and interaction interesting, all of which are unstable and liable to unpredictable change. Social conditioning at least in part accounts for a never-ending, Faustian process of striving, the search for 'more and better' wants rather than resting contented with what one has, even if it is well over and above the level of subsistence. This bears on a related point: not only are wants not given; the same applies to the 'units', the individuals taking part in market exchange. The influence of family and a hierarchy of wider communities very largely frames their action. These account for the not insubstantial role of habit, conformity, unconscious imitation, sentiment and loyalty in behaviour.[8]

There is also an overlay of dark, although by no means fatalistic, pessimism in Knight's treatment of human motivations:

> He is perhaps less *homo sapiens*, the knower, than *homo mendax*, the liar, deceiver, hypocrite, pretender, practicer of make-believe. . . . Man alone prefers fiction to fact, with respect to the world and especially to himself.[9]

Pessimism aside, Knight pays special attention to the element of play in human interaction – the 'game' of life. The play interest – emulation, rivalry, and the craving for symbols of distinction and reward – strongly marks business activity. This he ranks alongside rational, purposive behaviour, even in the economic field of market exchange.[10]

Such considerations of the plurality, changeability and conventionality of wants cast more than a shadow over uninformed musing on 'economic motives' or 'lower' as opposed to 'higher' wants. It is a fiction to separate material wants from higher wants such as cultural pursuits. They intermingle, and both require a strong dose of economising behaviour in terms of utilising alternative means to attain ends in conditions of scarcity. Lastly, one should not forget the above-mentioned final wants that lie behind both material and higher wants.[11]

Given these realistic, hard-boiled assumptions that impose sweeping limitations on the range of economic analysis, it comes as no surprise to find Knight in dismissive and belittling mood with respect to *confrères*, particularly from the welfare economics camp, who do make unrealistic assumptions about real-life behaviour. Welfare functions do not express individual satisfactions; a social maximum is not a composite of correlated individual maxima; and happiness or the 'good life' is not synonymous with the amount and distribution of measurable goods and services. This 'balance sheet' view of life, drawn up in terms of measurable magnitudes, is 'an absurd oversimplification'. The comparison and aggregation of quantifiable individual utilities, used as a benchmark for proposed policy action, overstep the frontiers of positive economics. In concord with Lord Robbins, Knight argues that concrete proposals for action have to be based on normative criteria – judgements of value – that lie beyond the domain of economics.[12]

If theoretical economics cannot explain concrete behaviour, then what can? Knight argues that applied economics, using statistical and inductive methods to interpret actual data in a particular time and at a particular place, can modify the general laws of formal economics. However, even applied economics has severe limitations: the constantly changing data lack stability and measurability. Hence the importance of what Knight calls institutional and historical (or evolutionary) economics, whose main task is to study growth and change, using 'informed judgement' more than anything else. Clearly, to Knight, institutional-historical economics has a different set of tools compared to that of scientific formal economics. Closely allied to institutional economics are cognate disciplines, such as psychology, cultural history and ethics, which are also concerned with the *longue durée*. In particular, ethics focuses on a criticism of values and their mutation over time. In two seminal articles, *Ethics and the Economic Interpretation* and *The Ethics of Competition,* Knight goes out of his way to decry the crude nineteenth-century utilitarian method (the precursor of twentieth-century welfare economics) which reduces ethics to the attainment of impersonal goods and services. Behind and undergirding the means/ends rationality of market exchange are final wants that can be interpreted only suggestively and sympathetically, not by objective scientific treatment.[13]

Manifestly, Knight's social thought is dichotomous, perhaps even a touch schizoid. He staunchly defends neoclassical rigour as the starting-point of analysis, but applies very different, realistic criteria to the political economy of concrete action in real-world markets. Lord Robbins has a similar, although not quite the same, distinction between economic and political economy.[14] At least in this respect, Knight does not follow the classical political economy tradition of Smith and Hume, for, as chapter two showed, they never make such an artificial distinction and on the whole employ realistic assumptions of man in his economic environment. Theirs is a science of political economy that studies how a system of interrelationships produces an economic order *in the service of* better (or less unsuccessful) policy. There is no hint of a conceptual separation of extreme abstraction from questions of policy analysis and prescription.[15] As Knight recognises, Adam Smith neither writes about, nor advocates, a perfectly competitive system divorced from pragmatic considerations of policy, law and pre-existing traditions.[16]

Similarly, some legatees of the classical liberal tradition in the twentieth century, notably Hayek, adhere to realistic assumptions of actor behaviour (e.g. an element of irrationality, lack of knowledge, error, erroneous expectations, competition as a dynamic process rather than a static equilibrium device). They use realistic assumptions *as part and parcel of economics* in order to study the working properties of rules and institutions in real-world political economy.[17] As we shall see in the following chapter, Jacob Viner is another classicist who pleads for less abstraction and more realism in economics so that the discipline can serve as a better guide to policy.

On the other hand, Knight's working assumptions of concrete behaviour in political economy, as opposed to idealised economic behaviour, are four square in the classical liberal tradition. As mentioned above, Adam Smith and David Hume, as well as a number of their successors in twentieth-century classical political economy, are not purveyors of *homo oeconomicus* and his rarefied world. Assumptions of rational utility-maximisation under conditions of full knowledge and competitive equilibrium are not part of their scheme. To repeat the argument in chapter two, their generalisations are based on complex interactions in real-life markets, taking humans to be fallible, capricious and in partial ignorance of their environment. To them, relatively free markets do not presuppose an *ex ante* rationality; rather, they provide propitious institutional conditions that make people *gradually* more rational in adjusting means to ends.[18] Knight's assumptions of concrete actor behaviour are in accordance with the classical liberal canon, as is his pessimistic view of human nature. In a long line of 'critical rationalists' (to use Sir Karl Popper's term), prominently including Edmund Burke and Alexis de Tocqueville, he considers men to be highly flawed, occasionally rather pathetic beings, a part of 'the coarse clay of which the bulk of mankind are formed', as Smith so aptly put it.[19]

Lastly, to complete the picture of Knight's classical liberalism with regard to his psychological assumptions, the play interest of the 'game', so prominent and recurrent in his work, closely resembles Smith's metaphor of the 'game of human society'. Smith couches his account of the social game in broad-based notions of 'interesting' activity; he does not restrict it to an instrumental means–ends rationality to produce and consume goods and services.[20]

The nature of liberalism

Knight, unlike Viner, did not write extensively on the intellectual history of liberalism, but there are plenty of *obiter dicta* on the subject sprinkled among his works. They serve as a useful introduction to his perspective on the nature of liberalism.

Knight argues that the liberal epoch emerged as a by-product of increasingly complex cultural evolution. It was not 'planned'; rather it 'just happened'. What little Knight has to say on this score fits in well enough with an evolutionary explanation of history that is the hallmark of the Scottish Enlightenment. Complex and spontaneous orders emerge 'as the result of human action, but not the execution of any human design', to borrow Adam Ferguson's famous phrase.[21]

The eighteenth and nineteenth centuries displayed as much intellectual, material and humanitarian progress as in all previous history, for the first time diffusing the means of achieving a decent existence among the masses. However, a fatal complacency plagued liberalism's Golden Age, the nineteenth century. This prepared the ground for collectivism.[22] Optimistic liberals in an optimistic age took certain principles, such as individualism and scientific intelligence, to extremes, and failed to appreciate the problems of defending liberalism in the long run. By the mid-twentieth century, collectivist public policy received succour from the new Keynesian economics, 'carrying economic thinking well back to the dark ages', as Knight derisively puts it.[23]

In light of liberalism's atrophy, beginning in the nineteenth century, Knight launches into an investigation of the content of liberalism and the envelope of social forces that sustain as well as threaten a free economic order in the long run. It is this strain of Knight's thought, perhaps more than any other, that connects him to the Smithian methodology of the classical liberal tradition.

The core of liberalism to Knight, as to Smith, is an 'orderly system of economic cooperation' that emerges from the apparent chaos of buying and selling in competitive markets. It presupposes individual freedom or *laissez faire* in the choice of ends and means in production and consumption.

The supreme and inestimable merit of the exchange mechanism is that it enables a vast number of people to cooperate in the use of means to achieve ends as far as their interests are mutual, without arguing or in any way agreeing about the ends or the methods of achieving them. It is the 'obvious and simple system of natural liberty'. The only agreement called for in market relations is acceptance of the one essentially negative ethical principle, that the units are not to prey upon one another through coercion or fraud.[24]

Quoted above, in a few sentences, is the essence of the classical 'system of economic freedom', as Alfred Marshall calls it. *Laissez faire* dispenses with the cumbersome, indeed Utopian, task of securing agreement on collective goals and the detailed means of achieving them in a complex society.[25] Rather, the negative principle, legally forbidding individuals from infringing others' rights but otherwise leaving them free to do as they wish – pursuing 'their own interests their own way', according to Smith – spontaneously brings about a vast and intricate system of *cooperation* that caters for reciprocal wants and renders mutual service. This is indeed Smith's 'obvious and simple system of natural liberty'.[26]

Like Smith, Knight constantly emphasises the *cooperative* nature of 'competitive' markets. This system of free cooperation prevails because it is more satisfactory to all parties concerned than alternative modes of cooperation: it combines the efficiency of production and consumption with individual freedom better than any other system. Knight's defence of free markets is similar to that of David Hume: this type of economic order displays long-run *utility* in promoting efficiency and progress, and it locates the exercise of choice in the individual, not in a collective authority.[27] Knight's economic liberalism rests, ultimately, on normative postulates of utility based on individual choice (in the Humean rather than the more simplistic nineteenth-century sense), not on positivist analysis. Moreover, Knight, following Smith, prefers leaving choice to individuals, not so much on the grounds of individual competence but due to the stupidity of governments: even 'irrational' individuals are better at making their own decisions than having decisions made for them by an outside agency of control. Here the classical liberal case for economic freedom rests on sceptical and empirical arguments (the critical rationalism previously alluded to), without recourse to hubristic assumptions of human rationality.[28]

In keeping with the classical liberal tradition, Knight, far from confining his study to 'economic' liberalism, consistently relates it to its 'political' twin. 'Negativism' applies as much to the political sphere as it does to the economic sphere if government is to uphold a free economic order. Political negativism entails government refraining from interventions in the market process: it should not eat into the freedoms of producers and consumers, which are fundamental to social activity and basic to all other freedoms. Government should restrict itself to foreign defence, the maintenance of law and order (the prevention of force and fraud) and the provision of public goods, if there is general agreement that government should supply such public goods or services – the three functions of government laid out in *The Wealth of Nations*.[29]

Knight emphasises that political negativism does not imply an absolutist *laissez faire* nor a minimalist 'nightwatchman' state. He is clearly aware of the doctrinal extremes and journalistic excesses of other elements of nineteenth-century liberalism, none of which were part of the classical liberal tradition. Furthermore, Knight recognises that the role of the state as 'umpire', upholding the 'rules of the game', is an infinitely and eternally complex task. This conception of the state's functions, however, differs fundamentally from any notion that the state should directly engage in, or take charge of, market activity.[30]

Freedom and order

From the above account it should be transparent that Knight, in common with other classical liberals (as opposed to liberals of the John Bright and Richard Cobden variety, or even some modern contractarian liberals), does not consider economic freedom as an *ex nihilo* creation,[31] nor does he believe that it can survive and flourish *in vacuo*. Far from existing in an autonomous sphere, freedom in the economic order is highly dependent on a favourable social consensus and an appropriate political and legal framework. What further distinguishes Knight as a classical liberal is his deep concern for the fabric of social order and the problematic nexus between individual freedom and order.

To Knight, the maintenance of order in society is a 'categorical imperative', prior even to freedom. 'A large part of the social problem centres just here. Especially, freedom and progress, the distinctive values of modern civilisation, conflict with the older values of order and security'. The 'older values' are those of the bygone, 'stationary' times, reliant on custom, habit and, not least, supernatural beliefs, with little or no sense of individuality. Modern progress builds on the perception of society as an association of deliberative individuals endowed with free choice who force the pace of change, which is highly disruptive of order. Progressive conditions also bring in their wake new social problems: conflicts over the distribution of the fruits of the free market system detract from the efficiency gains from that very system.[32]

This leads on to a rather Burkean conservative disposition in matters of public policy.[33] Knight argues that conservatism is not antithetical to liberalism but another aspect of it, inasmuch as it recommends gradual, piecemeal change that is respectful of custom, habit and traditions – the continuing moral basis of order. Not only is the social order more dependent on these 'informal constraints' than the 'formal rules' of law (to borrow Douglass North's terminology), the organised framework of 'made' law is itself primarily drawn from the accumulated 'moral sentiments' of society.

Knight insists on the narrow bounds of critical deliberation, even in modern progressive times. Social behaviour continues to be largely based on habit, sentiment and loyalty. Indeed, it must have some kind of irrational 'opiate', such as religion, to preserve order, in lieu of the inability of man to recognise the limitations of his reason and his predilection to escape the evils he knows for those he has no knowledge of. Precipitate, unreflective legislative action not only involves compulsion but also has moral and material costs, straining the limited resources of government and doing untold damage to the preexisting institutions of society, particularly the family. The sudden transfer of age-old social functions and responsibilities to the state morally weakens the institution of the family, traditionally the strongest bulwark of social order. Hence Knight's conservative emphasis on the 'slow and silent forces' of change, sticking to the order that is and undertaking reform only when there is reasonable agreement that changes will on balance be beneficial.[34]

Prima facie, Knight's conservative streak seems rather illiberal, and could easily serve as an argument against liberal reforms that, inevitably, upset the pre-existing order. Assuredly, there is no hope of reconciling this facet of his thought with the ahistorical contractarianism of Rawls or the (equally ahistorical) utilitarianism of Nozick.

On reflection, however, Knight's concerns about social order fit quite well with the thinking of classical liberalism. Knight remains radical when it is a question of political negativism, that is to say, when the task of public policy is to remove artificial restraints on private entrepreneurial activity by rolling back the frontiers of excessive government. The objective is, of course, to establish 'the obvious and simple system of natural liberty'. Whether these artificial restraints should be removed quickly or gradually is a question Knight does not quite get round to answering directly, reflecting the touch of ambivalence among the classical economists on the same issue.

However, Knight's conservatism mainly displays itself with respect to government's active, 'positive' functions: here, in light of the deficiencies of human intelligence and the requirement of preserving social order, he recommends caution in undertaking new ventures. Thus, in common with all the classical economists, Knight has a broad presumption against government interference, without taking the argument to doctrinal extremes (as argued in the previous section).[35]

Knight's wider emphasis on the order-maintaining role of traditions and conventions is eminently classical and, moreover, quintessentially 'Scottish', although it might be foreign to modern liberals unacquainted with *The Theory of Moral Sentiments*, *The Wealth of Nations* and *The Treatise of Human Nature*.[36] As argued in chapter two, Hume's theory of utility, and his principles of justice, particularly in regard to property, are founded on the evolution of tried-and-tested morals and traditions. To him the 'wise magistrate . . . will bear a reverence to what carries the marks of age: and though he may attempt some improvements for the public good, yet he will adjust his innovations, as much as possible, to the ancient fabric'.[37] Smith's *Theory of Moral Sentiments* is overwhelmingly concerned with extralegal norms that generate and maintain social order, and it would be a cardinal mistake to interpret *The Wealth of Nations* as a contradiction of his previous work on this score. The following quotation suggests Smith's preference for what Hayek, after Popper, calls 'immanent criticism', that is, gradual change on the basis of the existing order as opposed to *tabula rasa* rationalist designs that destroy an accumulated fund of morals and traditions:[38]

> Therefore he will content himself with moderating what he often cannot annihilate without great violence. When he cannot conquer the rooted prejudices of the people by reason and persuasion, he will not attempt to subdue them by force; but he will religiously observe what, by Cicero, is justly called the divine maxim of Plato, never to use violence to his country no more than to his parents. He will accommodate as well as he can, his public arrangements to the confirmed habits and prejudices of his people. . . . When he cannot establish the right, he will not disdain to ameliorate the wrong; but like Solon, when he cannot establish the best system of laws, he will endeavour to establish the best that the people can bear.[39]

Democracy and 'government by discussion'

The final aspect of Knight's work considered in this discussion – the role of democratic politics in modern societies – is less directly related to the classical liberal tradition, although it does bear some resemblance to passages in Hume's *Political Essays*. Whereas Knight takes political democracy as given and seeks to reconcile it with economic liberalism, Smith and Hume did not explicitly advocate a democratic form of government (although some nineteenth-century utilitarians did).[40]

A key insight of this part of the Knightian *oeuvre* is the similarity of competitive politics with competitive economics: demand and supply in open competition, with the consumer as the final judge, are common to both. The political and economic 'games' share the same weaknesses, but democratic politics vastly amplifies these weaknesses. It is true that market exchange not only involves 'economic' power – the power or means to acquire material things, but it also involves the 'political' power – 'power for power's sake', 'prestige power' or 'power over other men' – that lurks behind the surface of economic power as a 'final want'.[41] The difference is that political power only partially taints business life, which does provide desired goods and services. However, political power constitutes 'virtually the whole' of politics. And it is this 'power for power's sake', for reasons of reputation and prestige, that is the scarcest good (or 'bad'), with an inestimably greater rarity value than tangible goods and services. Furthermore, such power does not tend to saturation or stability, rendering the political sphere more volatile than its economic counterpart. There are other characteristics of politics that exacerbate this tendency: first, unlike market exchange, politics is highly personalised; and second, whereas the (impersonal) market minimises the scope for coming to collective agreement on means and ends, politics is centrally concerned with discovering complex agreements that apply to society as a whole. Thus, the principal–agent problem in politics is of a different order and magnitude compared to that in economics.[42]

Knight's identification of the *competitive* element in politics is a foretaste of the rational choice theories of the second half of the twentieth century, applying economic methods to the study of politics. The following generations, prominently including his students George Stigler and James Buchanan, elaborated a system in which politics, like economics, is motivated by self-interested competitive behaviour under constraints. Like them, Knight is all too aware of the propensity of private agents to resort to manipulation in political markets, using governments to gain personal, group or class advantage. This results in economic markets rigged and protected against domestic and foreign competition.[43] However, there seems to be one major difference between Knight and the later generations of the Chicago School: as explained before in this discussion, Knight employed realistic psychological assumptions in dealing with real-life, as opposed to abstract, political and economic behaviour; later members of the Chicago School, notably George Stigler and Gary Becker, rigidly applied the rational utility-maximisation paradigm to concrete economic *and* political markets.[44]

Alongside the attention devoted to political competition, there is another, arguably more important, aspect of Knight's work on democracy that emphasises *cooperation*. This logically follows from his cardinal emphasis on cooperation or mutual consent in market exchange. Democratic politics equally requires cooperative relations, not to exchange goods and services but to structure and conduct a 'discussion', for Knight considers the supreme function of politics to be, to use Lord Bryce's term, 'government by discussion'. It is a collective, cooperative quest, involving the participation of the citizenry, to define and elaborate the means and ends of government. It is also a deliberative, 'intelligent' search for consensus on the 'rules of the political game'. Not least, it is a constant, never-ending exploration of how these rules change and improve, for the political observer or the policy-maker cannot assume the fixity or finality of the laws.[45]

The first task at hand is to agree on a mechanism to structure the discussion, that is, a 'constitution'. On this score, Knight does not elaborate. He is less concerned with the makeup of government and how it relates to the 'consumer', that is, the voter, through electoral systems; rather, he is primarily concerned with the 'office' of government[46] – the nature and content of its activity – and how this relates to a social discussion. Once a constitution is in place, the content of the discussion necessarily revolves around the functions of government: fixing its appropriate sphere of activity, making sure that it has a monopoly of coercion in its own sphere, and leaving all that lies outside this delimited space to the free activity of individuals.[47]

Somewhat more specifically, Knight argues that one major task of government, in addition to preventing coercion of one individual by another, is to restrict the activities of groups 'organised for power'. By this he means that government should not allow itself to fall into the hands of private groups lobbying to deform or close markets in their favour but against the general interest. This ties in with Knight's views on the breadth or range of an appropriate collective discussion. He does not confuse it with rampant pluralism: it is not a gigantic arena in which a plethora of organised interests 'fight it out', with government acting as a mere referee seeking some kind of manageable accommodation between contending or countervailing interests. The latter is a game of 'interests'; there is no guiding light of 'public interest'.[48]

Knight is adamant that a proper discussion cannot sort out myriad and subjective individual or group wants; it has to focus exclusively on 'rights', not 'wants'. There can be collective agreement only on the content of individual rights embodied in procedural rules of law, whereas common agreement on subjective wants in complex societies is an impossibility, a will-o'-the-wisp.[49] Finally, the discussion should not be an excuse for majorities to lord it over minorities: where there is a serious difference of opinion to a rule, individual liberty must prevail, that is to say, there must be a presumption against government interference.[50]

Knight does consider a 'government by discussion' to be an essential complement to a free market order in modern societies. In this sense, democracy and economic liberalism are two sides of the same coin, which does not necessarily follow from the teachings of the Scottish Enlightenment. None the less, Knight, in his pessimistic incarnation, remains markedly circumscribed in his expectations of democratic discussion. In addition to differences of interest and genuine differences of opinion, collective discussion has to contend with the ignorance and apathy of the mass of the populace. Furthermore, the 'game' of discussion, without a sufficient degree of mutual restraint, is liable to degeneration and could easily disrupt social order.[51]

Restraint is essential. Here again one encounters Knight's conservative disposition. It is crucial that there is a general awareness of the complexities, and the narrow range of possibilities, of group action. Legislative and/or executive action should occur only after, first, a thorough appraisal of the questions, problems and possible alternative solutions, and second, on the basis of a reasonable knowledge of the consequences of action. Such public action presupposes an appreciation of the limits of knowledge; action should not take place randomly on the basis of ignorance or false knowledge. In such circumstances, there should be a presumption against government action. 'The possibilities of freedom have sweeping limitations, but accepting them and working within their bounds . . . is the price of the residual freedom that is possible, and that is still the most precious boon in life'.[52]

In his fixation with a collective discussion Knight follows in the footsteps of David Hume, who was intensely concerned with the collective formulation of public opinion. To Hume, 'opinion' has to transcend mere assertion and point-scoring in political processes infested with factionalism. It is all too easy for men to get carried away with their 'passions' in situations of uncertainty and flux, in the process inciting dogmatism and factional strife in politics. This endangers commercial society, which requires competent, level-headed government and a certain degree of institutional stability for its effective functioning. Institutional stability should be a paramount concern for thought and action in politics. Sound public opinion, based on collective experience, should favour and encourage rule-bound government, for the only kind of government that is stable and predictable is one that follows publicly known and clearly understood general rules. 'Good' opinion inculcated by a sensible collective discussion leads to good government. 'Bad' opinion resulting from faction-ridden politics leads to bad government and rocks the very foundations of commercial society. Hence Hume's assertion that 'it is therefore, on opinion only that government is founded'.[53]

Knight is rather vague on the precise constitutional and governmental structures that are supposed to facilitate a collective discussion. For a continuation and elaboration of this very political side of Knight's work, attention has to be directed to the 'constitutional political economy' of his distinguished student, James Buchanan. The latter's focus is not the 'choice within constraints' normally assumed in orthodox economics, that is, looking at maximising behaviour under given conditions (e.g. given public policy frameworks and political constitutions); rather it is the 'choice between constraints' or 'choice between rules' that engages his attention. Such *constitutional choice* presupposes a cooperative venture on the part of the citizenry to conduct a political discussion on the suitability of existing rules and the possibilities of their modification. Constitutional political economy's end-objective is to change or improve the rules governing the political order, which in turn govern the rules of market exchange.[54]

To conclude this section it is appropriate to mention the late Jan Tumlir, who took his inspiration from Knight and who incorporated the latter's ideas on 'government by discussion' into his own constitutional perspective on international economic order. Tumlir argues that the discussion, as envisaged by Knight and the American Founding Fathers before him, has suffered deterioration since the 1930s. The neglect of constitutional due process on economic policy matters in the democracies of the West has downgraded the role of the legislature and the scrutinising powers of the judiciary, favouring instead executive and administrative discretion. Governance has largely become a matter of informal bargaining between the executive and private interest groups, tantamount to a 'refeudalisation of the economy'. Protectionism in international trade relations is but an outward manifestation of this degeneration of democratic constitutionalism. The most damaging effect of more discretionary economic policy is the curtailing of 'government by discussion' and its corrosive effect on the Rule of Law: policy is conducted away from the public gaze in secretive dealings between privileged actors; less effective deliberation and scrutiny of legislation take place in legislatures; and the courts do not monitor the implementation of legislation by the executive to make sure that due process is followed.[55] Chapter eight concentrates on Tumlir's democratic constitutionalism as applied to the international economic order.

Conclusion

Frank Knight is one of the towering political economists of the twentieth century, and one of the Pleiad who have renewed the classical liberal tradition in modern times. This overview of Knight's political economy has sought to locate him in the stream of thought that finds its source in the great Scotsmen of the eighteenth century, Adam Smith and David Hume. It has argued that Knight's classical liberalism is manifest in his realistic assumptions of actor behaviour in real-life market exchange, his multifaceted and institutionally sensitive treatment of liberalism, subsuming a role for the state well beyond the limited survey of the nightwatchman, and his attention to the evolving morals and traditions that maintain order in society. Lastly, his thoughts on democracy are largely comple-mentary to the classical liberal tradition, if not quite a logical derivation of it, for he qualifies his firm advocacy of democratic constitutionalism (as Tumlir calls it) with a ringing reminder of the limitations of deliberative and intelligent group action and, relatedly, the dangers of assuming and expecting too much of human intelligence. Those at home in the classical political economy tradi-tion will, no doubt, detect Knight's inspiration in his Scottish and English intellectual antecedents, but the political philosopher should also notice more than a passing resemblance in Knight's thought to the scepticism and critical rationalism of Edmund Burke, Alexis de Tocqueville and, more recently, Michael Oakeshott and Bertrand de Jouvenel.

Notes

1 Jacob Viner, whose work crops up in chapter 5, was a colleague of Knight for many years at the University of Chicago, but, unlike Knight, a coterie of students who would carry on the Chicago economics tradition did not form around him. Thus it was Knight, not Viner, who founded the Chicago School. However, Viner shared a general value orientation with Knight and most members of the following gener-ations of the Chicago School: all adhered to the tenets of neoclassical price theory, were strongly in favour of free markets, and were correspondingly sceptical of govern-ment intervention. Nevertheless, there were differences between Viner and most Chicago economists, including Knight, especially in that Viner was more 'pragmatic' in allowing greater scope for government activism, for example in antitrust and counter cyclical policies. One final difference between Knight and Viner is worthy of mention: Knight was almost exclusively a theory man, whereas Viner combined theoretical knowledge with an enduring applied interest and expertise in policy matters. See M.W. Reder, 'Chicago School', in Eatwell et al. (1987a), pp. 40–43; Henry W. Spiegel, 'Jacob Viner', in Eatwell et al. (1987b), p. 814.

2 Hayek explicitly acknowledges Knight's theory of risk in his (Hayek's) landmark article 'Economics and knowledge' in Economica (1937), reprinted in Buchanan and Thirlby (1981), p. 46.

3 For an identification of the main twentieth-century centres of economic liberalism, see Egon Tuchtfeld and Hans Willgerodt, 'Wilhelm Röpke: Leben und Werk', in Röpke (1994 [1965]), pp. 368–369. In the most comprehensive recent restatement of classical liberalism, F.A. Hayek acknowledges his indebtedness to the 'two intel-lectual leaders' of modern liberalism, Knight and von Mises. See Hayek (1960), p. 416.

4 Frank H. Knight, 'Economics', p. 25, 'Social science', p. 127, 'Social causation', p. 145, 'Statics and dynamics', pp. 180, 185, and 'The role of principles in economics', p. 250, all in Knight (1956); Frank H. Knight, 'Ethics and the economic interpretation', p. 36, 'The ethics of competition', pp. 47, 50, and 'Economic theory and nationalism', pp. 282–283, all in Knight (1935); Frank H. Knight, 'Economics and human action', in Hausman (1994), p. 114; Frank H. Knight, 'Economics, political science and education', in Knight (1947), p. 329.

For a similar and concise definition of economics, see Robbins (1935), p. 16. For a critical scrutiny of the accepted assumptions of economic behaviour and organisation, see F.A. Hayek, 'Economics and knowledge' and 'The meaning of competition', both in Hayek (1949).

5 'Economics', in Knight (1956), p. 26; 'Economic theory and nationalism', in Knight (1935), p. 279.

6 'What is truth in economics?' in Knight (1956), p. 157; 'Economic theory and nationalism', in Knight (1935), pp. 336–337. To Knight, this scientism 'without recognition of the intellectual and moral limitations of the project, would appear as the outstanding intellectual event of the age, the supreme catastrophe in the history of freedom, the suicide, or attempt at suicide, of intelligence itself'. See 'Economic theory and nationalism', p. 344. Compare this statement to Hayek's closing remarks in *Law, Legislation and Liberty*:

> An age of superstition is a time when people imagine that they know more than they do. In this sense the twentieth century was certainly an outstanding age of superstition, and the cause of this is an overestimation of what science has achieved – not in the field of comparatively simple phenomena, where it has of course been extraordinarily successful, but in the field of complex phenomena, where the application of the techniques which proved so helpful with essentially simple phenomena has proved to be very misleading.
>
> (Hayek (1982), vol. 3, p. 176)

7 'Fact and value in social science', in Knight (1947), p. 233; 'Ethics and the economic interpretation', in Knight (1935), p. 21; 'What is truth in economics?' in Knight (1956), p. 172.

8 'Economic theory and nationalism', in Knight (1935), p. 347; 'Freedom as fact and criterion', pp. 10, 25, 'The meaning of democracy: its politico-economic structure and ideals', p. 188, both in Knight (1947); 'The role of principles in economics and politics', in Knight (1956), pp. 261, 271, 295.

9 'The planful act', in Knight (1947), p. 341.

10 Ibid., p. 374; 'The ethics of competition', in Knight (1935), pp. 46–47.

11 'Ethics and the economic interpretation', in Knight (1935), pp. 26, 28, 32–33.

12 'What is truth in economics?' pp. 176–177, 'The role of principles in economics and politics', p. 269, both in Knight (1956). Also see Robbins (1981), pp. 1–11. There is much in this, one of Lionel Robbins's last publications, that mirrors the Knightian treatment of the scope and limitations of economics. Like Knight, Robbins is wary of importing natural science wholesale into social science, of wildly unrealistic assumptions of human behaviour, and of quantitative predictions with a scientific label. And in common with Knight, Robbins makes a rigid distinction between value-free economics and the 'oughts' that lie in the realm of political economy. Interpersonal comparisons can only be based on value judgements; they are not 'scientific'. Questions and recommendations of distribution flowing from them, that is, matters of policy, form part of 'political economy' but not 'economics'.

13 'Ethics and the economic interpretation', pp. 36, 40, 'The limitations of scientific method in economics', p. 143, both in Knight (1935).

14 See note 12.

15 Robbins (1952), pp. 16, 171, 174; Terence Hutchison, 'From William Petty to Adam Smith', p. 18, 'A methodological crisis?', p. 244, and 'The uses and abuses of academic economics', p. 289, all in Hutchison (1994).

16 'The ethics of competition', p. 47, and 'Economic theory and nationalism', p. 286, both in Knight (1935).

17 See the chapter 'The market order or catallaxy' in Hayek (1982), vol. 2, p. 107 f.; and refer to note 4 for Hayek (1949).

18 Hayek (1982), vol. 3, pp. 75–76. Ronald Coase confirms this point in his typically succinct manner:

> It is wrong to believe, as is commonly done, that Adam Smith had as his view of man an abstraction, an 'economic man', rationally pursuing his self-interest in a singleminded way. Smith would not have thought it sensible to treat man as a rational utility-maximiser. He thinks of man as he actually is.
>
> (See R.H. Coase, 'Adam Smith's view of man', in Coase (1994), p. 116)

19 Smith (1982 [1759]), Part III, pp. 162–163. Hayek frequently draws the distinction between 'critical rationalists', with scaled-down expectations of human rationality, and 'rational constructivists', with a heroic faith in the rational powers of man. The Scots belong to the former camp and the *philosophes* of the French Enlightenment to the latter. Hayek argues that most social thought in the nineteenth and twentieth centuries, including economics, has followed the track of rational constructivism. See his essay, 'Individualism: true and false', in Hayek (1949). Also see chapter two of this book.

20 Smith (1982 [1759]), Part VI, p. 234.

21 Quoted in F.A. Hayek, 'Dr. Bernard Mandeville', in Hayek (1991), p. 96. Also see Michael Oakeshott's very similar account of the evolution of political ideas in Oakeshott (1993), p. 7.

22 Knight has much to say apropos collectivist doctrines, including Marxism and the socialist planning experiments of the twentieth century. This discussion will not address this side of his work. However, the following quotation merits reproduction and is indicative of his implacable attitude to Marxists:

> they are morally earnest, even to a fault – in fact, to a degree which makes it a serious ethical problem whether moral earnestness can be assumed to be a virtue at all. For in a plain factual appraisal, what they are doing is more catastrophically evil than treason, or the poisoning of wells, or other acts commonly placed at the head of the list of crimes. The moralisation of destruction, and of combat with a view to destruction, goes with the kind of hero-worship that merges into devil-worship. Such phenomena show that human nature has potentialities that are horrible, in full match for all those that are noble and fine.
>
> See 'Ethics and economic reform', in Knight (1947), pp. 98–99.

'Do-gooding' Christian socialists are also on the receiving end of his biting polemic:

> and the kind of legislation which results from the clamour of idealistic preachers . . . is especially bad. All this is the natural consequence of exhortation without knowledge and understanding – of well-meaning people

attempting to meddle with the workings of extremely complicated and sensitive machinery which they do not understand.

(See Frank H. Knight 'Ethics and economic reform', in Knight (1935) p. 123)

23 'Economic theory and nationalism', in Knight (1935), pp. 293–294, 305, 326; 'Freedom as fact and criterion', p. 40, and 'The planful act', p. 368, both in Knight (1947); 'The role of principles in economics and politics', in Knight (1956), pp. 252–253; Knight (1960), pp. 47–48.

24 'Economics', p. 9, and 'The role of principles in economics and politics', pp. 263, 267, both in Knight (1956).

25 This is a point most effectively developed by Bertrand de Jouvenel. Collective agreement on goals is the chief trait of small, primitive societies, 'but . . . any attempt to graft the same features on a large society is utopian and leads to tyranny'. See de Jouvenel (1957), p. 136.

26 The emphasis on cooperation or 'mutual service' is found in Edwin Cannan, 'Adam Smith as economist: the gospel of mutual service', in Cannan (1927), p. 429.

27 Knight (1960), pp. 87, 95; 'The role of principles in economics and politics', in Knight (1956), p. 259; 'The meaning of democracy: its structure and ideals', in Knight (1947), pp. 193, 199–200. Also see Hume (1978 [1740]), Book III, Part II, chs I–VI. A favourable treatment of Hume's utilitarian doctrine is found in Robbins (1952), pp. 49–55, 176–181, 187.

28 'Freedom as fact and criterion', in Knight (1947), p. 2.

29 'Economic theory and nationalism', in Knight (1935), p. 289; 'Ethics and economic reform', p. 52, 'The meaning of democracy', p. 193, both in Knight (1947); 'Free society: its basic nature and problem', in Knight (1956), p. 289. On Smith's three functions of government, see Smith (1976 [1776]), Book IV, ch. IX, pp. 208–209.

30 'The meaning of democracy', in Knight (1947), p. 202; 'Economics', pp. 17, 32, and 'The role of principles in economics and politics', p. 267, both in Knight (1956).

31 In fact, like David Hume, he dismisses notions of an original social contract between rational, deliberative men as arrant nonsense. See Knight, 'Economic objectives in a changing world', in Smithies et al. (1955), p. 62. Also refer to David Hume's essay, 'Of the original contract', in Hume (1994 [1752]).

32 'Economic theory and nationalism', in Knight (1935), pp. 310, 332; Frank H. Knight, 'Economic objectives in a changing world', in Smithies et al. (1955), p. 51; 'Free society: its basic nature and problem', in Knight (1956), p. 293; 'Meaning of democracy: its structure and ideals', in Knight (1947), p. 199.

33 I use the term 'conservative' here in a broad, impressionistic sense, not in any way exclusive to those who have a rigid adherence to the status quo. In contrast, Hayek defines conservatism more narrowly in the latter sense. See his chapter 'Why I am not a conservative' in Hayek (1960), p. 397 f.

34 Knight, 'Economic objectives in a changing world', in Smithies et al. (1955), pp. 276–277; 'Social science and the political trend', p. 25, and 'Ethics and economic reform', pp. 74, 120–121, both in Knight (1947); Knight (1960), pp. 14, 34–35, 117, 139.

35 On the classical presumption against government interference, see F.A. Hayek, 'The trend of economic thinking', in Hayek (1991), pp. 17–34. For those few interested in the rich history of economics at the LSE, it might be worth recalling that this was Hayek's inaugural lecture at the School in 1931.

36 John Gray was one of the few who was keenly aware of the chasms that divide much of modern liberalism from classical liberalism. See 'After liberalism' in Gray (1989), pp. 261, 262.

37 See note 27 and the essays 'Of the first principles of government' and 'Idea of a perfect commonwealth', both in Hume (1994 [1752]).

38 Hayek (1988), p. 69. The following Burkean statements by Hayek correspond perfectly to the sentiments of Smith and Hume:

> There probably never has existed a genuine belief in freedom, and there certainly has been no successful attempt to operate a free society, without a genuine reverence for grown institutions, for customs and habits. ... Paradoxical as it may appear, it is probably true that a successful free society will always in large measure be a tradition-bound society.
>
> (Hayek (1960), p. 61)

Further: 'Virtually all the benefits of civilisation, and indeed our very existence, rest, I believe, on our continued willingness to shoulder the burden of tradition'. Hayek (1988), p. 63.

39 Smith (1982 [1759]), Part VI, p. 233.
40 Robbins (1952), p. 194 f.
41 Much of political science, and political science-based political economy, overlook the conceptual distinction between economic and political power, collapsing them into a unified form of power that appears to be more 'political' than 'economic'.
42 Knight, 'Economic objectives in a changing world', in Smithies *et al.* (1955), p. 57; 'Economic theory and nationalism', in Knight (1935), pp. 295–298; Knight (1960), pp. 113, 162–163, 166.
43 Knight, 'Economic objectives in a changing world', in Smithies *et al.* (1955), p. 75.
44 Becker (1976), p. 5; Stigler (1968), pp. 181–182. Ronald Coase, another distinguished economist from Chicago (and earlier the LSE), is more in the Knightian and classical tradition. He has little time for the strict application of *homo oeconomicus* to the operation of political and economic institutions. See the selection of essays in Coase (1994) and Posner (1993), pp. 196–209.
45 Knight (1960), pp. 118, 131; 'The sickness of liberal society', in Knight (1947), p. 391.
46 See Oakeshott (1993), p. 8 f.
47 'Economic theory and nationalism', in Knight (1935), pp. 342–343.
48 Knight (1960), pp. 124–125; also see Tumlir (1980), p. 178.
49 See note 25; also 'Meaning of democracy', in Knight (1947), p. 191.
50 Ibid., p. 197.
51 'Economics, political science and education', in Knight (1947), p. 333; 'Economic theory and nationalism', in Knight (1935), pp. 350, 352–353.
52 Knight (1960), pp. 145–146, 172.
53 David Hume, 'Of the first principles of government', p. 16, and Knud Haakonssen, 'Introduction', pp. xxvii–xxviii, both in Hume (1994 [1752]).
54 Buchanan (1990), pp. 1–18.
55 Tumlir (1983a), p. 79; Tumlir (1985a), pp. 16, 42, 48, 71; Tumlir (1984).

5

JACOB VINER AS HISTORIAN OF IDEAS AND INTERNATIONAL POLITICAL ECONOMIST IN THE CLASSICAL LIBERAL TRADITION

But I do not fear much contradiction if I describe Jack Viner as being in this age the outstanding all-rounder in our profession. He has made important contributions to theoretical analysis. He has written works which are classics of their kind on applied economics and the theory of policy, especially in regard to international economic relations. In the history of thought, he is surely hors concours: *there are others with achievements of like quality, but none with his range and scope.*

Lord Robbins

Historians of economic thought and some of the more historically minded international economists know of Jacob Viner's work, but he remains largely unknown to most students of international political economy, with the singular exception of his widely acclaimed essay on mercantilist thought, *Power Versus Plenty as Objectives of Foreign Policy in the Seventeenth and Eighteenth Centuries*. This chapter seeks to survey, and interpret, some of the many facets of Viner's life-work that are of central importance to international political economy.

The introduction to the book made the point that international political economy, like many compartments of study, is manifestly not *au fait* with its own *tradition*, that is to say, the history of its diverse strands of thought. This particularly applies to the liberal tradition. There can be no better way of rectifying this weakness than by recourse to Viner, perhaps the leading twentieth-century authority on the classical liberal tradition and its approach to political economy and economic policy, especially in international economic relations (as Lord Robbins opines in the quotation at the head of this discussion). Further, an improved grasp of the history of classical liberalism, through Viner's lenses, is not only or merely worthwhile as a scholarly indulgence in the ideas of sages long dead-and-buried; it is also of use, in the negative sense, in countering the many jejune remarks, the glaring misapprehensions, of what classical liberalism stood for; and it is essential, in the positive sense, in intimating what classical liberalism (as opposed to other versions of liberalism) has to say on questions of *modern* theory and policy in international political economy. Hence the two objectives of this discussion: first, to scrutinise Viner's treatment of the history of classical political economy; and second, to present Viner, the twentieth-century political economist, as someone who, in modern times, has substantially renewed the tradition of Adam Smith and David Hume with respect to both theory and policy, *particularly* in international political economy.

The first section deals with Viner's history of thought, with special regard to classical liberalism. The following section looks at his general orientation on questions of contemporary theory and policy, highly influenced by his scholarship as an intellectual historian. The last section views his work on modern international (political) economic theory and policy, again infused with his rich fund of insights into the classical liberal tradition. The focus throughout is on Jacob Viner's 'political economy' in the classical liberal context, with correspondingly less emphasis on his more technical 'economic' analysis.

The history of classical liberal thought

The centrality of Viner's intellectual history is his unrivalled appreciation of Adam Smith's political economy, and his broad-ranging perspective on the English classical economists of the nineteenth century, particularly their theories of international trade. In these, as in other respects, Viner intricately weaves economic ideas into a tapestry of intellectual and institutional context. He relates the 'technicality', the mechanisms, of economic analysis to wider intellectual currents, political, philosophical and psychological, and to their 'fit' with political and legal institutions. This is political economy in the mode of Adam Smith; it has an eminently 'Smithian' methodology. In contrast, the other great historian of economic thought in the twentieth century, Joseph Schumpeter, adopts a more 'Ricardian' methodology: he regards economic analysis as a technical device within a bounded space, strictly divorcing it from noneconomic intellectual cross-currents as well as entanglements with institutional analysis in other social sciences.[1]

Viner is as sensitive to the genesis of liberalism and *laissez faire* pre-Adam Smith as he is to the great Scotsman and his classical followers.[2] Smith himself was more influenced by social philosophy, through Shaftesbury, Cumberland, his own teacher Frances Hutcheson, and not least Mandeville, with his notions of the beneficial operation of self-interested activity, than he was by antecedent economic thought.[3] In light of the marvellous eclecticism and intellectual ancestry of his work, it would be wrong to view Smith as the founder of political economy. Rather, Viner locates Smith's originality, his genius, in the elaboration, for the first time, of a *system* of mutually interdependent economic relations based on the concept of a unified natural order that, if left to its own devices, would produce results beneficial to mankind. Thus, Smith detected an underlying order beneath the surface chaos of the economic process.[4]

It is a common fault of the political economist to separate *The Wealth of Nations* from the rest of the Smithian *oeuvre*, notably the *Theory of Moral Sentiments*, assuming a contradiction between the 'sympathy principle' in the *Theory of Moral Sentiments* – man's fellow-feeling for those around him – and the self-interested activity around which *The Wealth of Nations* revolves. While acknowledging some discrepancies between the two books, Viner, especially in his later work, rejects this assumption of a basic inconsistency. To Viner, Smith alternates between 'partial models' applicable to different compartments of human action. Sentiments of benevolence and sympathy motivate nonmarket relations in proximate communities (the family, church, profession, village, etc.), but they do not apply in impersonal relations of market exchange, for these take place between strangers in vast and expansive areas. Market exchange is the sphere of *The Wealth of Nations*, in which self-interest is the more realistic expectation. As 'social distance' increases, that is, as relations become more impersonal, feelings normally reserved for family, friends, neighbours and colleagues are correspondingly attenuated.[5] As Ronald Coase most appropriately observes in a gem of an essay on Adam Smith, self-interest, not sympathy or benevolence, has to be the motivating force in a complex society (what Adam Smith calls the Great Society) with necessarily impersonal relations in an extensive division of labour.[6]

Moreover, there are themes common to both *The Wealth of Nations* and *The Theory of Moral Sentiments*. In market and nonmarket spheres, social order, not chaos or anarchy, emerges spontaneously and without detailed government intervention, although it is dependent on the enforcement of 'justice', that is, a legal framework. Apropos justice, the system outlined in *The Theory of Moral Sentiments* is key to an understanding of *The Wealth of Nations*. Smith emphasises the procedural and 'negative' functions of justice in protecting individual freedoms while maintaining order. He rejects more encompassing notions of justice (nowadays travelling under the labels of distributive or social justice) that enjoin government to play a more extensive role in the economic activity of society.[7]

The misconceptions about the link between Smith's moral philosophy and his political economy pale in comparison to those that concern his political economy in *The Wealth of Nations*, not least in the discipline of international political economy. Commentators assume, more often than not, that *homo oeconomicus* is the lifeblood of economic liberalism, including its classical incarnation. According to this version, free markets depend on the following: rational utility-maximising actors with a given and stable ordering of preferences; perfect knowledge of relevant facts in order to make optimising choices between given, competing alternatives; costless and instantaneous exchange; and market-clearing equilibrium outcomes that are predictable and controllable. The whole apparatus outlined here is rather ahistorical and mechanistic. An additional assumption is that there is a long-run harmony of interests between the self-serving actions of actors in a competitive market and the public good. Lastly, this supposedly classical liberal scheme has the economic order operating under its own laws, autonomous of the legal and sociopolitical framework, which is treated as exogenous to economic activity. In sum, economic liberalism, beginning with the classical liberal tradition, has the appearance of a programme of *laissez faire* bounded only by a 'nightwatchman' state. This interpretation of economic liberalism, Adam Smith included, is common to most, if not all, prominent international relations theorists, from E.H. Carr and Karl Polanyi to Robert Gilpin and Robert Keohane.[8]

E.H. Carr, whose knowledge of economics appears to have been at best rudimentary, typified this view of classical liberalism: 'It was the *laissez faire* school of political economy created by Adam Smith which was in the main responsible for popularising the doctrine of the harmony of interests. The purpose of this school was to promote the removal of state control in economic matters'. And he went on to say: 'But Marx believed, just as firmly as did the *laissez faire* liberal, in an economic system with laws of its own working independently of the state'.[9] It is a pity that others – the Gentlemen Amateurs of international relations – have largely followed Carr's precedent, leading them to expatiate on matters political-economic without requisite knowledge of the subject. They should take careful note of what Lionel Robbins has to say about bastardisers of the classical canon:

> Popular writing in this connexion is far below the zero of knowledge or common decency. On this plane, not only is any real knowledge of the classical writers nonexistent but, further, their place has been taken by a set of mythological figures, passing by the same names, but not infrequently invested with attitudes almost the exact reverse of those which the originals adopted.[10]

Lord Robbins certainly contributes to setting the record straight on the subject of the classical economists, but it is also to Viner that we must turn to counter the egregious stereotyping of Adam Smith by those, one suspects, who have, at the very best, only a passing acquaintance with *The Wealth of Nations*.

First, Viner makes it crystal clear that *The Wealth of Nations* does not propound a harmony of interests doctrine by which a self-regulating Invisible Hand automatically reconciles individual and general interests. On the contrary, Smith points to the defects of a totally unregulated order and the existence of a partial, highly imperfect harmony between individual and general interests. He presents a catalogue of conflicts of interest between groups, and between certain groups and the general interest, for example, conflicts between agricultural, labouring and merchant interests, and especially between self-serving merchants and the public good.[11]

Given such considerations, Smith's case for individual liberty does not rely on a natural harmony of interests; rather on the existence of an appropriate, mediating institutional framework, and above all a legal framework of general rules, which can overcome intergroup conflicts and reconcile individual with general interests. The self-interested activity of individuals in market exchange does bring forth an order of beneficial cooperation or mutual service. This order arises spontaneously, that is to say, it is an unplanned by-product of human action, symbolised by a (metaphorical) Invisible Hand 'to promote an end which was no part of his intention'.[12] But these forces do not exist *in vacuo*; they are circumscribed and guided by the law, *inter alia*. In short, this is a programme of 'liberty under the law', not the anarchy or license of unbounded *laissez faire*.[13]

Viner proceeds to underline the superlative institutional analysis in the *The Wealth of Nations* – much of it firmly grounded in inferences from detailed observation – that searches for an appropriate institutional framework to facilitate the efficient coordination of economic activities. At the heart of such a framework is Smith's 'obvious and simple system of natural liberty', allowing individuals to pursue 'their own interests their own way' under the law and unhampered by pre-existing systems of (mercantilist) government intervention.[14]

However, to reiterate, this 'natural liberty' is in the form of a *qualified*, not an absolutist, *laissez faire*, operating within the law and presupposing an important role for the state. This brings Viner to another major point: the classical system in Smith's work has no truck with a minimalist or nightwatchman state. The complexity and range of public office in Smith's three functions of government go well beyond the restricted survey of the nightwatchman, as previous chapters highlighted.

No wonder then that the leading classical economists *en masse*, from Ricardo and Malthus to McCulloch, Torrens, John Stuart Mill, Senior and Cairnes, and later Jevons, Marshall and Edgeworth, sharply dissociated themselves from the extreme *laissez faire* advocated with theological fervour by the Manchester School and others, such as Bastiat in France, none of whom were trained economists.[15]

The above points, expounded with force and verve by Viner (and others with a knowledge of the relevant literature, such as Frank Knight, Lord Robbins and F.A. Hayek), surely rule out of court the accusations of a harmony of interests, extreme *laissez faire*, the minimalist state and the exogenous treatment of sociopolitical and legal institutions, levelled against Smith and his followers. But that is not the end of it; there are additional points that merit consideration.

The case for economic liberty in Smith and classical political economy does not rely on purely abstract speculation in the form of a metaphysical natural rights doctrine, as is the case with the Manchester tradition. On the contrary, very much in keeping with the tenor of the Scottish Enlightenment, the classical economists advocate economic liberty on the empirical and policy grounds of *utility*, with the aim of promoting social efficiency and progress. *Individual choice* is the basis of such utility, in the belief that even fallible individuals are better at making their own decisions than having decisions made for them by stupid and incompetent governments. There is in fact a strong vein of policy relevance in the classical liberal scheme, relating the theoretical system developed to concrete, practical questions of public policy. In the final analysis, Viner argues that Smith draws the line between the legitimate and illegitimate activities of government, that is to say, those that accord with the natural order and those that do not, based on empirical data, not metaphysics.[16]

Viner further contends that Smith, in keeping with a political economy model tailored to complex reality, does not mechanically conceive a theoretical maximum of welfare engineered by a perfect market; rather, he believes that a higher level of economic welfare would materialise under conditions of qualified *laissez faire* than would be the case if government, inefficient, ignorant and profligate, tried to direct economic activity.[17] This is vintage Scottish political economy, engaging in a concrete institutional comparison between the working properties of viable alternative systems, not the neoclassical method of comparing real-life situations to a fictional state of perfectly competitive equilibrium.[18] Adam Smith (and David Hume) is (are) dealing with the deep and wide psychological motivations of real people in complex, real-life conditions, not with *homo oeconomicus* in a perfect market.[19]

Intermezzo: economic method and economic policy

Viner's deep and extensive analysis of, and evident sympathy for, the classical liberal system informs his own approach to economic method and economic policy in modern times. He constantly emphasises the cardinal importance of keeping theoretical models relatively flexible and elastic with realistic assumptions of actor behaviour and market process, in order to firmly maintain the relevance of theory to policy. Hence it is not surprising to find him wary of the tendency to greater logical and mathematical abstraction in economics that, in an increasingly complex world, removes theory from the coal-face to the distant horizons of policy. Like Alfred Marshall, he argues that the mathematical method can only handle most significant variables with simple, stable interrelationships between them, and with fixed and stable parameters; whereas reality consists of a great number of significant variables with a great number of varying, complex interrelationships, and without fixed and stable parameters. With respect to modern welfare analysis, he cannot be more to the point:

> The idea, for instance, of being able to determine the optimal level of a tariff by a relatively simple geometry on the face invites the type of incredulity that, in another context, led Coleridge to ask: 'What should we think of one who said that his love of his wife was North-West-by-West of his passion for roast beef?'.[20]

One criticism Viner makes of Keynesian and neoKeynesian economics is precisely that they rely on unrealistic and often fantastic assumptions of economic organisation. However, there is a deeper divide between, on the one hand, Viner's defence of the 'old economics' and, on the other hand, the rise of the 'new economics' in the wake of Lord Keynes's *General Theory*. The classical system takes the 'long view' of theory and policy – the classical economists from Smith to Mill, and indeed neoclassical economists after them, devoted relatively little attention to short-run considerations (with the notable exception of Malthus). In contrast, Keynesian/neoKeynesian economics, in response to the Depression, concentrated on the 'short view', which has always been the preoccupation of governments and the lay public. To Viner, 'the short view and the long' (to borrow the title of one of his famous essays) are not opposing alternatives, as they should properly deal with different time-periods and different problem-sets of policy. The 'new economics', however, makes precisely this mistake, abandoning the traditional doctrines and *replacing* the 'short view' for the 'long view'. Thus, recommendations for government activism are not confined to short-run extreme and unique situations of depression, but are intended to apply generally and in the long run, in the process ditching the classical presumption in favour of free enterprise and against government activism. Here lie the main parallels between old-style mercantilism and Keynesianism – 'old poison in new bottles', according to Viner.[21]

In the above respects Viner is in substantial agreement with other classically inspired *confrères*, but there are one or two areas that bring out differences between Viner and classical political economists of the Hayekian variety, and, in particular, Hayek himself. These divergences are not unimportant, for Hayek is (at least in the humble opinion of this author) the leading exponent of classical liberal political economy in recent generations. Furthermore, the areas of incompatibility between Viner and Hayek shed some light on Viner's occasionally activist stances on international economic policy (dealt with in the following section).

First, Hayek's political economy centres in the 'knowledge problem' – the 'constitutional ignorance' of actors engaging in economic (and political) activity that renders them incapable of behaving in a fully rational manner. However, this hardly figures at all in Viner's work. In the Hayekian scheme, knowledge of relevant facts in complex social orders is highly fragmented and dispersed among millions of actors; no one has sufficient knowledge of the present to choose rationally between competing means to attain set goals; and everyone is ignorant of the future. Nevertheless, the 'spontaneous order' of the market economy emerges imperceptibly from the decentralised coordination of existing (fragmented and partial) knowledge, and the discovery of new knowledge, in myriad relations of exchange.

The rules of general conduct embodied in the legal framework enable the spontaneous order of market exchange to survive and flourish. On the other hand, that very order suffers from the rampant use of specific government interventions that go beyond the framework of general rules and eat into the individual's freedom to 'use his own knowledge for his own purposes'. Governments may assume or pretend that they have relevant knowledge at their fingertips to plan or design, and subsequently execute, interventionist policies. The fact is, however, that they cannot possibly have access to or marshal such an enormous critical mass of fragmented knowledge in complex social orders.

In the final analysis, the 'extended order' of market society can only emerge from the spontaneous and decentralised coordination of knowledge that lies at the heart of the competitive process. The centralised coordination of knowledge by an outside agency of control (read government) is infinitely inferior and doomed to failure. Hayek uses these insights to argue the case for individual liberty under the Rule of Law, with a presumption against *ad hoc* government interference that distorts and weakens a framework of general rules.[22]

Viner almost completely overlooks the knowledge problem, which perhaps partially accounts for his guarded optimism in governments knowing better than the individual what he wants and how to satisfy his wants in limited and defined sets of circumstances. (This Hayek would regard as a 'pretence of knowledge'.) This goes some way to explain Viner's pragmatic policy activism in certain areas, especially antitrust policy. Overall, Viner, unlike Hayek, is reticent to commit himself to 'universal principles' as a hard-and-fast guide to policy action. He prefers 'information' and 'wisdom' to make 'reasonable' decisions in particular cases, compatible with wide acceptance in democratic society.[23]

Here Viner, like Robbins, fits into a pragmatic Anglo-Saxon mould, not exactly comfortable with the constitutionalism of Hayek. From the latter standpoint, one could venture that the vague and catch-all benchmarks for policy applied by Viner, bereft of 'universal principles', are but open invitations to creeping and then spiralling government interventions in democratic societies.

International political economy: theory and policy

In his day, Viner was one of the leading international economic theorists and policy analysts. His main book in the field is *Studies in the Theory of International Trade* (1937), still the leading reference text on mercantilist and classical theories of international trade and payments. *The Customs Union Issue* (1950) is *the* pioneering analytical study on the political economy of regional trading arrangements in the world economy. *International Economics* (1951) is a collection of his papers on international economic theory and policy over a period of more than twenty years. Finally, *International Trade and Economic Development* (1953), resulting from a series of lectures delivered in Brazil, provides a useful overview of his approach to international economics, with chapters related to development policy, an area otherwise not covered in great detail in his work.[24]

There are several distinctive features of Viner's international economics, all of which relate to the preceding two sections of this discussion: first, the firm commitment to the classical theory of international trade; second, the expert and deft use of the history of classical economics to inform Viner's own approach to trade and payments issues; third, the constant emphasis on the necessity of relating international economic theory to practical policy; fourth, the embedding of international economic analysis in a wider framework of sociopolitical institutional relevance and intellectual discourse, following the Smithian methodology alluded to earlier.

The classical theory and policy of international trade

The magisterial *Studies in the Theory of International Trade* epitomises Viner's effective combination of all four factors mentioned above. However, there is one noticeable omission in Viner's analysis: he does not delve into the dynamic gains from trade, and their institutional underpinning, which are of first-order importance to Smith and Hume, if not to the nineteenth-century English economists (as indicated in chapter three); rather, he concentrates on the static, allocative efficiency gains that run through the classical tradition from beginning to end.

Viner traces the beginnings of classical trade theory to, first, the explanation of an automatic, self-regulating mechanism in the balance of payments and the international flow of specie, and second, the doctrine of comparative costs, holding that, under free trade, each country would specialise in the production and export of commodities in which it had a comparative real cost advantage. David Hume and David Ricardo respectively were first to clearly and synthetically outline these two core elements of trade theory. They drew on scattered and partial previous treatments (on which Viner's historical research is astounding in its breadth and depth), and prepared the ground for future elaboration by Torrens, James Mill, McCulloch, Senior, John Stuart Mill, Marshall, Edgeworth, Taussig and others.[25]

A fixture of both classical and neoclassical trade theory has been the essential argument that the gains from trade, that is, a better allocation of national and world resources, arise from specialisation according to comparative costs. What has changed is the definition of comparative costs. Viner is superb at exposing the transition from a 'real cost' definition, adhered to from Ricardo through to Taussig and Viner himself, to the neoclassical attention to factor proportions and prices, pioneered by the work of Hecksher and his student Ohlin, and the Austrian focus on alternative or opportunity costs, introduced to trade theory by Haberler. Viner, while sticking to the classical real-cost principle, argues that the insights of Hecksher, Ohlin and Haberler supplement rather than contradict the main body of classical trade theory (whereas Ohlin and Haberler present their theories as a refutation and replacement of comparative real costs). To Viner, the main weakness of accumulated trade theory (at the time of writing in 1937) is its inattention to factor (labour and capital) mobility across borders.[26]

Above all, Viner underlines the generality of analysis in classical trade theory, taking into account a range of significant variables in macro- and microeconomic functions simultaneously. He also lauds its effort to be relevant to policy realities. He finds fault with neoKeynesian as well as some neoclassical trade theories because of their unrealistic assumptions and excessive abstraction, serving as a poor or misleading guide to policy. NeoKeynesian analysis abstracts from money and banking policies and price elasticities (which are central to classical theory), essentially relying on income elasticities. Its anti-free trade policy recommendations, such as quantitative controls on exports, imports and foreign exchange, serve the function of protecting domestic interventionist and inflationary policies by engineering a rather artificial equilibrium in the balance of payments. Viner also reproaches Ohlin's neoclassical theory for assuming that factors are homogeneous or identical in quality between industries and regions. The classical economists, in contrast, recognise the heterogeneity in the quality or 'effectiveness' of factors, especially labour, due to national and regional variations in health, education, management skills and other matters – all at least in part a product of public policies.[27]

Viner also dwells on the theoretical and policy arguments pro and contra free trade, typically drawing on the rich nineteenth-century discussion. His arguments are of great relevance to current debates on the matter in international political economy. The recent and continuing exchanges between neoclassical free traders and votaries of the New Trade Theory (or 'strategic trade policy') would gain much from the not-too-dissimilar debates in the nineteenth century so lucidly analysed by Viner.

Viner comments that there has always been 'a protectionist skeleton in the free trade closet': the classical economists made a powerful case for free trade while clearly recognising some sound theoretical arguments for protection. All the classical economists began their analyses with a theoretical statement on the static and dynamic gains that issued from unimpeded cross-border trade. Nevertheless, their clinching argument against the imposition of trade barriers relied primarily on the 'political economy' of empirical and policy observations.

The terms of trade/optimal tariff controversy is a suitable illustration of the range of political-economic arguments deployed by the classical economists in defence of free trade. *A priori*, the imposition or increase of a tariff can shift a country's (commodity) terms of trade (the ratio of export to import prices) to national advantage if the country's exports have market power in influencing international demand. The result is that the country gains a monopoly profit at the expense of the outside world. Correspondingly, a unilateral reduction or removal of a tariff can worsen a country's terms of trade and, ultimately, reduce national welfare. From the 1830s, Robert Torrens used this theoretical realisation to make a clear-cut policy argument in favour of British reciprocity, not unilateral free trade: Britain should not unilaterally reduce or remove tariff barriers; rather it should negotiate tariff reductions on the basis of like concessions by other countries; and it should retaliate against the imposition of tariffs by other countries.

Some of the other leading classical economists, and especially John Stuart Mill, gradually came round to accepting Torrens's theoretical premises, but on the whole vehemently disagreed with his policy conclusions. They came to recognise that the terms of trade argument was the most powerful theoretical exception to the established presumption in favour of free trade, but provided plenty of counterarguments that tilted the balance back in the direction of free trade. More specifically, they continued to recommend *unilateral* free trade, that is, the reduction or removal of trade barriers even if others continue with protection.

First, the argument for unilateral protection (the imposition or increase of a trade barrier) collapses if there is aggressive retaliation, or the gradual imitation of protectionist policies, by other countries. The result is either no change in the terms of trade or, more likely, an all-round loss compared to the benefits of a free trade policy. Second, once a trade barrier is imposed, it is very difficult to get rid of as it invariably serves the interest of particular import-competing producers. Third, the imposition and administration of a trade barrier is rarely likely to be efficient (on terms of trade, infant industry, increasing returns, macroeconomic or other grounds); rather policy-makers are likely to impose and administer it in an arbitrary and promiscuous fashion to cater to particular interest groups. Fourth, the improved terms of trade from protection should be measured against the welfare loss, that is, the uneconomic allocation of domestic resources, which results from the trade barrier. Free trade engenders a better allocation of national resources with cheaper imports replacing comparatively costly domestic production, releasing domestic resources for more productive uses. The trade barrier (or its increase) nullifies that gain. Thus Viner opines, on policy grounds, 'that these conclusions are sufficiently restrictive in combination to guarantee, I am convinced, that the scope for nationally profitable long-run protection is, in practice, very narrowly limited'.[28]

All the above points are very germane to current discussions on trade theory and policy. One could press home the argument that, in spite of an accumulation of theoretical cases for protection, and in spite of recent developments in the industrial organisation-based New Trade Theory, there are still powerful reasons to favour free trade *on political economy and policy grounds*. A protectionist policy will always suffer heavily from the threat of retaliation, the likelihood of trade policy capture by import-competing producers, the incompetence of, and lack of sufficient information available to, governments (to carry out an effective policy of protection), and the distortion of domestic resource allocation that results from trade barriers. Indeed, though Paul Krugman, from the strategic trade policy camp, disagrees with established neoclassical trade theorists like Gottfried Haberler and Jagdish Bhagwati on some theoretical issues, he agrees with them that political economy and policy arguments favour free trade, not protection.[29]

This is exactly the point made by Viner and the nineteenth-century classical economists before him. It is highly unfortunate that the esotericism of extremely formal and abstract modern trade theory, on both sides of the argument, leads theorists and policy-makers to either blithely ignore the policy and institutional realities, or make very misleading inferences from theory to policy application. One cannot reproach Viner on this score.

On a related point, many insights of modern public choice theory on imperfect 'political markets', as applied to international trade policy, mirror Viner's conclusions. Discretionary and protectionist trade policies, however well designed by policy-makers, are beset by 'government failure' and the 'rent-seeking' activity of organised producer interests. This not only stymies enterprise, innovation and growth within national economies, but also fuels the flames of conflict in relations between states.[30]

Viner on international relations

Viner has distinctly 'political' views on interstate relations, incorporating a judicious mixture of economic liberalism and political realism, which should be of interest to the international relations scholar.

First, he dismisses as juvenile the Marxist-Leninist and Hobsonian theses that business interests create friction in interstate relations. To him, the empirical record suggests the very reverse: bankers and industrialists have by and large exercised a pacific influence on governments, for they have a direct interest in stable, not conflictual, interstate relations; it is governments who have been bellicose, frequently putting pressure on business interests to come into line with their (governments') political, not economic, objectives. Hence the use of private financial negotiations by continental governments in the nineteenth century to pursue political and military objectives in the balance of power diplomacy of the time.[31]

This is Viner in his realist incarnation, emphasising the primacy of politics in international relations. But this is his appreciation of what existed in his day and age; it is not his personal preference. As a liberal, he regards interference by governments in international economic relations as extremely damaging and inherently more conflictual than exchanges between private agents across borders. The supercession of the *jure gestiones* of the nineteenth century by the twentieth century *jure imperii* of international politics injected a poisonous dose of instability, ill-feeling, uncertainty and friction into international affairs. Arbitrary diplomacy, political and economic reprisals, the imposition of quotas and exchange controls, and the use of force, took over from unconditional Most Favoured Nation status, the equality of treatment of foreigners in national commercial law, and the *lex mercatoria* of international commerce. Viner believes that the rise of blanket government intervention in the twentieth century, inevitably spilling over into foreign economic policy, has an enormously high political, as well as economic, price.[32]

International economic policy post-1945

Viner's writings on postwar international economic relations (from the mid-1940s to the early 1950s) are characterised by a curious and not wholly consistent combination of economic liberalism and policy activism, and of savvy realism and unrealistic optimism.

A large measure of pessimism pervades this side of his work. He is not overly optimistic about the prospects for an enlightened US leadership role in the world economy. This role suited Britain well in the nineteenth century, and it performed its duties excellently. However, the highly suspect record of US foreign economic policy over a century-and-a-half, especially in its predilection for conditional Most Favoured Nation (MFN) status and reciprocity (as opposed to British unilateral free trade and unconditional MFN in the nineteenth century), did not augur well for the future. Further, Viner is on the whole realistic on the subject of intergovernmental collaboration, deriding the naïveté of those who put so much faith in the United Nations and 'world government', and making the odd reference to 'the futility of textual exercises' and 'the happiness of wishful thinkers'.[33]

Viner's basic economic liberalism also comes to the fore. He wishes to see a relatively speedy transition from the sorry and bleak circumstances of 1945 – planned economies, distorted prices, wages, money costs and exchange rates – to a situation in which international economic cooperation is, at bottom, brought about spontaneously by letting people produce and buy each others' goods and services freely at competitive prices. Of course, this scheme presupposes a policy switch from arbitrary and heavy-handed regulation to the removal of trade barriers and capital controls.[34]

Nevertheless, Viner's pronouncements on the concrete policy measures of the day accord only partially with his political realism and economic liberalism. While not quite going to the silly and Utopian extremes of Lord Robbins in advocating world government,[35] Viner supports a major role for intergovernmental agreements and international organisations in the postwar order. He sees no prospect of a return to pre-1914 conditions, given widespread government intervention in domestic and foreign economic affairs in the pursuit of 'full employment' and other 'social' goals. Therefore, reciprocal international agreement is the only way forward to gradually bring about freer trade and capital mobility. In this vein, he broadly approves of the Keynes and White Plans, the resulting Bretton Woods agreements on payments and development, and the Havana Charter on the establishment of an International Trade Organisation. He does seem to put considerable faith in discretionary powers given to international organisations (to manage exchange rates, a multilateral clearing system, supervise countries' disturbances of international equilibrium, provide international liquidity, channel funds to developing countries and manage international trading relations). In his most glaring and inexcusable deviation from the classical liberal path, he even goes to the extreme of proposing an international organisation to take charge of countercyclical lending. The major redeeming feature of his views on the international economic policies of the time is his implacable opposition to the continuation of capital controls as found, for example, in the 'scarce currency' clause of the International Monetary Fund (IMF) agreement. This he sees as preventing the restoration of private international capital flows and giving the green light to the use by governments of highly damaging protectionist instruments, particularly exchange controls.[36]

Viner's policy activism and optimistic belief in the efficacy of international organisations do not sit at all comfortably with the classical liberal tradition. As Viner is well aware, the classical economists, from Smith down to Marshall, made their case for free trade in terms of national, especially British,

unilateralism, and they were not in the least keen on the reciprotarian management of the world economy by means of intergovernmental negotiations and
agreements. In response to the Depression and the Second World War, many
economic liberals, including Viner, Hayek and Robbins, departed from the
classical liberal track and turned their attention to 'reciprotarian' thinking.
Unfortunately, they overlooked the pitfalls of a heavy emphasis on intergovernmental collaboration and international organisations. They were not particularly
attentive to the potential for bureaucratic expansion and the risk of makeshift
political compromises that legitimate and prolong market-nonconforming behaviour within nation-states – manifestations of political cartellisation and government failure at the international level.

In contrast, as we shall see in chapter seven, Wilhelm Röpke was one of the
very few liberals of the time who remained highly suspicious of such a 'liberalism from above'. He continued to advocate a classical liberal presumption in
favour of unilateral liberalising action by one or a number of nation-states
in the context of a 'light', not 'heavy', organisational setup at the international
level – more a 'liberalism from below'.[37] In the scenario of the 1990s, in which
capital is increasingly mobile across borders, and with proliferating unilateral
measures of trade liberalisation and domestic deregulation (especially by developing and transition economies), Viner's faith in international institutions seems
somewhat overblown and outdated. It is Röpke's classical liberalism that has
stood the test of time much better.

That said, Viner's policy activism and optimism in international institutions
form only part of his policy analyses of the early postwar years. By the end of
the 1940s and early 1950s, he does seem to have veered to a more realistic and
balanced appraisal of international agreements and organisations. He argues
that, in the context of government intervention in the immediate postwar period,
one could not really speak of hard-and-fast international rules:

> As long as national boundaries persist and constitute frontiers of
> predominant interest and loyalty, and as long as nations plan their
> economies along lines which involve rigidities in price structures, it
> will not be feasible or practicable to formulate precise rules to govern
> international economic relations; and order in international economic
> relations, insofar as it will not arise spontaneously and more or less
> fortuitously, will be established, if it is to prevail at all, by means of
> day-to-day negotiation, whose outstanding characteristic will be its
> dependence on compromise, on piecemeal adjustments where the pres-
> sures are greatest, and on avowed or disguised improvisation.

And further:

> Where rules of some degree of precision are proposed, they are invari-
> ably qualified by exceptions and escape clauses necessary to make them

generally acceptable but easily capable of becoming more important than the rules to which they are attached.

Here Viner is not exactly full of optimism that this cumbersome and very politicised mechanism will proceed from palliatives to the underlying cause of the malaise – the persistence of excessive government intervention. Moreover, his remarks quoted above capture the essence of political action in intergovernmental fora and international organisations remarkably well.[38]

Conclusion

It is perhaps too much to contend that Jacob Viner is one of the twentieth century's most original economists. He does not possess the originality of a Knight, a Mises, a Hayek or a Coase, all economists who have, in their own heteredox and idiosyncratic ways, pushed back the frontiers of knowledge in social science. But he is, like Robbins and Schumpeter, a great synthesising economist, with a synoptic overview of a vast expanse of interrelated phenomena and a fine skill in literary and pedagogical exposition.[39]

Viner is one of the truly outstanding all-rounders of twentieth century political economy. His deeply learned and cultivated scholarship ranges breathtakingly from the nooks and crannies of the history of thought, through the controversial debates on the nature and scope of modern economic theory, to the nitty-gritty of international economic policy analysis. In all these departments, with the possible exception of some of his *dicta* on postwar international economic policy, he remains a classical liberal, true to the tradition of Adam Smith and, later, the nineteenth-century English economists. Based on his unsurpassed interpretation of the Smithian *oeuvre* and of nineteenth-century classical trade theory, he restates and renews classical liberalism in the twentieth century. This is evident in his insistence on realistic assumptions of actor behaviour and market process, on aligning theory with the complexity and change of contemporary policy, and on relating economic analysis to the political economy of ideology and institutions. All of this is plain to see in his application of theory to both domestic and international economic policy.

International political economy, poor in its basic knowledge of the history of ideas and the classical liberal tradition, which it falsely believes to be minimalist and *passé*, would gain substantially from a reading of Viner. He would indeed provide a rather different perspective on what passes for the liberal paradigm in the discipline.

Notes

1 Jacob Viner, 'Schumpeter's *History of Economic Analysis*', in Viner (1958), pp. 346–347; Douglas A. Irwin, 'Introduction', in Viner (1991), p. 12.
2 Viner is, of course, an expert on the mercantilist literature pre-Adam Smith, which does not figure in this discussion. For those interested in this area, see 'Power and

plenty as objectives of foreign policy in the seventeenth and eighteenth centuries', in Viner (1958); Douglas Irwin, 'Introduction', pp. 26–30, 'The Wabash Lectures: Lecture II: The nation-state and private enterprise', pp. 46–53, 'Mercantilist thought', pp. 262–276, all in Viner (1991).

3　'The Wabash Lectures: Lecture III: The emergence of free trade and the *laissez faire* doctrine', in Viner (1991), p. 59. On the influence of Mandeville on the Scottish Enlightenment, see F.A. Hayek, 'Dr. Bernard Mandeville', in Hayek (1991), pp. 79–100.

4　'Adam Smith and *laissez faire*', in Viner (1958), pp. 213–215. Also refer to Terence Hutchison, 'From William Petty to Adam Smith and the English Classicals', in Hutchison (1994), p. 19.

5　'Adam Smith', in Viner (1991), p. 253; Irwin, 'Introduction', in Viner (1991), pp. 19–20.

6　Ronald Coase, 'Wealth of Nations', in Coase (1994), pp. 81–82.

7　Irwin, 'Introduction', in Viner (1991), p. 20; 'The Wabash Lectures: Lecture V: The "economic man" or the place of economic self-interest in a "good society"', in Viner (1991), p. 74.

8　See, for example, Polanyi (1944), pp. 68–69, 73, 141; Gilpin (1986), pp. 28–31, 45, 82; Keohane (1984), pp. 51, 89; Moravcsik, (1993), pp. 7, 14.

9　Carr (1939), pp. 43, 116.

10　Robbins (1952), p. 5.

11

> People of the same trade seldom meet together, even for merriment and diversion, but the conversation ends in a conspiracy against the public, or in some contrivance to raise prices. . . . The proposal of any new law or regulation of commerce which comes from this order, ought always be listened to with great precaution. . . . It comes from an order of men, whose interest is never the same with that of the public, who have generally an interest to oppress and deceive the public.
>
> Smith (1976 [1776]), Book I, ch. XI, p. 278.

12　On the Invisible Hand, see Smith (1976 [1776]), Book IV, ch. II, p. 477. On the economic order as a cooperative system of 'mutual service', see Edwin Cannan, 'Adam Smith as economist: the gospel of mutual service', in Cannan (1927), p. 429.

13　On the lack of a harmony of interests doctrine in Smith, see 'Adam Smith and *laissez faire*', in Viner (1958), pp. 216, 220–222, 228. Also refer to Hayek (1960), p. 434; Robbins (1952), pp. 22–26.

14　'Adam Smith and *laissez faire*', in Viner (1958), pp. 227–228.

15　On the role of the state in the Smithian and wider classical system, see 'Marshall's economics, in relation to the man and to his times', pp. 248–249, and 'Bentham and J.S. Mill: the utilitarian background', pp. 330–331, both in Viner (1958); 'The intellectual history of *laissez faire*', in Viner (1991), pp. 200, 217. Also see F.H. Knight, 'Economics', pp. 17, 32, 'Free society: its basic nature and problem', p. 288, both Knight (1956); Hayek (1960), pp. 60, 434; Robbins (1952), pp. 3, 22 f., 34 f., 169 f.

16　'The economist in history', p. 231, and 'Adam Smith', p. 258, both in Viner (1991); 'Adam Smith and *laissez faire*', in Viner (1958), p. 234. Also refer to F.H. Knight, 'Freedom as fact and criterion', in Knight (1947), p. 2; Robbins (1952), pp. 174, 176 f.

17　'The Wabash Lectures: Lecture III: The emergence of free trade and *laissez faire*', in Viner (1991), p. 62.

18　This is the approach that Hayek employs. See his 'The meaning of competition', in Hayek (1949), p. 100.

19 'The Wabash Lectures: Lecture V: The "economic man" or the place of economic self-interest in a "good society"', in Viner (1991), p. 75.

20 'The relation between economics and ethics [discussion]', p. 9, 'Marshall's economics, in relation to the man and to his times', pp. 256, 258, both in Viner (1958); Jacob Viner, 'International trade theory and its present day relevance', in Smithies *et al.* (1955), p. 105; Viner (1953), p. 3; Terence Hutchison, 'The wisdom of Jacob Viner: "outstanding all-rounder", and profound and persistent methodological critic', in Hutchison (1994), pp. 269–270.

21 'The short view and the long in economic policy', in Viner (1958), pp. 108, 112, 115, 120; Viner (1953), pp. 8–9.

22 The 'knowledge problem' is the *leitmotif* of Hayek's work and can be traced back to a seminal article, 'Economics and knowledge', written at the LSE in 1937. It is reproduced in Hayek (1949). The theoretical and policy implications of the knowledge problem are extensively elaborated in his subsequent works, *The Road to Serfdom*, his *chef d'oeuvre The Constitution of Liberty*, his three volume *Law, Legislation and Liberty*, his last book *The Fatal Conceit*, and many, many shorter studies.

23 'Hayek on freedom and coercion', pp. 352, 355, and 'The history of *laissez faire*', pp. 218–219, 221, 223, both in Viner (1991).

24 For a wide-ranging survey of Viner's international economic theory and policy, see Arthur I. Bloomfield, 'On the centenary of Jacob Viner's birth: a retrospective view of the man and his work', in Bloomfield (1994), pp. 145–204. This essay covers some aspects of Viner's international economics, such as dumping, customs unions and exchange rates, that are not broached in this chapter.

25 Viner (1937), pp. 71, 84, 290, 292, 438–440.

26 Ibid., pp. 501–509, 518–519, 600.

27 Viner, 'International trade theory and its present day relevance', in Smithies *et al.* (1955), pp. 111–112; Viner (1953), pp. 14–15; 'Introduction', in Viner (1951a), pp. 13–15.

28 Viner (1937), p. 298; Viner (1953), pp. 40–42; 'Introduction', in Viner (1951a), pp. 10–11. For another useful and illuminating discussion of what the classical economists and others in the nineteenth century had to say on these matters, see Bhagwati (1988), p. 26 f.; Jagdish Bhagwati and Douglas Irwin, 'The return of the reciprotarians: US trade policy today', in Bhagwati (1991), p. 87 f.

On the terms of trade argument, also see Irwin (1996), pp. 101–115; Robbins (1958), pp. 182–231.

29 See Krugman (1987); Jagdish Bhagwati, 'Is free trade *passé* after all?' in Bhagwati (1991), pp. 3–26; Gottfried Haberler, 'Strategic trade policy and the New International Economics', in Jones and Krueger (1990), pp. 25–29.

Douglas Irwin makes the additional point that the underlying economic logic of most theoretical arguments for protection are open to question. This applies, for example, to the infant industry argument (a domestic subsidy is usually preferable to protection to correct the offending market failure) and strategic trade policy (a very slight modification of the basic assumptions on market structure and strategic behaviour by firms and governments can change outcomes and cast serious doubt on the protectionist policy inference). See Irwin (1996), p. 220 f.

30 On modern public choice approaches to trade policy, see the references in note 27 and Patricia Dillon, James Lehmann and Thomas D. Willett, 'Assessing the usefulness of international trade theory for policy analysis', in Odell and Willett (1990), pp. 32, 38–39; Baldwin (1988), pp. 102–103, 121–122, 129–134; Anne O. Krueger, 'The political economy of the rent-seeking society', in Bhagwati (1987), p. 291; Olson (1982), p. 118 f.

31 'International finance and balance of power diplomacy 1880–1914', pp. 82–84, 'International relations between state-controlled national economies', pp. 224–231, both in Viner (1951a).

32 'The Most Favoured Nation clause in American commercial treaties', pp. 17, 20, 22, 25, 'The Most Favoured Nation clause', p. 96, 'Memoranda on commercial policy', pp. 170–171, 'International relations between state-controlled national economies', pp. 219–220, all in Viner (1951a).

For a rather similar interpretation of the transition from nineteenth- to twentieth-century conditions in international economic relations, see Röpke (1959a), pp. 74–79, 96–102, 157–158, 194–220; and chapter seven in this book.

33 'International economic cooperation', in Viner (1951a), pp. 283–284, 286, 289–290.

34 Ibid., p. 289, 'Economic foundations of international organisation', pp. 375–376, 378, both in Viner (1951a).

35 Robbins (1936); Lord Robbins, 'Liberalism and the international problem', in Robbins (1963), pp. 134–155. Hayek, following Robbins, makes a similar plea for 'international authorities'. See Hayek (1944), pp. 163–176. What little Hayek has to say about the international order in his later work quite sensibly strikes a more realistic chord and does not advocate a major role for international organisations.

36 'Two plans for international monetary stabilisation', pp. 195–196, 211, 'The Bretton Woods agreement', pp. 236–237, 'International finance in the post-war world', pp. 328–329, all in Viner (1951a); Viner (1947), p. 628.

37 See chapter seven; Röpke (1959a); Röpke (1951).

38 'Economic foundations of international organisation', in Viner (1951a), pp. 378, 381; Viner (1947), p. 627; Viner (1953), p. 93.

39 Hayek makes the distinction between the 'master of his subject', the all-rounder, and the 'puzzler', the original thinker, in economics, akin to Sir Isaiah Berlin's distinction between the 'hedgehog' and the 'fox'. See 'Two types of mind' in Hayek (1991), pp. 49–55.

Part III

GERMAN NEOLIBERALISM: EUCKEN, BÖHM, RÖPKE

6

ORDOLIBERALISM AND THE SOCIAL MARKET

Classical political economy from Germany

Moreover, while various tributaries to the broad flow of ideas about economic individualism and free markets have, over the decades, come down from Manchester, Vienna, London, Chicago, Virginia and elsewhere, the distinctive Freiburg contribution, with its concern for the legal and institutional order, is much closest, methodologically, to the original Glasgow source of Adam Smith.

Terence Hutchison

German neoliberalism is a significant, albeit distressingly neglected, body of thought in the political economy of this century. Few of its main works have appeared in English translation. It shares with Adam Smith and David Hume, and more recently F.A. Hayek, a classical political economy that focuses on questions of order, institutions, law and ethics, notwithstanding the differences between these thinkers and their respective traditions. To re-employ Terence Hutchison's characterisation, a mainstream 'Ricardian' methodology in economics expresses itself in narrowly economic terms. The other 'Smithian' case for a free market economy goes beyond technical economic analysis to encompass the political and social context. This is the lineage in which German neoliberalism has to be placed.[1]

The seeds of ordoliberalism and what later came to be called social market economy germinated in the early 1930s, were nurtured during the Nazi period by 'internal exiles' at the universities of Freiburg and Münster, and by 'emigration exiles' in Switzerland and Turkey, bloomed in the immediate aftermath of the Second World War, having a great influence on the architect of West Germany's *Wirtschaftswunder* (economic miracle), Ludwig Erhard, and towered over West German economic debate in the 1950s. What Germans call *Neoliberalismus* became somewhat *demodée* from the 1960s, corresponding to the tidal wave of American social science that swept through the German university system. Furthermore, the German variety of neoliberalism has never struck a chord outside the German-speaking area.[2]

Quite apart from representing an important staging-post in the history of ideas in political economy, German neoliberalism continues to be a living and breathing body of thought in the German-speaking countries, where it still has influence in economic policy debates. Its normative and institutional dimensions anticipate breakthroughs in both contemporary institutional economics and rational choice-cum-constitutional economics. Perhaps most importantly, this is a corpus of thought that should be, alongside the works of Frank Knight, F.A. Hayek and others, an essential building-block for all those who wish to renew classical political economy, in the tradition of the Scottish Enlightenment, for our times and beyond.

It is useful, *ab initio*, to distinguish between at least two different groups of thinkers: first, the 'ordoliberal' economists and lawyers of the Freiburg School, centred on Walter Eucken and Franz Böhm; second, and the more sociologically inclined Alfred Müller-Armack, Wilhelm Röpke and Alexander Rüstow. All the above and Ludwig Erhard were associated with what was called 'social market economy'. Despite many unifying aspects, it is advisable to keep the terms ordoliberalism and social market economy conceptually apart, for there are substantial differences of emphasis, and some differences in content, between the Freiburg School and the 'sociological neoliberalism' of the others.

Walter Eucken, Franz Böhm and the Freiburg School: a theory of economic orders

Ordoliberalism is a holistic conception of political economy that goes some way beyond the mere economics of the market. One facet of it is explicitly normative, regarding the market mechanism as an instrument to assure freedom over the *longue durée*. Ordoliberalism does not regard the market exclusively as a utilitarian efficiency device or an end in itself; rather, it is a means of ensuring liberal outcomes, favouring decentralisation in the social, political and economic departments of life.[3]

The gestation of ordoliberalism corresponds to the turbulence of the 1930s. On the one hand, the Depression had seemingly discredited the prevailing liberal orthodoxy, on whose cross Chancellor Brüning's government was crucified; and the deepening social malaise served only to increase the magnetic attraction towards the Scylla and Charybdis of the competing totalitarian nostrums, fascism and communism. On the other hand, German political economy was in crisis: its dominant paradigm of historicism seemed to be in terminal decline. For some liberals of the time, liberalism itself needed to undergo reformation in order to present a 'third way' between *laissez faire* and totalitarianism.

One response to the situation came from a group of academics based at the University of Freiburg in Breisgau, whose writings attempted to fuse law with constitutional economics. To quote from the 'Ordo Manifesto':

[Our fundamental principle] consists of viewing individual economic questions as constituent parts of a greater whole. The treatment of all practical political-legal and political-economic questions must be keyed to the idea of the economic constitution. . . . *The economic constitution must be understood as a general political decision as to how the economic life of the nation is to be structured* [emphases added].[4]

The stage is now set to consider the work of Walter Eucken, the founding economist of the Freiburg School. His *Grundlagen der Nationalökonomie* (The Foundations of Economics), first published in the early years of the Second World War, is a significant landmark in the history of German economic thought. Here Eucken directs his gaze at the 'great antinomy' in economics between theory and empiricism. This found its most polemical expression in the heated and acrimonious *Methodenstreit* between Carl Menger, representing the Austrian neoclassical theoretical approach, and Gustav Schmoller, the leader of the German Historical School, who was more sceptical of speculative economic theory and advocated greater emphasis on time and space-bound empirical research. One should recall that the Historical School dominated German economics for about a century and cut itself off from the theoretical developments taking place in classical and then neoclassical economics. Eucken and his neoliberal colleagues, themselves schooled in the historical tradition, broke with the antitheoretical bias of their peers among German economists and sought to return to the international classical and neoclassical fold.[5]

The *Grundlagen* has *economic orders* as its unit of analysis, within which economic processes take place. Any plan, any act of economising by an actor (i.e. the use of alternative means to attain diverse ends), has sense only within a historically given economic order, without which no economic action is possible.[6] The identification and analysis of particular economic orders takes place through the method of 'isolated abstraction', borrowed from the phenomenology of Edmund Husserl. Eucken uses isolated abstraction to construct 'pure forms' or ideal types from real-life examples. He refers to two main ideal types of economic order: a centrally planned economy (*Zentralverwaltungswirtschaft*) and a market economy (*Verkehrswirtschaft*) based on the price mechanism with decentralised exchange relations, itself divided into twenty-five supply–demand 'market forms' between full competition and full monopoly. Associated with these economic orders are different types of monetary order. These ideal types relate to real-world economic orders across time and space, that is, they have *universal* application. Both centrally planned and market orders, together with the different types of monetary order, crop up in all periods of history and in all parts of the world, but the role and relative importance of each order differ according to time and place.[7]

In opting for general theory with universal application, Eucken rebels against the Historical School's antitheoretical bias. He also rejects the relativist theories of economic periods or styles in the works of Werner Sombart and Arthur Spiethoff, in which separate theories apply to discrete periods of history. With particular reference to Sombart, Eucken argues that the factitious cutting up of history into periods of precapitalism, early capitalism, high capitalism and late capitalism, each operating under different laws of development, is a gross oversimplification and distortion of the historical record. Market exchange orders, for example, did not sprout up under early capitalism in the sixteenth century, but flourished in ancient and medieval times, coexisting rather uneasily with command economy and mercantilist orders.[8] However, in directing general theory to concrete testing on reality, analysing the changing coexistence, combination and weighting of different orders across time and space, Eucken displays the sensitivity to historical and institutional differences that was the hallmark of the German historical economists and their strength in comparison to Anglo-Saxon and Austrian counterparts. In this way, Eucken attempts to overcome 'the great antinomy' in economics and engender a theory-history synthesis.

Thinking morphologically in terms of economic constitutions and orders is therefore the point of embarkation for the Freiburg School. The *Foundations of Economics* is primarily concerned with historically evolved economic orders *in concreto*. Only in the last pages of the book does Eucken allude to something much more normative: the search for a *willed* order that corresponds to 'reason and the nature of man'. This *Ordo* concept originates in the philosophy of antiquity and then recurs through Saint Augustine to the scholasticism of the late Middle Ages. It reappears in the thought of the seventeenth and eighteenth centuries, making the distinction between a given *ordre naturel* and a consciously instituted *ordre positif*.[9]

During the war years and in its chaotic aftermath, Eucken was principally concerned with laying the conceptual foundations for a new, consciously formed and instituted *Ordo* for postwar Germany.[10] The fruits of his thinking appeared in his *Grundsätze der Wirtschaftspolitik* (Principles of Economic Policy), the completion of which was cut short by his sudden death in 1950 (incidentally during a series of lectures delivered at the LSE at the invitation of his friend and fellow traveller, F.A. Hayek). The book was published posthumously by his wife.

The *Principles of Economic Policy* begins with a distinction between economic thinking in terms of functions and that in terms of orders. The former, a product of both academic specialisation and the 'experimental' economic policies beginning in the late nineteenth century, concentrates on particular policy areas, for example, agricultural policy, monetary policy, employment policy. The problem with such functional thinking is that it ignores the interaction of each policy area with all other policy areas that form part of an overarching economic order. This kind of thinking overlooks the repercussions of particular policies on each other and, by extension, on the order as a whole. One could well make this accusation against modern welfare economics, accustomed to thinking in terms of functional interventions rather than thinking about the knock-on effects of such interventions on the overall order.

Eucken clearly opts for thinking in terms of orders as opposed to functions: all acts of policy should be judged in terms of how they fit in with the total economic process and its steering mechanism, that is, with the 'order' of economic activities. This is particularly important given the complex interdependence brought about by an extensive division of labour in the modern economy. In such a complicated apparatus, the process of coordination of economic activities, that is, the 'steering mechanism' of the economy, is highly sensitive to particular measures in any one area of policy. Thus 'all economic policy questions get back to the question of economic order and have sense only in this context'. This is the core of Eucken's concept of the interdependence of policy within an economic order, which he extends to a political-economic 'interdependence of orders': the mutual dependence of the economic order with the other orders of society.[11]

Eucken then goes on to an evaluation of economic policy experience in the nineteenth and twentieth centuries. The first period he considers is that of *laissez faire*, lasting until the end of the 1870s. Free price formation, the steering mechanism of the economic process, tackled the main problem of order, that of reconciling the myriad plans of individual agents and overcoming the inescapable fact of scarcity. The resulting market order relied heavily on the institution of a legal order that guaranteed the autonomy of individual action *vis-à-vis* other individuals and the state.

Eucken criticises *laissez faire* for not constructing the rules of the game to govern the economic process, thus leaving the generation of order to uncontrolled and spontaneous development. This resulted in the emergence and rise of monopolies and oligopolies that progressively distorted both the market and legal orders of society. Without any mechanism to hinder and check monopolies, *laissez faire* contributed to the replacement of 'competition through achievement' (*Leistungswettbewerb*), which rewarded and punished entrepreneurs through the selection process of the market, by 'competition to prevent competition' (*Behinderungswettbewerb*), which entailed the use of predatory measures, such as boycotts, price discrimination and cartels, to drive out and close the gates to competition. This transition practically negated the formal legal guarantees of economic freedom such as the freedom of trade and the freedom of contract. An economic order dominated by the private power of monopolies and oligopolies emasculated the free domain of other individuals and thus made a mockery of the *Rechtsstaat* (the Rule of Law).[12]

Eucken is quite right to address the phenomenon of monopoly and its rise in the industrialisation of the nineteenth century, to which the classical economists paid insufficient attention. Nevertheless, the analysis is faulty in several respects. First, as the previous chapters have repeatedly emphasised, it is inaccurate to portray the classical liberal theory of the period in terms of unconditional *laissez faire*. None of the main classical economists believed in a totally automatic market mechanism or a universal harmony of interests. The Scots in particular thought in terms of liberty under the law, realising that conflicts of interest had to be checked and policed by a legal framework, and devoted considerable attention to the rules of the game that must underpin and accompany a free market order. In other words, order could not be left completely to the forces of *laissez faire;* it had to be a fundamental preoccupation of public policy.[13]

Second, Eucken overestimates the spontaneous emergence of monopoly in the private sector and its inimical impact on the Rule of Law. Correspondingly, he underestimates the creation and promotion of monopoly through discriminating acts of government. Moreover, such government intervention, more than private restraints on trade, vitiates the Rule of Law by granting privileges to some groups at the expense of others according to the dictates of political expediency.[14]

The second period covered by Eucken is that of 'experimental economic policy', with proliferating functional government intervention in a wide array of policy areas, especially in social legislation, tariff protection and the promotion of monopolies. This set in train a self-perpetuating process, without regard to the overall order of economic activities, whose result was the progressive replacement of a free market order and a functioning price system with increasing state direction. Such experimentation tended to move the economic order towards central planning. This is the danger of acting experimentally or functionally and ignoring the interconnections of economic policy – 'playing with fire and causing an explosion through the use of seemingly harmless measures'.[15]

Eucken then goes on to consider the workings of the command economy, which changed the character of all economic institutions. The freedoms of trade, movement, association and contract disappeared. Private property no longer conferred the right to plan and act autonomously. Contrary to the beliefs of many, including Joseph Schumpeter, Eucken argues that individual freedom under the Rule of Law is incompatible with the central direction of the economic process. The latter destroys fundamental economic freedoms in the sense that individuals no longer have the equal protection of the laws with regard to the use and disposal of their property. This eviscerates the *Rechtsstaat* for, in effect, political power comes to replace the law.[16]

All these historical considerations give us an indication of the fundamental problem in Eucken's eyes – that of *power*. The rise of private power in the nineteenth century led to a degeneration of market and legal orders and made its influence felt in the political sphere. This prepared the ground for experimental economic policy, resulting in the rise of state power and the collusion of public and private power in cartel-like, corporatist arrangements. This in turn paved the way for the final destruction of the market order through central planning. It is true to say that this interpretation has the German experience primarily in mind, but the *tendencies* referred to occurred elsewhere as well, if not in as extreme a form. The general argument, therefore, bears some relation to Hayek's *Road to Serfdom*.[17]

To Eucken, power in the economic order is evil in two senses. First, it cripples the price mechanism through private and public interventions, rendering the cardinal problem of economic order, that of scarcity, even worse. Second, it weakens and finally destroys the indivisible freedom of the individual. In modern industrial times, the main 'social problem' is the subservience of the individual to a massive state machine, in which the individual becomes a means to the achievement of the ends of the ruling elites. Centralising power in the state, or delegating it to interest groups so that they check and balance each other, cannot get rid of this malaise; rather the cure lies in decentralising and disarming power concentrations through a competitive market order. Moreover, a hybrid compromise between command economy and market economy principles is contradictory and inherently unstable: it is 'as if two conductors with two orchestras play in the same concert hall, until one gives way to the other'.[18]

The objectives of a free economic order are thus twofold: deal with the problem of scarcity as effectively as possible; and, in conjunction with the 'interdependent' social and legal orders, enable individuals, in the Kantian sense, to be ends in and of themselves, not means to the achievement of others' ends. Freedom in the economic sphere is, in this conception of the 'interdependence of orders', intimately linked to the Rule of Law and a society formed 'bottom up' and spontaneously by families, local associations and the like. It is incompatible with a 'top down' construct of a thin layer of powerful elites subjugating a mass of undifferentiated individuals. The economic order has to play its part in realising the Kantian ethic of ensuring the independence and freedom of the citizen from other citizens as well as from the state.[19]

This is the entry point to Eucken's conception of an *Ordo* for the economy, a competitive order (*Wettbewerbsordnung*) constituted and regulated by a 'policy of order' (*Ordnungspolitik*) compatible with the *Rechtsstaat*. We can now deal with Eucken's principles for a free market order, seeking a 'third way' between *laissez faire*, accused of exacerbating the accumulation of private power, and totalitarianism.

First, a 'general political decision' – the 'economic constitution' already alluded to, representing the 'guidance mechanism' for the economic process – is required to institute and enforce a free economic order with competitive markets. *Ordnungspolitik* 'seeks to construct the *forms* of the economy or to influence the *conditions* under which they come about. But it leaves within these forms the plans and actions of households and enterprises completely free' (emphases added).[20] Or as Eucken puts it in his last LSE lecture: 'State planning of forms – Yes; state planning and control of the economic process – No! The essential thing is to recognise the difference between form and process, and to act accordingly.'[21] In other words, it behoves the state to set up and maintain the *institutional framework* of the free economic order, but it should not intervene in the price-signalling and resource allocation mechanisms of the *competitive economic process*. This is the essence of *Ordnungspolitik*.

Eucken has eight *constitutive* and four *regulative* principles for such a 'policy of order'. The constitution of the order requires the realisation of the basic principle of setting up a functioning price system. Anything that hinders the working of this first constitutive principle, such as an anticyclical policy,[22] monopoly formation and exchange controls, should not figure in economic policy.[23]

The second principle concerns the 'primacy of currency policy' to safeguard the stability of the value of money. 'Open' inflation and deflation induce mismatches between the price relations of different goods and distort the cost calculations of individual agents. 'Repressed' inflation, that is, freezing prices and introducing rationing after the forced expansion of the money supply, as Hitler did in 1936, destroys the price mechanism altogether. With price stability in mind, Eucken favours a built-in automatic international stabiliser in the form of a fixed commodity standard. He is at the same time very critical of the Bretton Woods agreement with its compromise between different national monetary orders, but without the rule-bound automaticity and stability of both prices and currencies in a fixed 'commodity standard, such as that which operated under gold in the nineteenth century.[24]

The primacy of price stability in Eucken's scheme has been very influential in postwar West German monetary policy conducted by an independent Bundesbank. Given that nations have not been willing to commit themselves to the discipline of a fixed international commodity standard, Eucken's hopes for an automatic stabiliser have not, of course, achieved fruition.

The third principle is that of open markets, excluding discriminatory intervention by the state and guaranteeing the freedom of trade. Economic policy should prohibit the closure of markets by private actors – the *Behinderungswettbewerb* already referred to. Eucken argues that modern patent law has aided the process of concentration and monopoly formation, closing off competition from outsiders. His preference – an extreme one at that – is to replace exclusive patent rights by a compulsory licensing system that would enable others, for a fee, to make use of innovations and thus keep the supply-side of markets open.[25]

Private property is the fourth constitutive principle, an indispensable precondition to protect the private sphere of individuals in which they can act freely and remain uncoerced by others. Then comes the principle of the freedom of contract that should not, however, extend to the freedom to prevent others from exercising their freedom of contract.[26]

Next comes the principle of liability. The limitation of liability, notably through limited liability companies and publicly listed companies, has also contributed to the concentration process. Eucken argues that the board of directors or the majority shareholder should be responsible for full liability as the most effective means of tying risk to responsibility.[27]

The penultimate constitutive principle is that of the 'constancy of economic policy', avoiding policy experiments that habitually alter economic data and create a climate of insecurity that makes private actors balk at taking risks and making investments. The last principle concerns the interdependence of all the previous constitutive principles. All should apply in equal measure.[28]

The identification of the principles of policy interdependence and policy constancy is quite appropriate, but Eucken surely leaves himself open to the charge that he is really asking too much of both political intelligence and political practice in believing that these principles can be fully and rigidly implemented. There is an element of impracticability and perfectionism in the overall scheme. Having said that, most of the constitutive principles, namely open markets, private property, liability and the freedom of contract, are also the realistic ordering economic principles of the Scottish Enlightenment – the basic policy programme of classical liberalism.[29]

Regulative principles that maintain the functioning of the order should supplement the aforementioned constitutive principles. The main regulative principle is competition policy. It is important at this juncture to point out that Eucken's economic model is one of perfect or 'complete' competition – what he terms *vollständige Konkurrenz* – in which supply and demand clear at equilibrium prices that in turn equal marginal cost. Any deviation from such equilibrium, that is, when price is above marginal cost, represents a monopoly situation in which one or many actors have market power. Government action should correct this disequilibrium and return the market to equilibrium prices. In this respect, Eucken agrees with the industrial organisation/imperfect competition literature[30] as well as the early writings of some of his Freiburg colleagues, notably Franz Böhm and Leonhard Miksch.[31]

Most forms of monopoly would be hindered by the effective application of the constitutive principles of economic policy. However, antitrust policy in the guise of monopoly supervision comes into play for those monopolies that somehow or other slip through the net and remain in existence. An independent antitrust authority should break up monopolies where possible and supervise the natural monopolies (e.g. the utilities) that remain. The law not only should forbid competition-preventing practices such as boycotts, price discrimination and cartel contracts, but also should empower the antitrust authority to set prices for the remaining monopolies and make them act 'as if' full competition were in operation.[32]

This is perhaps the most unrealistic and faulty aspect of Eucken's work and that of the early Freiburg School. At least in this respect, they rely more on hyperabstract neoclassical models than the more realistic, rough-and-ready conception of market order immanent in classical political economy (as argued in chapter two in particular as well as in the following chapters). As Hayek has argued, the assumption of equilibrium-based perfect competition, and associated with it the assumptions that full knowledge is available, that costs are readily calculable, and that the results of competition can be adequately predicted, are unrealistic yardsticks for real-life competition. It is therefore pie-in-the-sky to insist that monopolists behave 'as if' perfect competition were in operation. Monopoly is bound to exist in large measure in the real world, especially in short-run situations.

The problem is not one of monopoly *per se*, but of the prevention of competition. Competition enforcement is the task of general rules that should prevent discriminatory and monopoly-inducing acts of government intervention. General rules should also remove the legal protection of private parties engaged in anti-competitive practices such as price discrimination and cartel contracts. The perfect competition assumption, however, can serve illiberal ends, for it leads to a policy recommendation in favour of discretionary powers for governments and antitrust authorities to 'correct' market imperfections. Such discretion, far from reducing the prevention of competition, is frequently arbitrary, privileging some actors at the expense of others and often reinforcing some government-favoured monopolies. By departing from the framework of general rules, whose principle is the reduction or minimisation of discretionary power, such a conception of antitrust is difficult to reconcile with the Rule of Law.[33]

The later generations of German neoliberalism have, to some extent, taken on board these criticisms. Indeed, Wilhelm Röpke, one of the neoliberal founding fathers, argues that the 'chemical purity' of perfect competition, theorised to perfection, should give way to the concept of 'active' competition. In a dynamic reality producers should continuously struggle to gain the custom of the consumer, even if there are frequent short-run monopoly situations.[34] Arguably, this is more in keeping with the classical recognition that decentralised exchange is inherently imperfect, and that perfect competition models are thoroughly inappropriate measuring-rods of real-life competition.

Eucken, and indeed his colleagues of the Freiburg School, have little to say about social policy. Apart from progressive income taxation and a basic safety net, it is clear that Eucken regards social policy first and foremost in terms of *Ordnungspolitik*, whose proper application should enable the economic order to function well and reduce social problems to a minimum.[35]

Eucken's work is a rich and many-sided political economy. At the forefront of his concerns is the interdependence of orders, particularly the institutional interdependence of the economic and the legal orders, both historically given and normatively proposed. To repeat, the fundamental aim of these orders is to ensure the freedom of the individual. The final section of the *Grundsätze* reflects these lines of thought by touching on the question of the authority of the state. To undertake its *Ordnungspolitik* functions the state requires 'authority', but this is precisely what it has in large measure lost in the twentieth century as a result of the increasing range of its activities. As it expands its intervention in the market process, it becomes beholden to an array of private interest groups, some of whom come to exercise competencies previously reserved to the state. This occurred in the interwar period, for example with syndicates and pools organising international markets in sugar, rubber and wheat. The state thus loses its impartiality and capacity to conduct an *Ordnungspolitik* in the general interest.[36] In the context of a wide-ranging political economy, Eucken outlines an argument that resonates with Frank Knight's thoughts on the pros and cons of democratic politics in modern times (see chapter four). It is also an argument that anticipates more narrow, neoclassical-based rational choice theories of government failure from the late 1950s onwards.[37]

The Freiburg School clearly has classical liberal concerns of order, its institutional underpinning and liberty under the law uppermost on its research agenda. If there is one general and fundamental accusation that one can level against it, particularly in its first generation incarnation, it is that its leading lights are rather *constructivist* in the Hayekian sense of the term. There is a faith in human intelligence and knowledge to design or make a new order or *Ordo*, and in the subsequent ability of the state to regulate such an order. The tendency to place an unrealistic model of perfect competition at the heart of such an order, and to allow public authorities considerable discretionary room for manoeuvre, as in competition policy, have already been noted. Eucken chides the classical economists for their 'negative' economic policy, that is, the presumption against government intervention. His argument does take the latter case on board but adds a 'positive' component of government action, perhaps most evident in competition policy. Correspondingly, he seems to have little faith in 'spontaneous orders' and their self-generating properties. Rather ordoliberalism points to the endogenous degenerating tendencies of spontaneous orders (especially the rise of private monopoly power), and recommends the 'constructivist' correction of those tendencies.[38] Furthermore, the Freiburg approach has a rigid and not wholly plausible distinction between the spontaneity of the economic process, based on freely forming prices, and the rational-constructivist design and control features of the order, as if the *process* and the *order* are two strictly separable spheres.

As argued earlier in the book, the thinkers of the classical liberal tradition, most notably the Scots and more recently Hayek, have a rather different evolutionary conception of the generation and maintenance of order. Our key institutions of language, law, money and the market, are complex spontaneous orders, the result of the unintended consequences of human action but not the result of human design. A society based on individual freedom, and that remains 'open' to future development, cannot dispense with these spontaneous orders. Furthermore, this conception has much more emphasis on the irrationality and fallibility of the individual in conditions of partial knowledge and uncertainty. There is a role for human design and government action, but mostly to modify the general features of the order, such as the framework of general rules, rather than to control specific processes and outcomes (e.g. resource allocation in markets).[39] For these reasons, the work of Walter Eucken and his contemporaries of the Freiburg School, in spite of their commendable and indispensable role in renewing the classical liberal tradition, is in some respects a 'restrained' liberalism, as Hayek puts it.[40]

Eucken's Freiburg legal colleagues, notably Franz Böhm, enormously influence his ordoliberalism. In a superbly vivid and pellucid exposition, Böhm elaborates a theory of 'private law society' (*Privatrechtsgesellschaft*) based on a system of private (or civil) law, applied universally and impartially to protect the individual from interference by other individuals, groups and the state. His emphasis is on guaranteeing the individual's civil liberties and autonomy as an economic agent. It is a private law society, subsuming the legally protected freedom of the individual to use his property to enter into transactions and strike contracts with others, which is the legal bedrock of a free market economy. The state exercises political authority to lay down and operate the ground rules – the 'rules of the game' – to realise free market conditions and act as a neutral arbitrator, but it should not venture any further by interfering with the economic process.[41]

As with Eucken, Böhm aims to minimise power formations in the state and society. Deliberate limitation of the functions of the state, and its independence of the *volontés particulières* of private interests, allow it to exercise qualitatively more effective action where required, especially in upholding the framework of general rules and maintaining the order as a whole. The increasing dependence of the state on 'intermediary powers' in industrial societies (large industrial firms, banks, insurance firms, industry associations, trade unions) represents a weakening of the state's constitutional mandate in acting impartially and upholding a free order. The *volonté générale* is thus sacrificed on the altar of the various *volontés particulières*: some actors are privileged over others, weakening the 'rules of the game' and undermining the order itself. Political intervention in the form of subsidies, tax breaks, the protection of monopolies, price fixing and trade protectionism, offends against the private law society. This kind of selective intervention favours particular interest groups and departs from the cardinal principle of the equality of all individuals before the law.[42] Once again there are similarities with the conclusions of more recent public choice theory, although Böhm attacks the problem from a legal-constitutional angle and not primarily from the perspective of neoclassical economics.

This classic essay shows off Böhm at his very best, and strikes a different, evolutionary note compared to the more rigid and constructivist designs of the early Freiburg School. There is indeed much correspondence between Böhm's private law society and the legal base of Hayek's spontaneous order, particularly as developed in his major work, *Law, Legislation and Liberty*. Like Hayek and the Scots before him, Böhm defines the rules of private law in a general, abstract and negative sense, telling individuals what *not* to do and otherwise leaving them free to pursue their own interests and discover new actions. Only in this manner is the system itself open-ended to future evolution. Like the price mechanism, rules of private law provide information and a framework for experimentation by individual agents who would otherwise have to 'grope in the dark'. As with prices and speech, rules are 'signals' that steer or coordinate the actions of autonomous but not autarchic individuals who have incomplete information. In such a world of dispersed and fragmented information, the complex coordination of millions of individual plans proceeds not on the basis of leadership and an overall plan, but by means of market price signals and the exchange of goods *according to private law contracts*. Böhm emphasises that acts of state did not design or put in place private law as well as two of the other major social institutions, speech and the market price system; rather they evolved in a nonlinear and spontaneous fashion over a long period of time.[43]

As Jan Tumlir remarks, Böhm's experience as a civil servant in the Weimar Republic of the 1920s coloured his antipositivist conception of the law. Böhm had witnessed at close quarters the power of cartels and business associations, a phenomenon that had spread since the second half of the nineteenth century through combinations of financial and industrial capital, with the connivance of the state and the passive acceptance of the law. Economic power had grown and come to direct political power to its own ends.

Drawing on these lessons of history, Böhm believes that the law, and private law in particular, far from being the mere instrument of political decisions, should actively shape collective action through juridically enforced general rules. Such rules of private law and their impartial enforcement serve the function of separating the powers of the state from those of society, as well as arbitrating state–society and intrasocietal conflicts. Thus, the law should be a bulwark defending individual liberty against the tyranny of both majorities and minority interests. These conclusions to some extent mirror those of 'constitutional economics' in the work of James Buchanan.[44] The conceptual and constitutional distinction between state and society is central to Böhm's liberal thought and goes against the grain of one influential strand of German legal thought, from Hegel through to Carl Schmitt, which seeks to dissolve the state–society distinction.[45]

In his concluding remarks, Tumlir links Böhm's thought to his own constitutional thinking on foreign economic policy. Given that an antiliberal foreign economic policy makes the enforcement of competition at home much more difficult, an economic constitution is incomplete without the legal control of foreign economic policy. The law should guarantee the freedom to trade across borders rather than leave the issue to the discretion of executive judgement and international diplomacy (see chapter eight).[46]

Wilhelm Röpke and Alexander Rüstow: the sociological underpinning of liberalism

With Röpke and Rüstow the scene shifts from legal-economic constitutionalism to the philosophy of history, historical sociology and a piercing cultural critique. As Daniel Johnson points out, Röpke and Rüstow are quite clearly the major influences on each other's work, a particularly fruitful intellectual exchange forged in the years of emigration from Nazi rule – Röpke settling in Switzerland and Rüstow going to Turkey, returning to Germany only after the Second World War.[47]

Wilhelm Röpke was in his heyday one of the most famous and controversial political economists in the world. He was the only German neoliberal with an international reputation, carried far and wide by his extraordinary literary flair with the German language, mastery of several other languages, a vast learning, a biting polemic and a volcanic energy for work (by the time of his death in 1966 he had notched up about 900 publications). From his intellectual pulpit in Geneva, he retained close contacts to Eucken, Hayek, Erhard and others, indeed co-founding the Mont Pelérin Society with Hayek in 1947. Like Hayek, he started out as a precocious technical economist but, during the long years of painful exile, underwent a transformation into a political economist.[48] The much-acclaimed wartime trilogy, *Gesellschaftskrisis der Gegenwart* (The Societal Crisis of Our Time), *Civitas Humana* and *Internationale Ordnung* (International Order), was his *rite de passage* from economics to political economy, ethics and sociology, culminating in his sociocultural work, *Jenseits von Angebot und Nachfrage* (Beyond Supply and Demand).[49] Röpke was also one of the few leading German neoliberals to specialise in questions of international political economy (dealt with in the following chapter).

As Kathrin Meier-Rust argues in her intellectual biography of Alexander Rüstow, the latter was the last in the line of the epic German historical sociologists, whose leading lights included Max Scheler, Max and Alfred Weber, Franz Oppenheimer (teacher to both Rüstow and Ludwig Erhard), Karl Mannheim, Walter Benjamin, Max Horkheimer and Theodor W. Adorno. Their passion was the contemplation of society in its universal and multifarious dimensions, on the breathtakingly vast canvas of the history of civilisations. Rüstow's monumental three-volume *opus magnum, Ortsbestimmung der Gegenwart* (The Localisation of the Present), is a historical-philosophical treatment of force, domination, liberty, rationalism and irrationalism, in the genesis and turbulent development of the state and society, from ancient times to the present day.[50]

Röpke and Rüstow are concerned with the sociological preconditions for successful economic reform, the ethical environment required for a sustainable market order and, at base, the noneconomic foundations of society – 'what lies beyond supply and demand', according to Röpke. Rüstow in particular accuses a 'paleoliberal' *laissez faire* of 'sociological blindness' to the institutional prerequisites, the political, social, legal and moral crutches, of a market order. (Here one could make the same reproach I have already made with respect to Eucken, namely that commentators have egregiously caricatured the classical economists, and the Scots in particular, falsely accusing them of a wholesale attachment to *laissez faire*.) Röpke and Rüstow thus fault *laissez faire* for assuming that the economic order is autonomous of other social orders and operates under its own laws. Röpke makes the opposing point that the market order is an artefact of civilisation rather than an ethically neutral sphere, infused with Christian and pre-Christian morality and their secularised forms.[51]

Central to the work of Rüstow and Röpke is a merciless cultural critique of mass society, following in the footsteps of Burckhardt and Tocqueville, with a judicious mixture of liberalism and conservatism. Röpke's portrayal of the upheavals of modernity – the transformation of communities into anonymous societies through industrialisation and urbanisation, the destruction of crafts and independent existences and their replacement by a wage-dependent proletariat, the rise of modern bureaucracy in both public and private spheres, the pernicious use of modern technologies – is nothing short of dramatic. Nineteenth-century liberalism failed to arrest the degeneration and remove the feudal vestiges of capitalism – 'modern industrial and financial capitalism with its all-powerful accumulation of capital and power, its proletarian masses, its centralisation, the elephantiasis of the big cities and industrial areas', as Röpke describes it – leading inexorably to the crisis of the 1930s and the totalitarian nightmares that followed.[52]

What Röpke finds most alarming is the 'centralism' of our times: mechanical thinking in terms of grandiose organisation and construction, 'the cult of the colossal', as opposed to the 'decentralism' of respecting that which is given, grown, spontaneous and self-regulating. The blind optimism of centralist thinking, its zeal to construct a Brave New World and reach a New Jerusalem, leads to the destruction of historically grown social orders and with it the traditions of self-help and self-responsibility in the family, church and local communities. Big government, a welfare state, inflation, and the social traits of what we would call the permissive society, fill the resulting vacuum.[53] There is at least some resemblance here to Hayek's critique of rational constructivism and its after-effects.[54]

Röpke is especially scathing with respect to the 'new' economics, which he regards as a regrettable symptom of centralist thinking. The legacy of Lord Keynes and others is a quantity fetishism, forgetting the elementaries of economics, namely, that prices, savings, investment and other quantities form individually through marginal cost calculations, and that the manipulation of global aggregates in macroeconomics bears little relation to reality. Similarly, the use of mathematics conveys the misleading impression that political economy consists of steady relations between constants, whereas in reality it consists of changing relations between constantly varying quantities – something mathematics cannot capture. Worst of all, Keynesian macroeconomics is dangerously naive of the political economy implications of its technical prescriptions. In the political reality of mass democracies, it is easy to apply compensatory fiscal policy (i.e. boosting demand by deficit financing) during a slump, but it is quite another thing to slam on the brakes by cutting public expenditure when the economy is overheating. The net result is a long-term decline in the rate of savings and a corresponding rise in forced investment, credit, inflation, government expenditure and government debt.[55]

In many ways, Röpke speaks for his fellow German neoliberals when he lambasts the intellectual currents of modern times. All of them decry a *deformation professionelle* of the intellectual class, a replacement of an *esprit de finesse* with an *esprit géometrique*, to use Pascal's terminology. What Röpke and his colleagues find particularly irksome is the putative value freedom of modern economists and other scientists. To them this is irresponsible in the extreme: scientists cannot stand aside and fiddle like Nero while Rome burns; science is complete only when it serves cherished values. To illustrate the point Röpke is fond of quoting Rabelais's dictum, *'science sans conscience n'est que ruine de l'âme'* (science without conscience only ruins the soul).[56]

This is indeed a stance that marks out the generation of the founding fathers of German neoliberalism from later postwar generations. The former, after all, experienced the First World War, the disappointments of the Weimar Republic, the descent into Nazism, the wrench of exile and the daily fear of life within the Nazi Reich. Eucken, Böhm and other Freiburg colleagues were involved in resistance movements and had to live with the very real danger of arrest and even worse. No wonder then that this band of internal and external exiles – most of them, by the way, committed Christians – had a deep commitment to rebuild a humane and free order for Germany and Europe.[57]

The above account gives us an idea of Röpke and Rüstow's diagnosis of the problem. The solution to them is a return to eighteenth-century individualist *and* communitarian values for a harmonious and natural social order. Here the social vision of Röpke and Rüstow is somewhat more radical and romantically nostalgic, and sprinkled with a fair amount of pathos, compared to the more measured tones of their ordoliberal counterparts. Röpke and Rüstow advocate social microstructures of burghers and peasants in small towns and villages, with the economy based on small and medium-sized enterprises. These microstructures permit the combination of economic and social freedom with decentralised citizen politics. Furthermore, such small units should foster transeconomic values, geared to the nonmaterial happiness and contentment of men – their 'vital situation', as Rüstow puts it. Rüstow in particular idealistically longs for noncompetitive solidarity that should apply maximally outside the discrete sphere of economic competition.[58] With the benefit of hindsight, this is perhaps a rather optimistic, not to say somewhat anachronistic, view of the possibilities of modern societies, in Röpke's case at least in part based on a gilded perspective of social life in the Swiss countryside.

Rüstow is probably the most radical of all the neoliberals when it comes to the 'social' question, favouring steep inheritance taxes to achieve equal opportunity and 'just initial conditions for all'.[59] Many liberals, including Röpke, would, of course, object to such redistributive measures, partly on the grounds that they represent an unwarranted intrusion into the institution of the family and the socially valuable qualities of taste, knowledge and morals that inherited wealth confers and transmits through the generations.[60]

Rüstow also allows greater leeway and flexibility for state intervention than envisaged by Böhm and Eucken. For example, he advocates 'adaptation subsidies' (monetary transfers, training programmes and the like), particularly in agriculture but also for small business and handicrafts, with the intention of facilitating structural change and adjustment to world market conditions. The younger, more optimistic Röpke agreed with these measures, which he considered 'market-conforming' because they did not interfere directly with the price mechanism (unlike 'market-nonconforming' measures such as price controls, exchange controls and quotas).[61] The older, more conservative Röpke was somewhat more pessimistic about the efficacy of such state intervention, with the exception of state support for agriculture – the blind-spot of an otherwise steadfast liberal.[62]

Classical liberalism would reject such 'liberal intervention' – an oxymoron if ever there was one. First, subsidies inevitably involve favouring one group over another by means of discretionary state power, thus posing problems for the general rules of conduct in the classical conception of the law. And second, the state, or any other actor for that matter, does not have the foreknowledge to plan structural change from one situation to another in the market. This can be 'discovered' only by the market actors themselves in the process of engaging in competition.[63]

Having made these criticisms, however, it is important to underline the very large measure of agreement between, on the one hand, Röpke and Rüstow, and, on the other hand, the Freiburg ordoliberals. Like Eucken and Böhm, the former believe in a strong but limited state to defend a free market order. It is indeed Alexander Rüstow who made the initial neoliberal call for a neutral state unpolluted by the power of private interests – 'a strong state, a state above the economy, above the interests – there where it belongs in the interests of a liberal economic policy'.[64]

What the 'sociological neoliberals' do, in the hallowed tradition of the Scots, Edmund Burke and Tocqueville, and more recently, Knight and Hayek, is try to combine the liberal principle of freedom with the conservative requirement of order. The traditions and grown institutions of social order sustain freedom over the long term, but there is an unavoidable tension between the two concepts. Freedom without order leads to anarchy and libertinism. On the other hand, it is quite easy to smother freedom in the name of conserving order. Furthermore, their conception of mankind is similar to that of the Scots, Knight and Hayek (certainly true of the more pessimistic Röpke, perhaps somewhat less so of Rüstow). A free order should accommodate highly imperfect, irrational and fallible human beings; it should not rely on saints, virtuous human beings, or even rational and intelligent maximisers. The pitfalls of the latter, perfectionist and constructivist, approach are illustrated by a quotation from Pascal that Röpke uses in a number of his writings: '*Ni ange ni bête, et qui veut faire l'ange fait la bête*' (Neither angel nor beast, and he who wishes to create angels ends up by creating beasts).[65]

Social market economy

All the German neoliberals were closely associated with the *soziale Marktwirtschaft* (social market economy), the astonishingly successful political label used by Ludwig Erhard for his economic policy programme from 1948 onwards. There are indeed many who argue that the social market economy is not only a political programme, but also a theory of economic policy. Given this almost automatic association between 'ordoliberalism', 'neoliberalism' and 'social market economy', it is necessary to explore the meaning and content of social market economy, and evaluate its similarities and differences with the range of thought considered thus far in this discussion. One should begin with Alfred Müller-Armack, the originator of the concept of the social market economy.

Müller-Armack combines economics with ethical and sociological preoccupations. Central to his thought is a conception of 'social irenics', an attempt to reconcile and harmonise seeming conceptual opposites such as liberalism and socialism, and Catholic social ethics with the Protestant equivalent. From this philosophical basis, he thought up the idea of an 'irenic' order for postwar Germany, envisaging a *balance* between market freedom and social protection. In this order competition is the primary organising principle, but Müller-Armack aims for a 'new synthesis' that has a different accent from that of the ordoliberals. Indeed, he goes so far as to say that a 'complex and complete' system of social security should flank market-based competition.[66]

Müller-Armack is in some ways the odd man out in the German neoliberal tradition. He came to liberalism somewhat late in life and then only rather haltingly. His conception of the market economy is not at all 'classical' in the sense that he does not regard it as an artefact of selective cultural evolution governed by spontaneous forces; rather it is a manmade construct or design that one can manipulate much as an engineer tinkers with a machine. Hence the policymaker can 'engineer' the 'free' market to produce the required amount of wealth, which can then be redistributed in the name of social justice. Ultimately, an 'irenic' synthesis should reconcile the antithetical ordering principles of the 'social' and the 'market'.[67] There is more than a passing resemblance here to John Rawls's concept of distributive justice.[68]

Müller-Armack places emphasis on the principle of subsidiarity drawn from the social teaching of the Catholic Church, an ethic designed to coordinate the initiatives of individuals, groups and the state in modern industrial society. In the first instance, the principle is reliant on individual self-help, self-responsibility and auto-organised cooperation in small communities; and where this proves to be insufficient, public functions should come in as near as possible to the citizen at a decentralised level. Upper tiers of government should get involved only when lower government tiers and social groups are unable to perform the necessary functions. A large central bureaucracy to uniformly and impersonally administer a 'welfare state' should be avoided.[69] Nevertheless, Müller-Armack's programme of social policy goes much, much further than those of the other neoliberals. It includes state subsidies for small businesses and vocational training, codetermination in the workplace, with a 'social right to participate in the organisation of work', and the use of countercyclical macropolicy instruments to ensure full employment.[70]

Manifestly, this view of the social market economy has little in common with classical liberalism and sits rather uncomfortably with the views of the other neoliberals. Röpke and Rüstow, for instance, regard the 'social' as part of a wider, organic whole, along with the Rule of Law and the free market economy, not a redistributive device to 'correct' the imperfections of a mechanical market. Social policy is first and foremost *Ordnungspolitik*, integrating as many individuals as possible into market society, with a minimal safety net for those who fall by the wayside. To the other German neoliberals, social cohesion spontaneously emerges 'from below', nurtured by traditions and conventions in the natural communities of the family, church and localities. This facilitates self-help, self-responsibility and civic-mindedness, all of which form the moral framework conditions enveloping and sustaining economic activity in the market-place. This is the conception of the social market economy that Ludwig Erhard always had in mind, not a welfarist and bureaucratic social policy to be ireni-cally reconciled with the market exchange principle.[71]

There is another objection made trenchantly by Hayek. Any notion of social or distributive justice is conceptually vacuous in the spontaneous market order. Redistribution involves specific commands to obtain specific results, altering environmental conditions to procure particular goals for particular groups. This has meaning within an organisation, but not within a complex spontaneous order, for 'justice' in the spontaneous order, as conceived by the tradition issuing from the Scottish Enlightenment, restricts itself to general, procedural and purposeless rules of conduct, not specific commands to redistribute income. Furthermore, redistribution effectively confers privileges on some at the expense of others by means of discretionary government action, something difficult to reconcile with the classical conception of the Rule of Law. For these reasons Hayek contemp-tuously dismisses the adjective 'social' as the 'weasel word', not only devoid of meaning but also easily amenable to arbitrary political manipulation. The latter breeds government intervention to satisfy a plethora of interest group demands.[72] Hayek is therefore not at all surprised to see a massive and bloated welfare state taking shape in modern Germany in the name of a social market economy.

Social market economy is thus rather problematic as a theoretical construct. The Müller-Armack version, certainly in its policy implications, is in many ways incompatible with key features of the legal-economic constitutionalism of the Freiburg School. The Erhard-Röpke-Rüstow version of the social market economy highlights a sociological component that is largely compatible with ordoliberalism, although it is more explicit as a policy programme than a theo-retical model. And if one is to believe Hayek, social market economy really has no meaning in terms of theory.

German neoliberalism was very influential in West Germany in the late 1940s through to the early 1960s, mainly due to the close connections between the thinkers covered here and Ludwig Erhard. Erhard's currency and economic reforms in 1948, introducing a new and stable currency and removing a host of price and other controls to restore a market economy, were very much in line with the neoliberal message. Ordoliberal economists were prominent on the advisory boards attached to federal ministries, particularly Erhard's own Economics Ministry. Müller-Armack became Erhard's *compagnon de route* as a State Secretary in the Economics Ministry. Wilhelm Röpke exercised a signif-icant influence from Switzerland on the economic debate within West Germany, as did Franz Böhm as a member of the federal parliament. Neoliberal influ-ence guided the development of monetary, competition and trade policies, and to a partial extent it made its presence felt in the negotiations on European integration. From the 1960s, however, corresponding with Ludwig Erhard's political decline, the neoliberal influence waned, retreating into the penumbra of neoKeynesian economics, expanding government intervention and incipient countercyclical policies.[73]

Conclusion

German neoliberalism presents a distinctive variety of political economy with eminently classical liberal concerns, though some of its constructivist elements and willingness to accept discretionary government intervention run against the grain of the classical liberal tradition.

Adam Smith's work is constantly concerned with the appropriate institutional framework for the working of a market exchange system, taking his range of analysis deep into the political and legal domains. Both *The Theory of Moral Sentiments* and *The Wealth of Nations* accord first-order priority to (procedural) 'justice', the hinge of the economic system with negatively defined, general rules of conduct that prevent individuals from interfering with each others' rights. In essence, general rules of conduct provide the indispensable rules of the game for what Smith calls the Great Society.[74]

Similarly, as Hayek points out, David Hume's political and legal philosophy is an elaboration of the rules of law, particularly those protecting property rights and contractual obligations, which reconcile long-run stability with the open-endedness, flexibility and progress of the system.[75] Hayek's thought explicitly builds on Scottish classical liberalism, but the legal-economic constitutionalism of ordoliberalism is also a continuation of such thinking in twentieth-century conditions. The sociological concerns of Röpke and Rüstow, at least in part, also have a classical liberal inspiration.

German ordoliberalism (as opposed to the sociological side of neoliberalism) anticipates concerns and theoretical explorations that have recently been in vogue in the Anglo-American world. Ordoliberalism has much in common with the New Political Economy of rational choice and constitutional economics, as well as the New Institutional Economics with its legal-economic treatment of property rights and contract.

Rational or public choice is a burgeoning area of political economy based on neoclassical economics. Mancur Olson's pioneering work, for example, points to the incentives for enterprises and trade unions to organise in relatively tight-knit groups that maximise benefits to 'insiders' while excluding 'outsiders', especially consumers. Such organised interests have plenty of opportunity to lobby to obtain selective benefits from 'big government' engaged in large-scale redistributive activity. The result is the vast and opaque public and parapublic network of a political market, diverting time, talent and other resources from the business of wealth creation. Organised interests come to wield asymmetrical power and even dominate parts of government. Such corporatist practices serve particular interests at the expense of the general interest, for they freeze and entrench present privileges and structures. They delay, and even block outright, necessary economic adjustments.[76]

Although in a less formalised manner, the German neoliberals expounded insights that later cropped up in the works of Mancur Olson, Anne Krueger, George Stigler, Gary Becker, Gordon Tullock, James Buchanan and others on government failure in advanced industrial democracies. Eucken, Böhm and others very clearly saw from the German experience of the nineteenth and twentieth centuries that private power not only distorted the economic process, but also used discriminatory government action to close markets. Governments in mass democracies were and are amenable to capture by rent-seeking private interest groups at the expense of the general interest. Private collective action, for example in the form of industrial cartels and trade unions, easily undermines the free economic order. Collective action by organised interests, as well as government intervention, culminate in the corporatist conflation and collusion of public and private power. To public choice theorists, this suggests 'institutional sclerosis' and government failure. To Alexander Rüstow, writing in the early 1930s, this scenario is of a 'weak state' incapacitated by, and a prisoner to, rampant interest group activity. Paradoxically, as Eucken intimates, a government with expanding functions is 'weak', unable to conduct an *Ordnungspolitik* in the general interest.[77]

Rational choice is the stepping-stone to the more normative analysis embodied in constitutional economics, associated particularly with the work of James Buchanan. As indicated in the chapter on Knight, this approach studies the 'choice between rules', or the alternative constitutional structures that provide the legal-institutional framework of the market economy. Buchanan is primarily concerned with rules that counteract the deleterious effects of government failure predicted by public choice theory. His main emphasis is on rules that bind and limit the discretionary power of governments, in the expectation that a cap on government power will also cap the power of organised interests. Constitutional economics thus intends to arrest the expansion of, and indeed shrink, the political market.[78]

The normative conclusion of the Freiburg School is similar: the discretion of executives and legislatures has to be limited, although the earlier generations of ordoliberals do not explicitly investigate the political order, nor do they specify constitutional rules to contain government activity. The *leitmotif* of Franz Böhm's work is that rules of law have to be in place and properly enforced to limit public and private power formations – to constrain the *volontés particulières* and uphold the *volonté générale*. As with Hayek, Böhm is especially attentive to the rules of private law at the heart of a functioning market economy. Correspondingly, Eucken's economic analysis is 'constitutional': it is based on 'thinking in terms of orders' and, in its normative component, the state binds itself to the specified functions of an *Ordnungspolitik*, beyond which it should not trespass – akin to Jeremy Bentham's very classical distinction between the *agenda* and the *nonagenda* of government.[79]

Theories of property rights and transaction costs are part of a newly resurgent institutional economics, exemplified by the work of Ronald Coase, Oliver

Williamson, Stephen Cheung, Harold Demsetz and Douglass North, among others. Institutional economics, one should remember, was not particularly popular for most of the postwar period. Its leading light, Ronald Coase, has developed a path-breaking microeconomics, inspired by his teacher Arnold Plant and others in a rich institutional tradition cultivated at the LSE in the first half of this century. Coase's concern with the distribution of rights (to engage in market exchange) and the costs of their transference in transacting activity, leads right back to Smith and Hume, for what this line of analysis does is to link economic activity inextricably to the legal system and the wider institutional framework. His work on transaction costs in his seminal article, 'The Problem of Social Cost', is a stepping-stone to an investigation of regulatory failure that arises from overactive government. His normative search, in a continuation and reformulation of the Scottish tradition, is for an appropriate institutional framework that facilitates, or reduces the cost of, transacting activity.[80]

The Freiburg School, unbeknown to or overlooked by most Anglo-Saxons, centrally addresses the question of institutions and property rights in the order and process of economic activities. The connection between the rules of law and the economic order is clearest in Franz Böhm's scholarship. Although he does not explicitly deal with transaction costs, he does regard the legal framework as an institutional device to provide agents, armed with only fragments of relevant information, with signals and signposts that enable them to do better than 'grope in the dark'. This is akin to Douglass North's central point that institutions exist to reduce uncertainty and provide an element of stability to the structure of human interaction.[81]

North goes on to argue that a complex economy with inevitably high transaction costs requires the coercive third party authority of the state in protecting rights, and in policing and enforcing agreements. Obversely, the state should not arbitrarily interfere with property rights and radically alter the wealth and income of contracting parties. Relatively efficient institutions are those that promote productivity-raising activities by removing the impediments to low cost information and transacting, and by the same token discourage barriers to entry, monopolistic restrictions and the like. In the dynamic long run, this involves institutions being 'adaptively efficient'.[82]

Once again, this resonates with ordoliberalism. Perhaps the central and eminently classical liberal message of Eucken, Böhm and their followers is that the state has a legitimate, albeit circumscribed, function of order maintenance, involving policy and legal functions that are hardly simple or minimal. In other words, the state has an important role in assuring the stability of the institutional framework to facilitate flourishing market exchange, but there is a line in the sand beyond which it should not step, for then government activity weakens rather than strengthens an appropriate institutional framework.

The above comments give an indication of the similarities between German ordoliberalism, on the one hand, and the New Institutional Economics and the New Political Economy, on the other hand. There are, however, some differences, particularly with the public choice literature. *Homo oeconomicus* – the rational utility-maximising actor with a given, stable preference-ordering under conditions of full knowledge and instantaneous, costless exchange – is indispensable to public choice. The neoclassical apparatus used is ahistorical and mechanistic. There is the explicit theoretical assumption that the legal and political orders operate in much the same manner as the economic order, that is, with rational utility-maximisers.

The German neoliberal economists and lawyers have often used neoclassical tools of analysis (and have made too much use of the industrial organisation-market failure framework), but generally without taking unrealistic theoretical assumptions and ideal types to extremes in making a *political economy* argument. They do not automatically assume, for the purposes of theory, that the legal and political orders operate exactly along the lines of the economic order. The 'interdependence of orders' in the analyses of Eucken and others is much more differentiated. Ultimately, their case for free markets, like that of Adam Smith, is much more rounded and not dependent on the assumption of rational and self-interested utility-maximisation. Their argument for economic freedom forms part of the argument for a more encompassing, indivisible freedom. Philosophical, legal and historical reasoning blend with the rationale of economic efficiency. The sociological dimension of neoliberalism, admittedly without any real correspondence to the New Political Economy and the New Institutional Economics, adds another intellectual component to the case for individual liberty.

Two further points deserve mention. First, the ordoliberals do not lurch to the public choice extreme of regarding the state in the exclusively negative terms of a Leviathan or a Mafia-operation. They are attentive to both the upside and the downside of government activity, which again places them in the lineage of a sophisticated classical liberal tradition. Second, German neoliberalism is closer in some respects to those aspects of the New Institutional Economics that considerably modify neoclassical assumptions of actor rationality, perfect knowledge and instantaneous exchange, in order to better and more realistically account for the dynamic influence of institutions (as in North's work, for example).

Even so, German neoliberalism, like the political economy of Knight and Viner covered in Part II, remains a broader political economy, the legacy of its founding generation of cultivated Smithian classicists with a much more inclusive concern for order, its legal-institutional underpinning and individual freedom under the law. One should also mention their cultivation of a wider reading and a more 'literary' writing style compared to the dusty grey of modern social science. But then again, these scholars are products of a classical education in the liberal humanist tradition of Wilhelm von Humboldt. In Röpke's terms, they have more of an *esprit de finesse* and less of an *esprit géometrique*. To use Hutchison's distinction yet again, German neoliberalism was and is more 'Smithian' and correspondingly less 'Ricardian'. For those seeking more of a Smithian *esprit de finesse* in political economy in the late 1990s, German neoliberalism offers rich pickings.

127

Notes

1 Hutchison (1979), pp. 167–168.
2 Peacock and Willgerodt (1989a), p. 1.
3 Ibid., pp. 4–7; Peacock and Willgerodt (1989b), pp. 3, 6.
4 Walter Eucken, Franz Böhm and Hans Grossmann-Doerth, 'The Ordo Manifesto of 1936', in Peacock and Willgerodt (1989a), pp. 23–24.
5 Eucken (1989 [1941]), pp. 15–23.
6 Ibid., p. 50.
7 Ibid., pp. 70, 72, 110–111, 122.
8 Ibid., pp. 45, 48, 66.
9 Ibid., p. 239.
10 Eucken (1990 [1952]), p. 373.
11 Ibid., pp. 9, 11, 14.
12 Ibid., pp. 29, 41–43, 49–50, 52–55.
13 See Jacob Viner, 'Marshall's economics, in relation to the man and to his times', pp. 248–249, and 'Bentham and J.S. Mill: the utilitarian background', pp. 330–331, both in Viner (1958); Hayek, (1960), pp. 60, 434; Frank H. Knight, 'Economics', pp. 17, 32, and 'Free society: its basic nature and problem', p. 288, both in Knight (1956).
14 Hayek (1960), pp. 265–266.
15 Eucken (1990 [1952]), pp. 150, 152, 170, 186, 221.
16 Ibid., pp. 60, 62, 67, 70, 100–101, 103–104, 109–110, 127, 130.
17 Hayek (1944).
18 Eucken (1990 [1952]), pp. 144, 173, 187, 198.
19 Ibid., pp. 181, 188, 199.
20 Ibid., p. 242.
21 Eucken (1951), p. 96.
22 Eucken considers that anticyclical measures, for example, artificially low interest rates, deficit financing and credit expansion, accelerate the pace of investment but at the same time cripple the 'calculating machine' of the economy – the measurement of scarcity through marginal cost that efficiently allocates resources as long as prices freely form in the market. Central investment decisions can calculate only in terms of global quantities, not in terms of the individual proportioning of factors and products that are the basis of free price relationships. By blunting the price mechanism, 'full employment' policies lead to disequilibria and bottlenecks, which in turn create the pressure for further intervention, such as price freezes, rationing and exchange controls. See Eucken (1990 [1952]), pp. 140–143.
23 Ibid., pp. 254–255.
24 Ibid., pp. 168–169, 255–264.
25 Ibid., pp. 266–270.
26 Ibid., pp. 276, 278.
27 Ibid., pp. 279–280, 284–285.
28 Ibid., pp. 285–291.
29 Kasper and Streit (1993), p. 11.
30 See, for example, Chamberlin (1929); Robinson (1931).
31 Böhm (1933); Miksch (1948).
32 Eucken (1990 [1952]), pp. 291–299.
33 Hayek (1960), pp. 265–266; Hayek (1982), vol. 3, pp. 65–71, 79–88. Also see Streit (1992), pp. 682, 685–689.
34 Röpke (1962a), p. 33; Röpke (1994 [1965]), pp. 213, 217.
35 Eucken (1990 [1952]), pp. 300–301, 313.
36 Ibid., pp. 327–328.

37 See, for example, Mancur Olson, 'Collective action', in Eatwell *et al.* (1989), pp. 61–69.
38 Eucken (1990 [1952]), pp. 55, 255, 360, 373. Also see Giersch *et al.* (1992), p. 30.
39 Hayek (1982), vol. 1, pp. 29, 32, 37–54; vol. 2, pp. 26–28. Also see F.A. Hayek, 'True and false individualism', in Hayek (1949); F.A. Hayek, 'Dr. Bernard Mandeville', in Hayek (1991), pp. 79–100.
40 F.A. Hayek, 'The rediscovery of freedom: personal recollections', in Hayek (1992), p. 190.
41 Böhm (1966), pp. 75–76, 80–81, 85, 99–100. A shortened English translation of this article is entitled 'Rule of Law in a market economy', in Peacock and Willgerodt (1989a).
42 Böhm (1966), pp. 120, 138–141, 146–147.
43 Ibid., pp. 88–94.
44 See, for example, James M. Buchanan, 'Constitutional economics', in Eatwell *et al.* (1989), pp. 79–87.
45 Jan Tumlir, 'Franz Böhm and the development of economic-constitutional analysis', in Peacock and Willgerodt (1989b), pp. 127, 131, 134, 139.
46 Ibid., pp. 126, 128–129, 138, 140.
47 Daniel Johnson, 'Exiles and half-exiles: Wilhelm Röpke, Alexander Rüstow and Walter Eucken', in Peacock and Willgerodt (1989b).
48 See Egon Tuchtfeld and Hans Willgerodt, 'Wilhelm Röpke – Leben und Werk', in Röpke (1994 [1965]), pp. 340–371.
49 All volumes in Röpke (1980).
50 Meier-Rust (1993), pp. 10–11, 77–82, 200–210, 257–264.
51 Röpke (1942), pp. 6, 67–69; Alexander Rüstow, 'Appendix: general sociological causes of the economic disintegration and possibilities of reconstruction', in Röpke (1942), pp. 268–272.
52 This is the general argument in *Gesellschaftskrisis der Gegenwart*. Also refer to the review of the latter by Einaudi (1954).
53 This is the general argument in *Jenseits von Angebot und Nachfrage*. See Egon Tuchtfeld, 'Jenseits von Angebot und Nachfrage: Wilhelm Röpke – Ökonom und Moralist', in Ludwig Erhard Stiftung (1980), pp. 23–37.
54 Hayek (1960), pp. 54–58, 60–61; Hayek (1982), vol. 1, pp. 9–14, 25–26.
55 Wilhelm Röpke, 'Alte und neue Ökonomie', in Hunold (1958), pp. 80, 82; Röpke (1960), pp. 225–226.
56 Röpke (1963a), p. 199.
57 Rieter and Schmolz (1993), pp. 105–106.
58 See references in note 51.
59 Rüstow, *op. cit.*, pp. 281–282.
60 Wilhelm Röpke, 'Gefahren des Wohlfartsstaates', in Ludwig Erhard Stiftung (1988), p. 257–258.
61 Alexander Rüstow, 'Liberal intervention', in Ludwig Erhard Stiftung (1982), pp. 184–185; Wilhelm Röpke, 'The guiding principles of the liberal programme', in Ludwig Erhard Stiftung (1982), p. 189; Röpke (1942), p. 153.
62 Röpke (1979), p. 6; Röpke (1965), p. 54, 58.
63 For an elaboration of competition as a 'discovery procedure', see Hayek (1982), vol. 3, pp. 117, 131, 158–159.
64 Rüstow, 'Liberal intervention', in Ludwig Erhard Stiftung (1982), p. 185; Meier-Rust (1993), p. 50.
65 Wilhelm Röpke, 'Ethics and economic life', in Ludwig Erhard Stiftung (1982), pp. 371–373; Röpke (1947), p. 522.
66 Alfred Müller-Armack, 'Social irenics', in Ludwig Erhard Stiftung (1982), pp. 347–365; also see Alfred Müller-Armack, 'The meaning of the social market economy', in Peacock and Willgerodt (1989a).

67 Wünsche (1994), pp. 162–163.
68 Rawls (1971).
69 Uertz (1993).
70 Alfred Müller-Armack, 'The second phase of the social market economy: an additional concept of a humane economy', in Ludwig Erhard Stiftung (1982), pp. 53–61.
71 Wünsche (1994); Kurt Biedenkopf, 'Ludwig Erhard und die politischen Parteien', in Ludwig Erhard Stiftung (1985), p. 71.
72 Hayek (1982), vol. 2, pp. 2, 38, 71, 88–89, 136, 139, 142, 182; vol. 3, pp. 15–16, 160. See also Streit (1992), op. cit., pp. 698–699.
73 For a detailed treatment of the neoliberal influence on policy, see Nicholls (1994); Sally (1995), pp. 541–553.
74 Jacob Viner, 'Adam Smith', in Viner (1991), p. 252; R.H. Coase, 'Wealth of Nations', p. 88, and 'Adam Smith's view of man', p. 100, both in Coase (1994); Hayek (1982), vol. 2, pp. 2, 71.
75 F.A. Hayek, 'The legal and political philosophy of David Hume', in Hayek (1991), pp. 101–118.
76 See Olson (1965) and (1982).
77 See notes 36 and 64.
78 Buchanan (1991); Vanberg (1994).
79 See notes 20, 21, 42, 44.
80 R.H. Coase, 'The institutional structure of production', p. 11, 'Economists and public policy', p. 62, 'Economics at the LSE in the 1930s: a personal view', p. 213, all in Coase (1994).
81 See notes 41–45. North (1990), p. 6.
82 North (1990), pp. 27, 58–59, 64–65, 80–81.

7

THE INTERNATIONAL POLITICAL ECONOMY OF WILHELM RÖPKE

Liberalism 'from below'

But Röpke realised at an early stage, perhaps earlier than most of his contemporaries, that an economist who is nothing but an economist cannot be a good economist.

F.A. Hayek

The outlook is bad, however, if nations strive after international order while at home they continue to pursue a policy contrary to what is required for it. . . . Is it not starting to build the house with the roof if we subscribe to a falsely understood internationalism, and should not the foundations come first?

Wilhelm Röpke

The previous chapter concentrated on the domestic (or national) political economy of German neoliberalism, both in its ordoliberal (legal-economic) and sociological incarnations. This chapter focuses on the *international* political economy of one of the prominent Founding Fathers of that tradition, Wilhelm Röpke. As intimated in chapter six, most of the German neoliberals deal with domestic political economy, and this is one significant aspect of Röpke's astonishingly vast, kaleidoscopic scholarship. However, of the very few German neoliberals who tackle questions of international economic order, it is Röpke alone who develops a comprehensive international political economy.

The previous chapter gave decent coverage to the sociological accent of Röpke's 'domestic' political economy. The chapter also emphasised that Röpke very largely shares the ordoliberal precepts of the Freiburg School, particularly the *Ordnungspolitik* of his friend Walter Eucken. This chapter uncovers another side of *Ordnungspolitik*, namely, its relevance to the international economic order in Röpke's writings. It also seeks to show that Röpke not only swims against the tide of received opinion in his day and age, but also is four square in the classical liberal tradition on issues of international economic order.

Two, not necessarily mutually exclusive, approaches have long dominated the modern liberal paradigm in international political economy: a neoclassical economics-based rational choice, and an international politics-based 'neoliberal institutionalism' (which partially incorporates game-theoretic and collective action aspects of rational choice theory). The latter in particular places heavy emphasis on mechanisms of intergovernmental cooperation, often with the mediation of international organisations, to achieve liberal economic outcomes while preserving systemic order. 'International regimes' driving reciprocal interstate negotiations and bargains are the foci of attention. Frequently, liberalism seems to be equated with cooperation in international regimes (see chapter nine).[1]

These conventional treatments in modern international political economy leave classical liberalism out of the picture. The latter, with its wellsprings in the Scottish Enlightenment of Adam Smith and David Hume, and carried forward in the work of the nineteenth-century English economists, accords pride of place to policy action at the *national,* not the international, level to further the progress of a liberal international economic order. Moreover, classical liberalism conceives such action in *unilateral* terms, not predicated on reciprocal bargaining in international organisations and intergovernmental fora. Chapter three partially covered this ground.

Röpke quite deliberately adopts the latter, classical liberal approach. An investigation of his work should present a striking contrast to what most observers take to be the 'liberal' paradigm in international political economy. In particular it should give much insight to a classical liberal approach that fixes the observer's gaze on *national unilateralism* to promote a liberal international economic order. With its focus on the national or domestic preconditions of international order rather than international policy coordination, I would call this perspective liberalism 'from below', as opposed to the liberalism 'from above' of neoliberal institutionalism. In this way the revival of Röpke's work should contribute to reconstructing classical liberalism, hitherto lacking, in international political economy.

One parenthetical comment is apposite at this stage apropos Röpke's characteristic style on questions of international (and domestic) political economy. Like many other highly cultured master-craftsmen of the written word, his writing is not dry or dispassionate, and he is hardly a cool and distant observer of events. The normative approach, with its merits and demerits, is evident all over his work. Indeed it is often difficult to distinguish his positive from his normative treatment of issues, and there is the more than occasional sweeping generalisation carried on the crest of literary *élan* and emotional engagement with one cause or another.

For all its drawbacks, the advantage of this style of thought and writing is the overt discussion of *values* as an integral component of political economy, a penchant for which is a hallmark more of the classical than the neoclassical tradition.[2] Röpke makes no bones about the fact that, in addition to major questions that require a technical competence in economics, there are borderline questions for which economic analysis has definite limits. More fundamentally, Röpke argues that framework institutions surrounding and interdependent with the market require broader interdisciplinary and synthetic observation, including an explicit consideration of values.[3] This is political economy *à la* Röpke.

Röpke and international political economy

Although Röpke had an early interest from the 1920s in questions of international economic order, his political economy of the field began to take shape only in the 1930s,[4] for example in his work *German Commercial Policy*. It subsequently filled out into a comprehensive and distinctive design, with reference publications such as *International Economic Disintegration, International Order and Economic Integration*, and many long articles in the German language journal *Ordo*. Besides his general work on international economic order, there are two related strands of his thought: the integration of postwar West Germany in the European and international economies, as well as European integration. In both areas of policy, particularly the latter, Röpke adopted clear and controversial positions in the thick of highly charged debates.

The next section outlines Röpke's general view of internationalism and his rather sceptical, 'realist' approach to international organisations and 'world government'. Then there is a detailed discussion of what I would call his liberal reference system for international economic order, followed by his interpretation of successive periods of economic history, from the nineteenth century to the post-1945 era. Also examined is his treatment of European economic integration. The conclusion contrasts his classical liberal approach to international political economy with more popular present-day approaches, especially what goes under the name of neoliberal institutionalism.

International crisis: true and false internationalism

The catalyst for Röpke's investigations into international order was the 'international crisis' ignited by the First World War, unextinguished in the 1920s, and spreading like wildfire before engulfing the planet in the Second World War.

To Röpke, the source of the problem was to be found 'from within and beneath' in the internal social dissolution of nation-states, although the aggravated symptoms of the malaise were first evident at the brittle international level with the failure of international organisations, diplomatic friction, protectionism, the breakdown of the gold standard, etc. Nations papered over the cracks of domestic volatility and embarked on the path of least resistance by manifesting outward aggression in international political and economic relations. Thus, it would be facile and misleading to attribute the causes of the crisis, rather than its symptoms, to the international level. If this analysis holds, then surely the cure to the problem should not have been administered at the international level; rather the cancer should have been treated where it started, that is to say, *within* nation-states.

Hence it comes as no surprise to find Röpke engaging in mordant criticism of the 'one-sided legalism', the 'false internationalism', of interwar idealism with its stress on amending the statutes of the League of Nations, holding conferences, negotiating pacts, treaties and conventions, and inventing Utopian blueprints for economic unions and federations. 'Is it not starting to build the house with the roof if we subscribe to a falsely understood internationalism, and should not the foundations come first?' he asks rhetorically.

Röpke's preference, in contrast, is for an internationalism that 'like charity, should begin at home'. The solution lies not in overstressing action at the international level (while pursuing a contrary policy at home), in the process overloading international organisations with their perpetual conferencitis, inevitable power fights and political compromises; rather it lies principally at the national level, for without good order there no good and lasting international order is possible. This is key to an understanding of Röpke's internationalism which, like the policy preferences of the eighteenth- and nineteenth-century classical economists before him, is a liberalism 'from below', emphasising unilateral liberalising action at the national level. It is not a liberalism 'from above' that emphasises an elaborate machinery of intergovernmental cooperation.[5]

To Röpke, the pathetic and foolhardy extreme of false internationalism is the notion of 'world government', a popular fashion among economic liberals during the 1930s and 1940s. It is to Röpke's lasting credit that he was one of the very few liberals of the time who remained steadfastly realistic, not falling prey like eminent contemporaries, including Hayek, Robbins and Viner, to the will-o'-the-wisp of world government.[6]

Röpke's realism on this score is not cynical or amoral in the Machiavellian sense. On the contrary, it recognises that the moral and political framework conditions for world government are nonexistent and likely to be so for the foreseeable future. It is quite simply naive to believe that nations will relinquish the necessary amount of sovereignty to international authorities. The key attachment to the *civitas* is and will remain at the national level.

The problem is not so much the (inescapable) existence of a system of nation-states as the centralisation of power *within* nation-states that spills over into international friction. Röpke likens the modern nation-state to an inverted pyramid with its apex resting on the 1651 folio edition of Hobbes's *Leviathan*. The aggrandisement of the political power of governments *vis-à-vis* their own citizens inexorably projects itself onto the international stage: internal power feeds into external power used against other states in conflictual international relations.[7]

A liberal reference system for international economic order

Like the other German neoliberals and indeed most classically inspired political economists, Röpke recognises the supreme importance, the categorical imperative (as Knight terms it), of *order*, necessary to support the intensive exchange and mutual dependence of an international division of labour. Central to this protective casing of order are moral, legal and political framework conditions that surround economic life. It was the mistake of a credulous nineteenth-century liberalism to assume that the economic order operates autonomously of other aspects of social life.

A recurring theme in this book is the distinction between a 'Smithian' and a 'Ricardian' methodology in political economy. By emphasising the link between the economic order and other social orders, Röpke clearly plumps for a Smithian methodology. Indeed, as we shall presently see, he, like Jacob Viner, extends such a Smithian methodology to his coverage of the international economic order.

Moral, legal and political framework conditions are definitely observable within nation-states with their more-or-less established governments, legal orders, and social integration in the form of extralegal norms, principles and values, not to mention the intangible moral attachment of the citizen to the *civitas*. All these factors facilitate the workings of unified national monetary systems, a complex division of labour and intranational free trade. However, these meta-economic conditions obtain to a much lesser degree, if they obtain at all, in international economic relations. This accounts for the fragile nature of an international order that is hypersensitive to ructions within nation-states.[8]

Given the weakness of such meta-economic framework conditions at the international level, a liberal international economic order needs some kind of 'working substitute' for nonexistent world government. This 'as-if world state', as Röpke labels it, has certain cardinal requirements. First, the cornerstone of a liberal reference system for international economic order is a firmly anchored market economy within nation-states, what Röpke, borrowing Renan's phraseology, calls the consumer plebiscite *de tous les jours*. Liberal international order also presupposes a minimum of constitutional order in the nation-state, consisting of a separation of the public-state sphere from the private-nonstate sphere, of the *Imperium* of state authority and public law from the *Dominium* of the market economy and private law that protects (private) property rights – in short, the separation of the domain of politics from the domain of economics *at the national level*. Like the classical economists, Röpke draws a sharp distinction between the *agenda* and the *nonagenda* of government, which he illustrates with a quotation from Benjamin Constant: *'Le gouvernement en dehors de sa sphère ne doit avoir aucun pouvoir; dans sa sphère il ne saurait en avoir trop'*.

Note that Röpke's reference system for international order begins, as he puts it, 'from within and beneath' at the national level, and particularly relies on the 'separation principle' (of the political sphere from the economic sphere). Only on this domestic *terra firma* can nations operationalise the external requirements of a liberal international economic order, which consist of stable and convertible currencies, multilateral free trade and the free movement of capital across borders (and labour too, if at all possible). This ensemble is essential for nations with increasing populations, immense material requirements and enormous differences of wealth and resources. Such an order not only is best suited to the growth and prosperity of the advanced countries, but also is *sine qua non* to the poorer, less developed countries with rising populations.

Essentially, it is the multilateral principle that is the hinge of liberal international economic order, just as it is the hinge of domestic economic order. In the domestic context, buying and selling is based on an extensive division of labour and interdependence between great numbers of economic agents. In the international context, a dense multilateral network of exchange between economic agents in a great many countries is brought about by the operation of comparative costs: imports are procured as cheaply as possible from all over the world, and to pay for them exports are dispatched all over the world as well. In this way nations meet their material needs best, that is, they ensure the availability of the widest range of goods and services and maximise national income.[9]

All the above features – the separation principle within nation-states, stable and convertible currencies, free international trade and capital mobility – are necessary conditions for a liberal international economic order, but they are not sufficient. There is a flanking meta-economic dimension: public and private actors must adhere to certain standards and moral codes of behaviour to ensure a minimum of mutual trust and a sense of security and continuity. Such 'unwritten international law', as Röpke terms it, encompasses the respect of private property, meeting contractual obligations, nondiscrimination of the foreigner in national commercial arrangements, and much else besides. These ideological components, corresponding closely to what Douglass North calls the 'informal constraints' of institutional behaviour, are the enabling conditions for the proper functioning of a sound international monetary order, multilateral trade and capital mobility.

If all these constituents of international order were realised, the 'working substitute' for world government would be up-and-running. The liberal features of national economic order – a sound system of public money and credit, the flexibility of prices and costs, the freedom of intranational trade and capital movement – would then be replicated at the international level. International transactions would assume the character of domestic transactions.[10]

It is striking that Röpke's reference system for a liberal international economic order has hardly any mention of international organisations. As he states clearly, providing the above conditions were fulfilled, there would be no need for any international machinery. *Prima facie* this appears to be pie-in-the-sky optimism, particularly in twentieth-century as opposed to nineteenth-century realities. A (supposed) liberal of the Lord Robbins variety would assuredly counter that there is precious little hope of nations returning to the straight-and-narrow path of free markets in lieu of strong institutional mechanisms at the international level to provide requisite incentives and deter errant behaviour.[11] Indeed, this was the position adopted by Jacob Viner in the immediate aftermath of the Second World War (see chapter five).

Röpke is dismissive of this liberalism 'from above', arguing that it does not get to the root of the problem. Moreover, it has its pitfalls in the inevitable politicisation and bureaucratic expansion of international organisations, with the attendant risk of makeshift compromises that legitimise and prolong market-nonconforming behaviour within nation-states. Although he is not averse to a modicum of institutionalised international cooperation, he stresses a liberalism 'from below' couched in rather realistic, not hopelessly idealistic, terms: the prospects for a liberal international economic order are that much better if change occurs 'from within and beneath'; a spate of follower nations would most likely emulate the unilateral action of one or a number of pioneering nations, with more progress made in the direction of international economic integration. Though Röpke admits that there is reciprocal conditioning between the national and international levels, it is change within the nation-state that is of paramount importance in the international system. As he argues: 'More important than international institutions and legal constructions are the moral-political forces behind the market that are only really effective within individual nations'.[12]

Although Röpke concentrates almost exclusively on unilateral liberalisation by nation-states, it is worth emphasising that he is not totally against intergov-ernmental policy cooperation. It is true that he adopts a sceptical, indeed scathing, tone on the subject of nearly all international organisations, castigating them for their interventionist tendencies that compound the malaise of *dirigisme* within nation-states. Nevertheless, he has a quite favourable attitude towards the General Agreement on Tariffs and Trade (GATT) – now the World Trade Organisation (WTO) – which, unlike many other international organisations, is relatively small and has traditionally focused on a discrete agenda of multilat-eral trade liberalisation.[13] To Röpke the GATT has its uses, particularly in gently nudging countries in the direction of liberalisation as well as legitimating and locking in liberalisation measures already undertaken by one or more countries. However, Röpke still considers the GATT as little more than a 'helpful auxiliary'; his prime emphasis continues to lie with unilateral national liberalisation.[14]

Röpke is pretty clear that there is no necessary incompatibility between unilat-eral liberalisation and reciprocal liberalisation through the GATT, but he gives no precise indication as to where and how the GATT fits into his overall scheme. While he is sensitive to an over-reliance on reciprocity, he glosses over the link between unilateralism, on the one hand, and multilateralised reciprocity in the GATT, on the other hand, as *potentially* compatible modes of trade liberalisa-tion under certain circumstances. This is indeed a major gap and weakness in his work, perhaps somewhat mitigated by the fact that very few, if any, scholars have paid much attention to this question.

Thus, to recapitulate, Röpke's position is that a liberal international economic order presupposes a liberal domestic order; free markets 'abroad' rest on the solid foundations of free markets 'at home'. By the same token he would unreservedly oppose the 'mixed systems' thinking that legitimises a combination of international liberalism, achieved through regimes of intergovernmental cooperation, and national illiberalism in the form of extensive government intervention within nation-states. Neoliberal institutionalists in the US, among others, believe that a liberal international economic order, maintained by intergovernmental negotiation, is compatible with demand-led macroeconomic policies, interventionist microeconomic policies, a generous welfare state and a certain amount of trade protectionism (see chapter nine).[15] Röpke shares the view of the other German neoliberals and Hayek that national mixed economies, with their unstable compromise between antithetical ordering principles (the market economy and collectivism), are the source of international illiberalism: interventionist domestic economic policies invariably spill over into interventionist foreign economic policies that eventuate in conflictual international relations and all-round damage. Corrective action, in the first instance, entails rolling back the frontiers of the mixed economy within nation-states.[16]

Periods of economic history

It is now time to put some flesh on the bones of this liberal reference system by examining Röpke's interpretation of different periods of economic history.

The nineteenth century

The period spanning most of the nineteenth century and ending abruptly in 1914 corresponds better to Röpke's requirements for a liberal international economic order than any subsequent period of economic history. The separation principle (of politics from economics) was pretty much adhered to within nation-states; capital flowed and labour roamed relatively freely across borders; international trade increased significantly on the back of tariff reductions and the operation of multilateral principles, with the nondiscriminatory Most Favoured Nation and National Treatment clauses built into bilateral treaties and national commercial codes; the property and investments of foreigners were also secured in bilateral treaties and/or national laws; and a massively expanding international commerce reposed on the firm ground of a gold standard with stable and convertible currencies.

That said, the economic record of the period was not all rosy. There was much incompetence in the management of national currencies and the regulation of domestic monetary and banking systems.[17] Tariffs also began to rise again in the last quarter of the nineteenth century. Even so, international trade continued to expand, not least because increases in tariffs were relatively modest and did not seriously interfere with the market mechanism.[18]

So much for the 'economic' features of a liberal international economic order in the nineteenth century. But Röpke does not stop there: he proceeds to uncover the ideological, meta-economic framework conditions that undergirded the efficient functioning of the system. There was a widespread belief in the cardinal tenets of a liberal ideology that rendered public and private actors willing to stand hard-and-fast to the gold standard, free trade, capital mobility and the protection of investments. National laws embodied much of this ideology, but it fundamentally depended on informal constraints, that is, extralegal standards, conventions and moral codes of behaviour. These formed the backbone of what Röpke calls an 'international open society' or a secularised *ordre public interna-tional* with its philosophical roots in the *Res Publica Christiana* of the Middle Ages. And such was the resilience of this international open society that it required *no organisational setup at the international level:* national laws and informal constraints more than sufficed as working substitutes for world government. In other words, the system sprouted and grew 'bottom-up', with its roots deeply embedded in the subsoil of nation-states.[19]

Once again, Röpke's evaluation of nineteenth-century conditions has a some-what different accent from the mainstream of recent work in international polit-ical economy. His explanation is neither purely dependent on 'economic' forces, nor is it one based on the power and interests of British hegemony (as in hegemonic stability perspectives),[20] although he would not deny the validity of either as a partial explanation; rather it continually emphasises the glue of ideol-ogy that held many actors, and not only the British, firmly to the liberal order.

The interwar period

According to Röpke the First World War, the 1920s and the 1930s witnessed the pulling down of 'the very structure of this [nineteenth century] integration by rip-ping the multilateral network into bilateral shreds'. The considerable expansion of government intervention within nation-states gradually dissolved the liberal principle of separation between the political and economic spheres. The politici-sation of national and international orders led to greater instability and arbi-trariness in economic transactions. The liberal ideology of the pre-1914 'international open society' was fast disappearing into thin air. The Depression accelerated the breakdown and collapse of the moral, political, legal and eco-nomic crutches of international order. On the trade front, modest tariff protec-tion was rudely replaced in the early 1930s by rampant contingent protection (e.g. quotas, bilateral barter and clearing arrangements, export subsidies, government foreign trade monopolies and exchange controls). First, these barriers falsified rel-ative prices and distorted transactions, and then predictably shrank international trade to miniscule proportions (compared to pre-1914 or even pre-1929 trade). On the payments front, one country after another departed from the gold standard and imposed exchange controls; the world economy no longer had a monetary anchor of any sort. Lastly, international capital flows virtually dried up.

In keeping with his liberalism 'from below' perspective, Röpke traces the collapse of the world economy to the rise of public Leviathans, that is, govern-ments, within nation-states. Spiralling *ad hoc* interventions by governments

rigidified prices and reinforced monopolies. Governments also pursued inflationary policies that put unbearable pressure on the balance of payments
(especially in Germany from 1933). In Germany, the government 'repressed'
increasing inflation in 1936 by fiat with the imposition of quantitative internal
and external controls.[21] In nearly all countries, governments artificially corrected
balance of payments disequilibria by resorting to quantitative trade protectionism
and exchange controls, effectively screening off the national economy from the
international economy.

Thus 'disintegration began at home' with an inevitable spillover to the world
economy. As Röpke comments:

> Without philosophising about which came first, the chicken or the egg,
> we would surely not make a great mistake in regarding the national
> changes as the really strategic factor that is ultimately responsible for
> having started the vicious circle.[22]

The post-1945 period

Röpke delineates the postwar period (up to his death in 1966) in terms of an
uneasy compromise between antinomic ordering principles: on the one hand,
the continuing 'international disintegration' of mercantilist government intervention, collective planning and inflation within nation-states, spilling over into
chronic balance of payments disequilibria, quantitative trade protectionism,
exchange controls and the freezing of cross-border private capital flows; and,
on the other hand, gradual 'international reintegration' based on halting moves
in the direction of trade liberalisation and currency convertibility. The pace-
setters of external liberalisation were countries such as West Germany and
Switzerland pursuing domestic liberal policy reforms (consisting of the decon-
trol of prices, production and capital markets, and anti-inflationary macroeconomic policies that avoided neoKeynesian demand management).[23]

Röpke casts a very sceptical glance at the new international regimes of cooperation, quite unlike the initial and almost unbounded optimism of fellow
liberals like Viner and Robbins (see chapter five). His criticism of the Bretton
Woods agreements is that they did not quite counteract, indeed went some way
towards rubber-stamping, the forces of international economic disintegration.
The new currency arrangements, in the absence of a gold standard along
nineteenth-century lines, could not restore stable exchanges and convertibility
(on current account transactions), and had no substantial means of enforcing
discipline in national monetary and banking policies. The agreement establishing
the International Monetary Fund also had specific provisions allowing countries
to devalue the currency, and impose quotas and exchange controls, when faced
with balance of payments problems that, for the most part, were the by-product
of domestic inflationary and interventionist policies. There was also no intention of restoring convertibility on capital account transactions – a concern that

Röpke shared with Viner. To Röpke all this was tantamount to 'quackery on the epidermis', not 'real treatment'. In short, he, unlike most liberals of the time, including Viner, had a rather disapproving and pessimistic view of the postwar design for a liberal international economic order, although, as mentioned before, he welcomed the establishment and work of the GATT in Geneva as a helpful auxiliary to trade liberalisation by nation-states.

The following quotation well illustrates his general evaluation of the postwar conventional wisdom on international economic policy cooperation:

> Neither the IMF – which, as an international credit institution, has up to the present been of very little use, and, as an international monetary authority, has done more harm than good – nor the IBRD, nor the Marshall Plan, however salutary it was as a political move, and bountiful as international poor relief, nor the efforts of the ITO with its one surviving live child, the GATT, nor the other institutions of one kind or another, almost too numerous to be counted, nor the Schuman Plan, are the real institutions of the relative progress of the last few years, and even the OEEC with its European Payments Union, which may, before most others, claim a not inconsiderable credit, can, at the best, be considered merely as an impermanent emergency structure.[24]

If international regimes were not primarily responsible for the very real progress on liberalisation that started to bear fruit in the 1950s, then what was responsible? Röpke argues that just as disintegration began 'at home' between the wars, reintegration also began 'at home'. In other words, the progressive liberalisation of the international economy from 1945 started 'from below' in a few nation-states; international regimes played, at best, a supporting role. Just as Britain undertook unilateral liberalisation in the nineteenth century, a few countries, notably West Germany from 1948 with the Erhard reforms, did the same after the Second World War, unleashing the 'ordered anarchy' of spontaneous market forces,[25] and setting an example which others followed. Finally, the landmark of international reintegration was not Bretton Woods in 1944, but the collective move of West European countries to currency convertibility in December 1958, itself unimaginable without the pioneering liberalisation in West Germany that other countries progressively imitated.[26]

It is worth underlining at this juncture Röpke's preference for unilateral, 'example-setting' action at the national level as the motor of liberalisation in the world economy. This is quite in harmony with the policy prescriptions of the classical trade theorists, advocating unilateral free trade policies to reap welfare gains, even in a generally protectionist world (see chapters three, five, eight and nine). This stands in sharp contrast to the emphasis of a liberalism 'from above' on interstate reciprocity and policy coordination to undertake liberalising measures, a line of reasoning propagated these days by US neoliberal institutionalists.[27]

By the 1960s Röpke was increasingly pessimistic about the prospects for a liberal international economic order, in spite of the progress made on most fronts in the 1950s. He continued to upbraid governments for their increasing intervention in economic life within nations, resulting in bloated welfare states, labour market rigidities, public sector deficits and inflation. The external corollary of internal mismanagement was persistent protectionism and unstable monetary conditions, with fuel thrown onto the flames by 'imported inflation' (into Europe from the US) from the late 1950s. Developing countries, following the precepts of economists like Raul Prebisch and Gunnar Myrdal, were particularly culpable of inflationism and collectivism. Aid from governments and international organisations for big capital projects only exacerbated the problem. Röpke was also a lifelong and scathing enemy of the Communist bloc, on economic and noneconomic grounds. He remained to his death an uncompromising Cold Warrior.[28]

From a liberal standpoint, Röpke correctly and trenchantly diagnosed many international economic problems of his time but, as Gerard Curzon argues, Röpke's pessimism was somewhat exaggerated. Flexible exchange rates since the early 1970s have worked reasonably well in lieu of a fixed commodity standard (comparable to the pre-1914 gold standard, not the post-1914 gold exchange standards), and arguably better than the hybrid and cumbersome Bretton Woods arrangements. Röpke's inflexible objection to flexible exchange rates, quite in contrast with fellow liberals like Milton Friedman, Gottfried Haberler and Albert Hahn, is difficult to justify. Trade and direct investment have continued to grow very fast, especially in services. Capital has once again become internationally mobile.[29] And since the 1970s a deregulatory trend, albeit partial, has set in across the globe. It is now emerging markets in developing countries and the new transition economies of Eastern Europe and the former Soviet Union that set the pace in both domestic deregulation and international liberalisation, much of it consisting of unilateral, example-setting policy measures not contingent on reciprocity and intergovernmental agreements.

European economic integration

Röpke's pronouncements on regional integration are in perfect symmetry with his pronouncements on the international economic order. Indeed the two aspects are tightly interwoven in his scheme.

Röpke's cultural conception of Europe is the backcloth to his conception of Europe as a political economist. To him, as to the great Swiss historian Jacob Burckhardt, Europe's common religious-philosophical heritage relies on a concrete diversity of life conditions in different nations and regions with different languages, customs and habits. Röpke advocates a European federalism, but very much along Helvetic lines. Power should be decentralised as much as possible and diversity encouraged, with little or no reliance on common institutions or a political-bureaucratic machinery at the supranational level. Those who advocate a centralised European 'institutionalism' with common institutions and a *Gleichschaltung* of uniform, standardised policies, are scorned by him as 'Jacobinist' *terribles simplificateurs*. They threaten the glory of Europe – its *sui generis* diversity. Hence Röpke opposed on cultural grounds plans for a European Community in the 1950s. Added to this is his defence of longstanding and culturally anchored national sovereignty, which should not be transferred to artificially created supranational institutions.[30]

This is the entry point to his stances on the great European policy issues of the day. First, he is rather ambivalent about the Marshall Aid programme and the clearing mechanism of the European Payments Union (EPU): both, at least in their initial phases, rewarded the profligate and punished the virtuous. Countries such as the UK, France and Sweden with inflationary and collectivist policies that plunged the balance of payments into deficit, received more Marshall Aid and were bailed out in the EPU by the main surplus country, West Germany, which was following quite different market-oriented policies.

Röpke flatly rejects the argument that the regimes of Marshall Aid and the EPU were primarily responsible for economic reconstruction, intraregional trade liberalisation and the gradual progress to currency convertibility in Western Europe. These regimes of cooperation were 'a helpful auxiliary . . . but not a sufficient condition of European recovery'. Rather what took place within nation-states, that is to say, change 'from below', made all the difference.

Throughout the period there were very great differences between European nations in their economic policies, speed of recovery and overall economic performance. In the minority market economy camp were first the Swiss and then the Germans, with Ludwig Erhard's pioneering liberal reforms from 1948, going against the grain of the times and pushed through in the face of Allied opposition, particularly from the British. Once the internal reforms were consolidated by 1951, Erhard embarked on a course of unilateral liberalisation of quotas and tariffs, and pressed hard for a speedy return to the convertibility of European currencies. He was assiduously and energetically supported in this effort by his friend and fellow traveller, Röpke.

In the majority camp were the French and the British, at first committed to national planning, neoKeynesian macroeconomic policies, trade protection and exchange controls. Only gradually did the German approach, bearing fruit in much superior economic performance compared to Britain and France (or any other advanced industrial country in the 1950s for that matter, including the US and Japan), gain other European converts: first the Austrians followed the Erhard model of June 1948 by removing controls on prices and production, and by sticking to tight monetary and fiscal policies; and then the British and the French followed, even if partially and fitfully. The process was capped by the French Rueff-Pinay reforms of December 1958, somewhat similar to, and inspired by, those carried out by Erhard in 1948: many controls were removed and an austerity programme introduced to control the money supply,

increase reserves and restore balance of payments equilibrium. With the devaluation and convertibility of the French Franc, all the currencies in the EPU
achieved convertibility on current account transactions with the dollar area.
Unlike most international organisations, the EPU, having fulfilled its temporary
technical function, folded up. With convertibility came a wholesale liberalisation of trade between Western Europe and the rest of the world. It is no wonder
that Röpke refers to December 1958 as the landmark of international economic
reintegration.

Röpke infers from this experience that *national change* 'from below' outweighed
institutionalised regional cooperation in bringing about spreading liberalisation.
At its core was the German 'beacon of light': its *unilateral* domestic and foreign
economic policy reforms that encouraged others to do likewise. December 1958
did not start with regional regimes and American benevolence, although they
played a very useful, facilitating role; rather it started with the Erhard reforms
of June 1948 in Germany.[31]

As previously stated Röpke was, from the beginning, adamantly opposed to
a European integration 'from above' based on supranational institutions with
potentially market-nonconforming policies. To him the European economy, like
the international economy, was hostage to the dogfight of two opposing ordering
principles: one based on the market economy with an 'open integration' with
respect to third countries, following policies of trade liberalisation, currency
convertibility and unhindered capital flows; the other based on planning within
the regional area and 'closed integration' with respect to third countries by
means of exchange controls, trade discrimination and the like.

The planning, trade discrimination and heavy organisational setup of the
European Coal and Steel Community (ECSC) confirmed his worst fears. Even
the plans for a European Economic Community (EEC) based on a customs
union bore the imprint of the 'closed integration' approach. First, the customs
union would most likely end up in a lowest-common-denominator political
compromise between countries with diverging economic policies and heteroge-
neous production structures. Politicisation was bound to set in with the
establishment of supranational institutions. Market-nonconforming common
policies in steel, coal, agriculture and other areas, once in place, would be very
difficult to remove. Following Viner, Röpke argued that the Common External
Tariff, given differing national economic structures within the EEC, would result
in trade discrimination against, and 'trade diversion' from, third countries,
distorting international specialisation according to comparative advantages.[32]
There would be ample room for the raucous play of protectionist interests in
an expanded political process. Lastly, the customs union was inherently discriminating within the European theatre of operations: it split free Europe in two
between the 'insiders' in the EEC and the 'outsiders', like Britain, Scandinavia
and Switzerland, in the European Free Trade Association (EFTA).

Röpke's preferred approach was that of the EFTA: an 'open integration'
based on a free trade area that obliged governments to comply with certain

rules and codes, without either transferring sovereignty to supranational institutions or discriminating against third countries. This was also the basic approach of Erhard in Germany, although the political consensus there, led by Chancellor Adenauer, swung in the other direction of a customs union, more on political than economic grounds.[33]

With the benefit of hindsight, Röpke's Cassandra-like warnings on the future course of European integration have not been without foundation. There is much that is market-nonconforming in the internal policy of the European Union (EU), with wider discretionary powers invested with the supranational authorities over a swathe of policy areas, a trend accelerated by the Single European Act and the Treaty on European Union. Furthermore, the Common Commercial Policy has very definite discriminatory traits with respect to third countries, especially in the application of the nontariff barriers of quantitative protection.

The record of European integration in the 1990s would have certainly met with Röpke's great displeasure and been the subject of his devastatingly cutting remarks. He would have regarded the obsession with 'deepening' the EU, subsuming attempts to centralise and standardise an increasingly wide range of issue-areas (e.g. research and development, regional/social policy, education, environment, culture, taxation), as a further departure from a free market and a free trade orientation, especially by preventing individual member-states from pursuing unilateral liberalisation and setting examples which others could follow.

The above stance would apply in particular to the present plans for European Monetary Union (EMU). In lieu of a fixed international commodity standard, Röpke would, in all probability, have preferred the decentralised management of monetary and exchange rate policies at the national level to the centralised arrangements proposed in EMU. Quite apart from other economic and political objections, a policy cartel based on EMU would replace the decentralised competition of monetary (and perhaps fiscal) policies, with the attendant risk that centralised policy would be a pretext for avoiding difficult but necessary domestic policy choices. Finally, Röpke would have been enraged that the fixation with EMU has diverted attention from the underlying sclerosis in the EU, particularly the structural rigidities of its labour markets. He would contend that this fixation has both delayed and compromised the historic objective that, from a free market standpoint, should be uppermost on the EU's present agenda – enlargement to bring in the transition economies of Eastern Europe along market-conforming lines as speedily as possible.

On the other hand, Röpke's pessimistic predictions were perhaps a little (and characteristically) overdone. For all its drawbacks, the Internal Market has made substantial progress on the road to full integration, reaping static and dynamic gains, and providing the basis of greater integration between the European and international economies through trade, direct investment, portfolio capital and technology flows.

Conclusion

Neoclassical rational choice economists and US political scientists from the neoliberal institutionalist school dominate the liberal paradigm in international political economy. Both approaches cut themselves off in many respects from the pulmonary artery of liberalism, the classical tradition founded by Adam Smith and David Hume. The international political economy of Wilhelm Röpke is a highly welcome antidote to rational choice and neoliberal institutionalism, above all in its classical liberal derivation.

First, unlike rational choice, Röpke's political economy, in common with that of his German neoliberal colleagues, is not fundamentally dependent on *homo oeconomicus* and perfect competition. On the contrary, Röpke's conservative streak leads him to have a rather pessimistic (and many would say realistic) view of man's 'irrational' behaviour in his social environment.

Second, Röpke's liberalism 'from below', in the lineage of a hallowed classical liberal tradition through the eighteenth and nineteenth centuries, points to the pitfalls of complex mechanisms of intergovernmental cooperation, with their tendency to degenerate into political cartels that encourage discretionary power and bureaucratic expansion while avoiding both domestic political accountability and market disciplines. Neoliberal institutionalist enthusiasts of intergovernmental cooperation almost wholly ignore such features of 'international government failure'.

Furthermore, Röpke stresses the wide scope for unilateralism – not the beggar-thy-neighbour unilateral mercantilism of the 1930s, but unilateral liberalisation at the national level that, through example-setting, imitation and trial-and-error in the law and policy-making of governments, has a market-opening ripple effect that spreads throughout the international system – without an over-reliance on established or newly created organisational complexes at the international or regional levels. It is change at the national level that is of prime importance, which does not obviate a *degree of* institutionalised international (or regional) cooperation; rather a liberalism 'from below' accords more emphasis to unilateral national action in and of itself, and, in an interaction between national policy and international (or regional) regimes of cooperation, tilts the balance more in the direction of the national level as the appropriate level of policy action. Given the inextricable connection between domestic and foreign economic policy, there can be no change in the mercantilist character of trade policies, for example, without market-led reforms in domestic (macro- and micro-economic) policies. In the absence of the latter, too much cannot be expected of multilateral negotiations.[34] Ultimately, it is national institutions, embodying both formal rules and informal constraints (to re-employ North's terminology), that are decisive in bringing about liberalisation in the international system. Röpke applies the same argument to European integration as well.

To reiterate, Röpke's preference for unilateral liberalisation does not deny a place in the sun for intergovernmental cooperation and international organisations. However, a major lacuna in his work is the glaring lack of any explanation about how intergovernmental cooperation fits into his schemata of a liberal international economic order. He does not really address the question of how unilateralism and reciprocity can fruitfully interconnect.

The Bretton Woods compromise subsumed strict national capital controls and much else besides that hindered international economic integration. The contemporary world economy has become much more 'open' with floating exchange rates and the restored mobility of international capital, not to mention the current neoliberal wave of deregulation and trade liberalisation. Since the 1970s, a considerable chunk of such deregulation and trade liberalisation has occurred unilaterally: governments have taken down barriers to internal and external trade on their own initiative, without the exchange of concessions that is the stuff of intergovernmental negotiations and that usually works its way into international agreements.

Those fixated with organisational setup at the international level to facilitate intergovernmental cooperation would find it difficult to theorise and analyse the enormous range of actual and potential unilateral liberalisation, perhaps greater now than at anytime since 1914. Furthermore, they do not adequately account for the potential of intergovernmental cooperation, if it inclines in the direction of a political cartel, to provide excuses for *not* undertaking liberalising measures at the national level (as was the case with Bretton Woods by retaining and legitimising capital controls). This argument applies equally to regional areas like the European Union.

In common with the other German neoliberals and the classical liberal tradition in general, Röpke emphasises the *national preconditions of international order*.[35] With this insight in mind, Röpke's *oeuvre* should be an inspiration to those who wish to inject a genuinely Smithian, classical liberalism into an international political economy whose present liberal paradigm is distinctly suspect.

Notes

1 Admittedly, Robert Keohane makes an analytical distinction between 'cooperation' and 'liberalism'. See Keohane (1984), p. 37. Nevertheless, he clearly regards *institutionalised* international cooperation as the necessary, if not quite sufficient, condition of preventing economic conflict (including protectionism) and promoting a liberal international economic order (including freer trade). See Keohane (1984), pp. 6, 10, 17.

  Keohane also distinguishes between 'cooperation', the result of national policies mutually adjusted to prevent discord, and 'regimes' of principles, norms, rules and decision-making procedures around which actors' expectations converge in given issue-areas. The former can take place unilaterally, i.e. without intergovernmental negotiation and bargaining. The latter habitually entails cooperation *with* intergovernmental negotiation and bargaining. Keohane's focus is on the latter. See Keohane (1984), pp. 51–59.

2 The frank admission that political economy, as opposed to technical economic analysis, is fundamentally concerned with the discussion of values, is also found in the works of other notable classical liberal political economists of the twentieth century. See, for example, Hayek (1960), p. vii; Knight (1960), pp. 118–119, 131–132, 139–140, 145, 154, 166.

3 Röpke (1938), p. 288.
4 Incidentally, it is worth noting that some of Röpke's early publications in international political economy, notably *German Commercial Policy*, gained international recognition when he was still in his early to mid-30s. More generally, Röpke was a highly precocious economist, becoming Germany's youngest professor while in his mid-20s.
5 Röpke (1959a), pp. 9–20. Also see Gerard Curzon, 'International economic order: contribution of ordoliberals', in Peacock and Willgerodt (1989b).
6 For arguments in favour of world government, see Robbins (1936); Hayek (1944), pp. 163–176; Jacob Viner, 'Peace as an economic problem', in Viner (1951a), pp. 265–266.
7 For Röpke's views on realism, idealism and world government, see Röpke (1959a), pp. 21–24, 31, 33–43, 248–249.
8 Röpke (1955), pp. 210–212, 218.
9 Ibid., pp. 224, 231–232; Röpke (1994 [1965]), pp. 71, 105, 232–233; Wilhelm Röpke, 'Guiding principles of a liberal programme', in Ludwig Erhard Stiftung (1982), p. 188.
10 Röpke (1959a), pp. 16, 72–73; Röpke (1951). A shortened version of the latter article in English translation is entitled 'Interdependence of domestic and international economic systems', in Peacock and Willgerodt (1989a).
11 See note 6. Also refer to Lord Robbins, 'Liberalism and the international problem', in Robbins (1963), p. 144.
12 Röpke (1962b), p. 239.
13 The WTO agenda is no longer that discrete, having widened considerably since the Uruguay Round. Nevertheless, it remains a relatively small outfit by the standards of most leading international organisations.
14 Röpke (1959a), p. 224.
15 For representative positions in neoliberal institutionalism, see Robert O. Keohane (1984); Ruggie (1982), pp. 379–415; Ruggie (1995), pp. 507–526.
16 See Röpke's foreword to the German edition (*Der Weg zur Knechtschaft*) of F.A. Hayek's *Road to Serfdom* (Hayek (1945)), p. 10. *The Road to Serfdom* in many ways echoes Röpke's reservations about the mixed economy.
17 Viner (1937), p. 218 f.
18 Röpke, following Haberler, argues that (modest) duties are more-or-less market-conforming as they resemble internal freight costs: they merely widen the cost margin between separate places without seriously distorting price calculations. Thus, tariff increases are extra data incorporated into the price signalling mechanism. Quotas, bilateral clearing arrangements and exchange controls, on the other hand, are market-nonconforming because they seriously interfere with prices, causing great damage to multilaterally based cross-border trade. See Röpke (1955), pp. 252–253; Haberler (1950), Part II: Trade Policy.
19 On the analysis of nineteenth-century conditions, see Röpke (1955), pp. 225, 227, 259–260; Röpke (1959a), pp. 74–79, 157–158.
20 See, for example, Gilpin (1981) and (1986), p. 72 f.
21 Germany led the way in forcing the pace of investment way beyond accumulated (voluntary) savings. The resulting inflation not only severely distorted value relations, but also led to an excess of demand over supply on the foreign exchange market, that is, a balance of payments deficit. The classical remedy of restrictive monetary and fiscal policies to restore equilibrium with the international economy was not, of course, followed; rather Germany opted for a mercantilist remedy of repressing inflation through price-fixing, goods rationing, import quotas and foreign exchange controls. As all the major countries followed the German example, although not in

all respects, international economic disintegration was inevitable. See Röpke (1959a), pp. 194–220; Röpke (1947b) and (1947c).

22 On the evaluation of the interwar period, see Röpke (1959a), pp. 96–102, 162, 214–215; Röpke (1942), pp. 36, 42, 48–49, 121, 143, 201, 204, 224.

23 Röpke (1959a), p. 168; Röpke (1963b), p. 1.

24 Röpke (1955), p. 262; Röpke (1959a), pp. 224–225.

25 Röpke characterises the market as a self-regulating mechanism that, through the interplay of free price relationships, produces a spontaneous order. Hence the reference to the 'ordered anarchy' of the market. See Röpke (1994 [1965]), pp. 13–17.

26 Ibid., pp. 150, 318–324.

27 For a related argument on reciprocity versus unilateralism, see Tumlir (1983a), p. 75. On the views of liberal institutionalists, see note 17. For a representative argument that postwar international liberalisation is a direct result of international regimes, see Barry Eichengreen and Peter Kenen, 'Managing the world economy under the Bretton Woods system: an overview', in Kenen (1994).

28 Röpke (1994 [1965]), p. 152; Röpke (1959a), pp. 238–239; Röpke (1964a); Wilhelm Röpke, 'Die Kampf gegen die inflationärer Zeit', in Hunold (1959).

29 Gerard Curzon, 'Die internationale Ordnung', in Ludwig Erhard Stiftung (1980), pp. 65–79. On Röpke's differences with other liberal economists on the fixed/flexible exchange rate question, see Röpke (1976), p. 169.

30 On Röpke's general cultural orientation on the European question, see Röpke (1959a), pp. 52, 56; Röpke (1966), pp. 47–48; Röpke (1976), p. 123.

31 On Röpke's views of European recovery and liberalisation, see Röpke (1959b), pp. 79–81, 92; Röpke (1959c), pp. 486–488; Wilhelm Röpke, 'Wege der Konvertibilität', in Hunold (1953), pp. 84–85, 89; Röpke (1964b), pp. 189–191.
For similar arguments that put the emphasis on change 'from below' in engendering liberalisation in the Europe of the 1950s, see Giersch et al. (1992), pp. 95–124.

32 See Viner (1951b).

33 On Röpke's views on European integration, especially the customs union, see Röpke (1955), pp. 256–257; Röpke (1964c), pp. 235–237; Röpke (1958), pp. 39, 45, 49–50, 52–53, 56, 58.
On the debate in Germany, see Sally (1995), pp. 549–550.

34 Willgerodt (1988), p. 32.

35 This is arguably an undercurrent in German ordoliberal thought, for example in Walter Eucken's *Grundlagen der Nationalökonomie* and *Grundsätze der Wirtschaftspolitik* (Euken 1989 [1941] and 1990 [1952]).

Part IV

CONSTITUTIONALISM AND INTERNATIONAL POLITICAL ECONOMY: TUMLIR

8

JAN TUMLIR

Democratic constitutionalism and international economic order

Western influence on the world, though still great, is declining. Eventually our societies will be the minor partner in the terrestrial enterprise. What do we want the majority to believe about the liberal idea that animated the West's historical achievement and that we continue to profess, but have, in recent decades, ceased to act upon? What kind of world will it be, if the majority comes to believe that the idea is a sham?

Jan Tumlir

Not much has been written about Jan Tumlir. Unlike all the other scholars covered in this book, he is not nationally or internationally renowned, although he was well known to the economists and lawyers who specialise in trade policy. Furthermore, he did not build up an extensive corpus of writing on political economy, and there is no single book left by him that ranks in the same league as Hayek's *Constitution of Liberty,* Eucken's *Grundsätze* or Viner's *Studies in the Theory of International Trade.*

Nevertheless, Tumlir fits hand-in-glove with the general theme of this book. He stands at the crossroads of the different traditions surveyed in the preceding chapters and, as I suggested in the introductory chapter, no one has come as tantalisingly close as Tumlir to making *the* twentieth-century statement on classical liberalism and international economic order. Regrettably, Tumlir did not quite arrive at this destination; if not for his sudden death in 1985, he might have gone on to write his *magnum opus* on the very subject covered by this book.

Tumlir was of Czech origin and studied law at the Charles University in Prague. He emigrated to the West in the 1940s and settled down in the US to graduate studies, and then teaching, in economics. He went on to head the research division of the GATT in Geneva, where he stayed until his untimely death.

Tumlir's writings in political economy came relatively late in life and are mostly in the form of articles, contributions to edited volumes and policy papers, without a single, fully elaborated book to his name. His publications in political economy were also packed into less than a decade of work (from the mid-1970s to the mid-1980s). Nevertheless, during that period his output became ever more substantial, and his 'take' on the international economic order became ever clearer, sharper, more comprehensive and, finally, very distinctive. Indeed, it is very difficult to think of any contemporary who even approximated the range and quality of Tumlir's classical liberal approach to questions of international economic order.

Tumlir was one-of-a-kind in his time. In his fine, chiselled prose – always delightful in its erudition, its poise, its acuity of insight and ingenuity of expression – he conveys a sense of the *order* underlying and surrounding international economic transactions like no one else in the past few decades. He weaves law and economics, spontaneous processes and deliberately designed rules, and the two-way flow between national and international levels of governance, into an intricate web of international economic order. Throughout his work he emphasises the domestic legal and policy foundations of international order – almost a lone voice in an international political economy that tends to abstract from the national underpinning of international arrangements.

Despite Tumlir's uniqueness in modern international political economy, his work owes a great deal to liberal forebears such as Henry Simons, Frank Knight, James Buchanan, F.A. Hayek, Walter Eucken and Franz Böhm. Indeed, the German ordoliberals' combination of law and economics initially inspired him to think of economic order in 'constitutional' terms.[1] As the introductory chapter mentioned, however, all the above operate with a 'closed economy' in mind, abstracting from the international economic order.[2] To his credit, Tumlir transplants their thinking to the arena of international order.

Knight, Hayek and the German ordoliberals are only part of the classical liberal context for Tumlir. As I will argue later in this chapter, he has much in common with Wilhelm Röpke in his appreciation of international economic order, and, ultimately, his work has its roots in the international political economy of Hume and Smith.

Before going on to examine Tumlir's work, I should like to point out one more telling sign of his classical, rather than neoclassical, liberalism. He has an evident sympathy for parts of the public choice literature, particularly the work of James Buchanan, but he does not rely on rational utility-maximisation or perfect competition models anywhere in his political economy. As I will endeavour to show, his conception of economic order is overwhelmingly evolutionary and dynamic, with hardly a mention of static 'maximisation and equilibrium'.

The next section investigates the foundation of Tumlir's thought in what he has to say about economic order in general, and domestic economic order in particular. This part of the discussion revolves around his thinking on 'democratic constitutionalism' as the basis of economic order. A theory of democratic constitutionalism and (domestic) economic order is the building block of Tumlir's theory of international economic order, which is examined in the following sections. After looking at his general conception of international economic order and disorder, the discussion addresses two specific aspects of this side of his work: first, the difference between his emphasis on negative, procedural international rules and the type of intergovernmental policy coordination advocated by 'interdependence' (or neoliberal institutionalist) theorists; and second, his evaluation of reciprocally negotiated international agreements and unilateral free trade.

Democratic constitutionalism and national economic order

Tumlir thinks of economic orders in a way that is foreign to neoclassical economic analysis. As he argues, neoclassical economics analyses the consequences for resource allocation of 'given' political frameworks. Tumlir, in common with other classical liberals and modern constitutional economists, looks at how economic activity feeds into the political system and changes political conditions. Thus, like James Buchanan, his constitutional approach focuses on alternative institutional arrangements that set the scene for, and are in turn modified by, transactions within the market economy.[3]

Going beyond conventional economics, Tumlir tries to grasp the essence of economic order by way of an amalgam of law and economics, drawing inspiration from the Freiburg ordoliberal School, and the work of Franz Böhm in particular. Like Böhm, Tumlir has an antipositivist conception of the law: law should not merely react or submit to the whims of political rulers, the interests of politically powerful organised interests or the 'will of the majority'; rather, it should proactively shape the process of collective decision-making. It should forcefully separate the public and private spheres, and protect individual rights so that they remain beyond the reach of political discretion. Tumlir's maxim that 'the order is the creation of the law', encapsulates this point of view.[4]

Like other classical liberals, Tumlir has two kinds of economic order in mind: one results from decentralised decision-making and private property rights, the other from government control. Economic policy delimited and governed by the law, particularly in terms of general rules of conduct that safeguard property rights and enforce contracts, regulates the first kind of order. Such a strictly circumscribed economic policy serves the function of ensuring the stability of the purchasing power of money and the maintenance of competition. This enables a price system to discharge its information function, emitting signals to individual agents so that they can speedily adjust their behaviour to changing external conditions.

In this scheme, general rules pertaining to property and contract shape market-based competition and facilitate the spontaneous adjustment of economic and social structures. Under such a rule-governed framework, society is an 'open-ended adventure', for individuals are left free to plan their own futures and there is no way in which governments can plan or preprogramme specific outcomes for society.[5]

Thus Tumlir proposes an economic policy subordinated to general rules, and he has a distinct preference for a market economy that operates within such a rule-governed order. This conception bears a remarkable similarity to the Hayekian theory of the spontaneous order and its legal underpinning. General rules of conduct are in part the product of deliberative design by legislators. However, the economic order itself, providing it is based on private property rights and decentralised decision-making, is predominantly a spontaneous organism open-ended to future development; it is not a mechanical construct controlled and steered by a single or group mind to achieve preset objectives. As Tumlir remarks, 'a market economy is more of an organism evolved to cope with errors, and robust enough to take a lot of punishment'. And as he goes on to say: 'Order is a system, the regularity of which is largely spontaneous, the result of general rules within which self-conscious choosing units – governments, firms, households, individuals carrying out their functions – act independently, but also interdependently'.[6]

One distinguishing feature of a liberal economic order is progress, that is, manifold and incessant change. However, Tumlir argues that sustainable, ongoing change cannot occur in a vacuum, for the result will be a chaos and anarchy that will destroy society. Rather, change requires some kind of stability or orderliness in its midst. In effect, it is this 'order' that allows individuals to adapt to change as speedily and as efficiently as possible, with the minimum waste of resources. This is where general rules come in, particularly in the form of private property rights, for they furnish that anchor of stability that facilitates adaptation to change.[7]

Tumlir drives home the point that it is a decentralised, market-based order governed by general rules of conduct that best enables adjustment. 'The point is that order, or at least some degree of orderliness, is a function of the promptness of adjustment. That, in turn, is a function of the degree of decentralisation in economic decision-making.' A large number of profit-motivated individual agents, in the context of general rules and with the aid of a price-signalling mechanism, adapt in a reasonably prompt manner. In contrast, an economic order riddled with government intervention slows down the process of adjustment, and stores up future problems and conflicts within and between nations (as following sections will discuss).[8]

What role does democratic politics play in the proper functioning of a liberal economic order? Is democratic politics at all compatible with such an order? These questions are absolutely central to Tumlir, just as they were to Frank Knight before him. In fact, Tumlir follows Knight very closely in answering both questions.

As mentioned in chapter four, Frank Knight emphasises *cooperation* in both economic and political spheres. In politics, cooperation centres in 'government by discussion': a collective effort on the part of the various branches of government, organised interests and the wider public to discuss thoroughly the means and ends of social action, and to deliberate on necessary collective choices.

What Tumlir calls 'democratic constitutionalism' fundamentally concerns itself with the effective structuring of such a political discussion. It aims to bring the maximum amount of latent knowledge in society to bear on the collective discussion of the laws. All elements of the state and society should be free to contribute to the public good of informed agreement, but they should all be equally bound by the law and none should be legally privileged above others.[9]

A keystone of democratic constitutionalism is the doctrine of constitutional due process that, *inter alia*, stipulates the proper delegation of legislative powers. Under this doctrine, the legislature can delegate powers to the executive only on the condition that it gives clear and precise guidelines as to how the executive should administer such powers. The judiciary can effectively monitor and control the actions of the executive only if the legislature provides detailed and transparent specification of delegated powers. This kind of judicial review is crucial, for Tumlir argues that an integral component of constitutional due process is the ability of the courts to prevent governments from infringing individual rights – including private property rights.[10]

To Tumlir, the political-economic history of the twentieth century is very largely a sorry tale of destroying the gains so painstakingly achieved in the course of the nineteenth century. Before the First World War, limited government and a relatively free market economy in the West prevailed. Constitutional due process, the cornerstone of which was the strict limitation and close scrutiny of delegated legislative power to executives, buttressed the nineteenth-century economic order. First Europe after 1918, and then the US during the New Deal, abandoned this liberal order. With the demise of judicial review over economic policy (particularly in the US in the 1930s), legislatures feverishly enacted more laws and delegated more of them to executives. By this stage, there was virtually no external control over executive discretion.[11]

The door was now open to almost unlimited executive action and improvisation in economic policy, heralding the era of Big Government. The onset of uncontrolled and expanding government subtly changed the process of democratic politics, sacrificing 'government by discussion' and the Rule of Law on the altar of greater discretionary powers exercised by politicians and bureaucrats. *Ad hoc* government intervention favoured the established and politically powerful organised interests, and encouraged other groups to organise and lobby in the political theatre of operations. 'Rent-seeking' became the order of the day: private interests channelled more resources to influence political decisions, and in turn more income was redistributed by political manipulation of the conditions of competition, that is, by interfering in resource allocation and distorting prices.

As Tumlir cuttingly remarks, these trends amounted to a 'wild refeudalisation of society': modern government came to resemble the old-style mercantilist conception of group rights, not individual rights. Direct transactions between government and interest groups became the norm, well hidden from the public gaze and unaccountable to the chief organs of democratic constitutionalism, the legislature and the judiciary. Rent-seeking by private actors, and rent-giving by governments, trampled on private property rights and made a mockery of equal treatment before the laws. Discretionary government won a resounding victory over an emasculated Rule of Law and a gutted democratic constitutionalism. As Tumlir says, policy 'by means of law' metamorphosed into politics 'without law'.

What suffered most was 'government by discussion'. The pluralist politics of rampant interest group lobbying and untrammelled governments replaced a careful and thorough airing of views in the legislature, as well as the effective review of the laws by the judiciary. The 'discussion' surreptitiously retreated from the classic public arenas of the *polis* to the back-rooms of private and public power.[12]

The New Pluralism conveniently coincided with the New Economics that surfaced in the interwar period. The latter, a combination of Keynesian macroeconomics and a reformed microeconomics (Pigovian welfare economics, public goods, externalities, etc.), provided greater justification for government intervention, in the belief that the economy could be collectively guided to a better future. This mind-set also assumed that governments held more and better knowledge of economic conditions than the totality of individuals in the marketplace.[13]

Tumlir argues that this confluence of interventionist politics and interventionist economics led directly to the *malaise* that became plain for all to see by the 1970s. The gamut of progressively more interventionist macro- and micro-economic policies had so distorted prices that national economic orders had become heavily sclerotic, slowing down the market economy's necessary adaptation to change. Indeed, it seemed that there was mounting inbuilt resistance to adaptation and change of any kind as far as economic activity was concerned.[14]

To conclude this section, one should reiterate that Tumlir's normative conception of domestic economic order blends law and economics, and highlights spontaneous evolution within a framework of general rules. Hayek and German ordoliberalism heavily influence his work; and, of course, these features of economic order can be traced back to the source of classical liberalism in Hume and Smith. Furthermore, Tumlir's views on democratic constitutionalism and its decline in the twentieth century mirror the account of one of his intellectual heroes, Frank Knight.

International economic order

The long excursion into the theory of domestic economic order was necessary because Tumlir, like Wilhelm Röpke, believes that international economic order – or disorder – is essentially an overspill of what happens within nation-states. Policy-induced intranational imbalances such as inflation, unemployment, fiscal and balance of payments deficits, are rapidly transmitted into the arena of international transactions, causing instability and conflict between nation-states.[15]

Tumlir accounts for the incidence and increase of international protectionism in the structural shift in intranational democratic politics that took place after 1913. As mentioned earlier, a number of factors – the downfall of constitutional due process, the rise and rise of unchecked executive power, and the rent-seeking activity of private interests – led to the rigidification of economic structures, and decreased the willingness of public and private actors to adjust to external changes. The predictable corollary of these secular trends was a 'fear of trade' and the resort to import protection. Thus, according to Tumlir, 'protectionism is the inherent logic of the redistributive state working itself out externally'.[16]

International economic relations mirrored the paradigmatic shift in intranational politics after the First World War. Limited government and a high degree of respect for private property rights internally guaranteed the stability and openness of the liberal international economic order. Externally, unilateral free trade and the *Système de Traités*, the patchwork of bilateral, nondiscriminatory trade and investment treaties, reinforced the internal constants of such an order. The latter was ripped to shreds in the interwar years, followed by an attempt at partial restoration post-1945. However, the new international rules in the IMF and the GATT contained a fatal contradiction: rules to limit government discretion were nevertheless full of exceptions and escape clauses designed to accommodate discretionary policy – reflecting the great distrust of markets at the time (not least on the part of Lord Keynes). Wide latitude for informal intergovernmental bargaining – what Tumlir calls 'fuzzy diplomacy' – compromised formal procedures (i.e. rules). Inevitably, this created uncertainty for firms engaged in international transactions. There is much in Tumlir's interpretation here that reflects Jacob Viner's ambivalence on the nature and viability of the rule-base for the post-1945 international economic order (see chapter five).[17]

Tumlir argues that the crises of the 1970s and early 1980s were the direct product of greater intranational government intervention, worsened by an increasing disrespect for, and flouting of, international rules. These intra- and international aspects of economic policy reflected the decreasing capacity for adaptation by sclerotic societies in the West. At first a slowdown in adjustment resulted in protection against developing country imports, but by the 1970s protection had spread to intra-industry trade with other developed countries. Here Tumlir counters the charge that modern protectionism is a cyclical phenomenon – a transitory response to an economic downturn that will recede with resumed growth. Rather, it is a structural feature of modern democratic politics, the *permanent* issue of discretionary government and rent-seeking activity.[18]

In his wide-ranging study on protectionism for the American Enterprise Institute, Tumlir surveys the international debris left by the cumulative trashing of intranational democratic constitutionalism in the twentieth century. This culminated in the New Protectionism that began to fester in the late 1960s and early 1970s.

The New Protectionism differs from both nineteenth-century protection, based on moderate tariffs, and the blanket protection of the 1930s that relied on global quotas. It is more bilateral, selective and systematic, targeting offending exporting sectors in particular countries and attempting to neutralise them with a panoply of nontariff instruments. Voluntary export restraints (VERs) are perhaps the most visible sign of recent protection in oligopolistic sectors such as automobiles, consumer electronics and steel. They accommodate a broader range of interests than old-style protection in a political cartel. The latter subsumes not only the government and import-competing producers in the importing country, but also exporters and the government in the exporting country. Established exporting firms have an incentive to form a cartel because part of the rent accrues to them; and the national bureaucracy of the exporting country connives to make sure that the export cartel functions as planned. The damage is compounded by the exemptions from antitrust law, in both importing and exporting countries, which enable such arrangements to work. Hence trade policy 'beyond the border' seriously compromises competition enforcement 'behind the border'. The whole effort is a perverse symptom of international cooperation between governments and firms.

These features of the New Protectionism are well known by now, but Tumlir is one of the very few trade policy analysts who goes beyond a 'political' or an 'economic' analysis of the New Protectionism to uncover its inimical impact on domestic constitutional arrangements and the Rule of Law.

Tumlir's argument is that the instruments of the New Protectionism – VERs, Orderly Marketing Arrangements (OMAs), subsidies, regulatory barriers, antidumping duties – do more harm to democratic constitutionalism and 'government by discussion' than almost any other aspect of modern economic policy. Nineteenth-century tariff protection had little distortive effect on the world price system and its relative transparency left domestic constitutional arrangements intact. In contrast, the selective instruments of the New Protectionism not only distort world prices, but also abridge and circumvent political discussion within nation-states. Given that they involve direct and largely hidden transactions between governments, between oligopolistic firms, and between governments and organised interests, they short-circuit a comprehensive and open discussion of these arrangements in the legislature and in wider public arenas. Furthermore, given exemptions from antitrust, they are shielded from prosecution. In fact, they are largely beyond any kind of judicial oversight and control. In essence, this kind of protection gives politicians and bureaucrats *carte blanche* to privilege some (politically powerful) groups over others. Consequently, the New Protectionism has a deeply corrosive effect on the law.[19]

The parallels between Tumlir and Röpke in their separate accounts of protectionism have already cropped up, but it is also worth stressing that the political economy of protection in Tumlir's work is very close to that of Adam Smith. Many political science versions of international political economy explain modern protectionism in terms of the decline of US 'hegemonic' power to keep the international economic order open.[20] Like Smith, Tumlir does not, in the first instance, see protectionism as the result of an unbalanced international political system or of declining US hegemonic power; rather, he thinks it is an overspill of mercantilist deals between government and organised interests within nation-states.[21] Also like Smith, Tumlir emphasises that discretionary politics, privileging politically powerful rent-seekers at the expense of the general interest, makes a mockery of 'justice' or equal treatment before the laws (see chapter three).

The above account shows how Tumlir views the international economic *disorder* of our times. Now it is time to gauge his explanation of international economic *order*.

Tumlir argues that, like domestic economic order, its international complement must manage to find a propitious mix of continuity and change. Change is the stuff of progress, but it has to be anchored in the still waters of stability or orderliness, the objective of which is to facilitate smooth and rapid adjustment to external change. Prompt adjustment is of first-order priority. Economic history is replete with examples of 'institutional' creative destruction *à la* Schumpeter: dynamic newcomer countries rapidly catch up with advanced countries; and newcomers put the onus on richer countries to weed out antiquated institutional practices, and innovate new and better ways of doing things. Such adaptation is feasible if decision-making becomes or remains decentralised, leaving action and interaction in the marketplace to individual agents within the framework of general rules of property and contract. But adaptation is retarded if government actively or hyperactively meddles in the price mechanism and the process of resource allocation. The main thing is to keep a functioning world price system intact so that appropriate signals about changes in demand and supply can be transmitted within and between national societies, enabling economic agents to anticipate change and modify their behaviour accordingly. Finally, for a world price system to function effectively, policymakers should maintain a liberal system of trade and payments, that is, they should keep international trade relatively free of restrictions and ensure currency convertibility.[22]

Note that Tumlir's conception of international economic order, like his conception of domestic economic order, is more classical-liberal than neoclassical. Rather than taking snapshots of the (static) allocation of resources at any one moment in time, he captures a moving landscape of dynamic, open-ended competition and spontaneous evolution within the context of general rules – a blend of Hume and Smith, and of Schumpeter and Hayek, in the international arena. Indeed, Tumlir is one of the very few in modern international political economy who judge relations between states according to the dynamic criteria of adjustment and resistance to change.

Within this evolutionary purview, Tumlir goes as far as to equate liberalism with order, hitching stability and change inextricably and permanently to each other's fortunes.

> We cannot imagine international order in any form that could not be essentially liberal. For only when economic activity is carried on by competing individual units can adjustment be sufficiently prompt, smooth and efficient for the world economy to be in a state of order.

To Tumlir, the alternative to a liberal international economic order is not a different kind of 'order', but only and invariably international economic disorder.[23]

In Tumlir's scheme, an international economic order, like a domestic economic order, requires *rules,* and this is the conceptual bridge to a discussion of his interpretation of international rules. If governments discharged their 'classical' functions of providing stable money and guaranteeing the freedom of contract, international order would spontaneously result without any need for international rules. The latter come into play precisely because governments are prone to inflation-creation and interference in resource allocation, thus stoking the flames of international disorder. Hence international rules, mostly in the form of proscriptions or 'negative ordinances', exist as a mechanism to protect the market *against* excessive government. Put another way, they are tools that enable governments to discharge their classical functions of stable money and competition-maintenance.

Tumlir therefore regards international rules as constituent elements of stability that, by limiting the political discretion of governments, assist national societies in adapting rapidly to external change. In the international context, they are signposts that enable national policies to mutually adjust to each other with the minimum of conflict. Like the rules of private law that safeguard individual rights within nations, they are bulwarks of constancy and predictability that are highly useful to efficient policy planning.[24]

Once one makes a case for international rules that proscribe errant behaviour by governments, the matter of their implementation arises. Now the question of *how* such rules can effectively apply is much more difficult to answer than the question of *why* they should exist in the first place. The reason for this is obvious: international rules have to function in a world without world government, that is, in an anarchical international system without effective and binding third-party enforcement (in contrast to such third-party enforcement within sovereign nation-states).

Given these realistic considerations, Tumlir points to the fatal flaw in Lord Robbins's naive quest for world government or 'international authorities' to stem the tide of international economic disorder. It is easy enough to say that new international authorities should impose binding, proscriptive rules on nation-states. But it is quixotic to expect national governments to disarm themselves *en masse* and create international authorities along these lines. New international organisations are more likely to be 'diplomatic authorities' than apolitical enforcers of an international Rule of Law: they are quite likely to furnish an extra arena in which intergovernmental power struggles are played out.[25]

Thus, Tumlir is sceptical of purely international mechanisms, that is, negotiations and agreements between governments, as the *primary* solution to the problem of international economic disorder. This stance informs his interpretation of postwar international economic law. The GATT, for instance, does contain commitments that enjoin governments to respect the rights of private agents to trade freely across borders. The nondiscriminatory traits of the Most Favoured Nation and National Treatment clauses are the legal embodiment of the freedom of international trade.[26] However, there is no truly authoritative third-party enforcement of these international rules. They are left to the vagaries of diplomacy and the willingness of governments to stick to them.[27] MFN and National Treatment lack force because, at the end of the day, they are not private rights within nation-states. In other words, individuals and firms cannot, as a rule, seek redress from national courts if they believe that home or host governments are obstructing their freedom to trade across borders. US and EU courts, for example, balk at giving direct effect to GATT law, that is, making it justiciable as part of national private law.

Judiciaries have traditionally made a rigid distinction between domestic and foreign policy. Much of the former is justiciable within nation-states (although, even in this sphere, this is less the case now than it used to be due to the decline of constitutional due process). On the other hand, the courts tend to leave foreign policy to the discretion of governments. They treat foreign economic policy as equivalent to security policy: both are thought of as a *rapport de force* between governments; they are policy domains that do not involve individual rights guaranteed by (private) law.

To Tumlir, this is the core of the problem. Governments make reciprocal commitments in international agreements, and then invest time and diplomacy in wholly or partially squirming out of them. This only exacerbates international disorder. Tumlir reiterates that order can come about only by taking foreign economic policy out of the uncertain and unstable domain of diplomacy and placing it in the domain of the law. Stable and predictable foreign economic policy requires a framework of binding rules – and such rules can be effective only if they take the form of private rights *within national jurisdictions*.[28]

This emphasis on the reorientation of national law shows that, for Tumlir, all international roads lead back to domestic-level solutions and domestic order. Like Wilhelm Röpke in earlier decades, he stresses the *domestic legal and policy foundations* of international economic order. Just as international disorder originates in greater government intervention within nation-states, so liberal international order emerges from governmental and constitutional reconstruction at the domestic level. At best, international-level arrangements between governments alleviate the symptoms of disorder; only domestic-level solutions – 'from below' or 'from within and beneath' in Röpke's terms – get to grips with root causes. Thus, Tumlir progresses along the same track as Röpke – 'internationalism, like charity, begins at home' (see chapter seven).

Moreover, Tumlir is in no doubt as to the classical liberal provenance of his approach. Unlike Robbins, he squarely defends the eighteenth- and nineteenth-century classical economists for saying little about international order *per se* and concentrating on domestic order. They regard proper constitutional observance within the nation-state as key: a liberal international economic order is a by-product, or an epiphenomenon, of a well-adjusted domestic order (see chapter three).[29]

This brings Tumlir to the policy recommendation for which he is best remembered. He urges the leading Western powers – the US, the EU, Canada and Japan – to incorporate the unconditional MFN clause into their separate national laws *as a private right*. If this strict and simple approach applied, home country citizens and foreigners would be able to insist on their freedom to trade across borders in national jurisdictions. The courts would have the solid backing of the law in nullifying public restraints on cross-border trade. Giving direct effect to unconditional MFN would make traditional export and import cartels, as well as the core elements of the New Protectionism – VERs, OMAs and the like – illegal under national law. It would also automatically extend the freedom to export and import to all GATT contracting parties on a nondiscriminatory basis. Consequently, this legal innovation would transport the bulk of foreign economic policy out of the orbit of discretionary diplomacy and into the rule-based sphere of the law.[30]

Whereas most trade policy analysts tend to fix their attention on the international level, especially on the GATT (now the WTO), Tumlir adopts a radically different tack. To him, the GATT is large, amorphous body with too many disparate and conflicting interests. Perhaps the best hope for the GATT is a lowest-common-denominator compromise of so many diverging views. Therefore, Tumlir believes that the GATT is not a suitable vehicle for an intrepid voyage to a free trade destination. It can never be the repository of a truly solid international Rule of Law, and it cannot avoid getting entangled with intergovernmental politics.[31]

Instead of concentrating on the GATT, Tumlir places his hopes with a coterie of advanced industrial democracies that have similar political and economic systems, and that account for the bulk of world trade. By embodying free trade where it counts – in *domestic* law – they would set an example that would arrest the groundswell of protectionism and persuade other countries to follow suit (in adopting free trade).[32]

Tumlir says he does not underestimate the political difficulties of such a move. Nor is he unaware of the legal obstacles involved. As mentioned earlier, judges tend to shy away from foreign economic policy. Comprehensive judicial oversight of foreign economic policy would take them into new and controversial pastures. Nevertheless, Tumlir takes heart from the fact that increasing interdependence intermeshes domestic and foreign economic policy to such an extent that judiciaries are ineluctably drawn into the adjudication of foreign economic policy.[33]

Thus far in this section of the discussion, it might seem that only international trade is in Tumlir's sights. This is far from the case, for he sees the implementation of unconditional MFN in national law as a means of overhauling domestic political processes. The resort to a legal solution serves to limit the surge of *ad hoc* government intervention and rent-seeking activity by interest groups. This leads Tumlir back to his starting-point – democratic constitutionalism. Legally guaranteed MFN is the international equivalent of fundamental guarantees of individual freedom in national law. Like domestic private rights, unconditional MFN relies on the principle of the equality of persons before the law. Its incorporation into national law would immediately reverse the shrinkage of private rights by enabling judiciaries to protect individual freedoms against discretionary government intervention. It would help to arrest the deterioration of constitutional due process in the politics of the West, and represent a step in the direction of domestic constitutional refurbishment. Thus 'an economic constitution is not complete without a theory of foreign economic policy and the legal control of it'. Furthermore, the legal control of foreign economic policy is 'the second line of national constitutional entrenchment'.[34]

Tumlir's argument has by now come full circle, linking international economic order to intranational democratic constitutionalism. As suggested earlier, Tumlir's emphasis on the domestic sphere resonates with Wilhelm Röpke's work, although Röpke concentrates more on advocating the 'right' sort of policies than the legal-constitutional control of domestic politics. Both Tumlir and Röpke follow Adam Smith in highlighting domestic order as the key to a liberal international economic order.[35]

It is easy to dismiss Tumlir's proposal on MFN as improbable and guilty of not a little political naïveté. On the one hand, the countries favoured by Tumlir for a joint pledge to implement unconditional MFN in national laws are highly unlikely to take his hint. This applies particularly to the two most powerful players, the US and the EU. Protectionism, reliant on discretionary government and rent-seeking activity, is deeply entrenched in the politics of both the US and the EU. They are the most ardent admirers of reciprocity, consenting to open their own markets only if other countries grant like concessions. Public authorities and politically powerful private interests would see unconditional MFN in national (and EU) law as an unwarranted internal intrusion into executive power. Externally, they would see such a move as tantamount to unilateral disarmament.

On the other hand, one could well imagine small developed and developing countries following Tumlir's advice. All countries suffer from the kind of domestic politics that Tumlir decries, but small countries usually depend much more on the international economy and therefore have greater sensitivity to the gains from open international commerce, as well as the costs of protection.

One should also remember that the most daring measures of trade liberalisation in recent years have not materialised in the developed world, but in developing and transition countries. The kind of legal anchor proposed by

Tumlir would logically and practically follow from programmes of policy reform in countries like Chile, Bolivia, Estonia, Poland and New Zealand. The legal guarantee of the freedom of international trade as a private right would lock in existing reforms and probably prevent them from being rolled back by discretionary politics in the present and the future.

This scenario is rather different from the one Tumlir envisaged in the 1970s and early 1980s. Then, developing countries were hell-bent on a *dirigiste* New International Economic Order, and the Second World was still in a command economy time-warp. In common with other trade policy experts, Tumlir was not optimistic that trade liberalisation would come from these quarters. The late 1980s and 1990s have proved him wrong (although, if alive today, he would probably be the first to welcome this turn of events).

Tumlir has also drawn criticism for his pessimism about the trend of policy in the West. To repeat an earlier point, his constitutional solutions, in the spirit of Buchanan and Hayek, flow from a structural interpretation of domestic political processes. In this scheme, a more active role for the law is essential to protect individual rights from the tyranny of majority and minority interests immanent in modern democratic politics. Perhaps Tumlir's pessimism rendered him partially blind to the ideological and policy changes of the recent liberal revival that has touched nearly all parts of the globe.[36]

Nevertheless, optimists need to be reminded that Tumlir pinpoints secular trends in modern democratic politics. The liberal gains since the late 1970s precariously balance on shifting sands precisely because the institutional features of policy-making have hardly changed, particularly in the developed world. Discretionary government and rent-seeking activity continue unabated. This threatens the momentum of policy reform and leaves the possibility of regression wide open, if internal and external conditions change for the worse. This is not something that unduly worries many contemporary economic liberals. They seem to share the complacency of nineteenth-century liberals in believing that present trends are cast in stone.

The constitutionalism of Tumlir is a welcome antidote to such excessive doses of optimism. The current policy climate has not vitiated the case for greater legal limits on politics; it remains in force, not least due to continuing flaws in policy-making that are bound to create serious problems in the not-so-distant future.

This section has covered the general features of international economic order in Tumlir's thinking. The following subsections home in on two specific aspects of it: the tussle between 'rules and discretion' in intergovernmental dealings; and the debate that confronts reciprocity with unilateral free trade.

International economic cooperation: rules or discretion?

The previous section showed that Tumlir conceives international cooperation in terms of negative, procedural rules that tie the hands of governments, preventing them from excessive intervention in private property rights. He then goes on to differentiate his approach from the more popular conception of international economic cooperation, which privileges government discretion over binding rules. To Tumlir, the latter is 'cooperation instead of rules'.[37]

Interdependence theorists (or neoliberal institutionalists) like Richard Cooper, Robert Keohane and Joseph Nye exemplify the discretionary approach Tumlir has no truck with. They oppose any notion of giving direct effect to international rules in national law, for they believe that this is an altogether unwarranted encroachment on national sovereignty. They prefer governments to have maximum leeway to pursue their own economic objectives within their sovereign jurisdictions. Consequently, they see international cooperation as an almost exclusive preserve for dealings between governments, with the aim of reducing the tension and conflict between often incompatible or clashing government policies. To Tumlir, this is the 'executive approach to world integration'.

Hence interdependence theorists tend to prefer flexibility in intergovernmental negotiations to strict and binding rules. In fact, international economic cooperation in the postwar era bears much resemblance to the interdependence approach. Cooperation has become the public policy equivalent of private cartels to a much greater extent than the rule-based international order Tumlir prefers.[38]

Implicit in the interdependence type of thinking is that the 'legitimate' exercise of government power, in the 'national interest', inevitably and appropriately results from pluralist political processes within nation-states. National objectives supposedly emerge from the lobbying of organised interests with political clout. Once these objectives have been set, governments supposedly seek to achieve the social welfare function of their societies.[39]

At its extreme, interdependence theory leads to an unconditional advocacy of discretionary international economic cooperation. As Tumlir says, 'international organisations, negotiations, agreements and functions seem to be favoured, wholesale and uncritically, more for their international character than for their substantive content'. International economic cooperation comes to cover so many things, with so many new executive and administrative functions. Cooperation ends up as an incantation rather than anything with intelligible meaning.[40]

Tumlir argues that interdependence theory's fatal flaw is its blind ignorance of pervasive government failure and rent-seeking within nation-states. It does not seem particularly concerned with the demise of democratic constitutionalism and the abrasion of private property rights. By implication, it is unaware of how such intranational trends retard adaptation to external change, and how they fuel the flames of international disorder. Hence 'the belief that rules of policy conduct can be bargained about, that national interests will conflict and can be compromised only in the choice of rules, ultimately denies the possibility of an international order'.[41]

Tumlir strikes a very different note by rejecting the assertion that legitimate government power, or legitimate national interest, is compatible with untrammelled pluralist politics within nation-states. The putative national interest issues from the short-term considerations of disparate sectional interests and shifting majoritarian political coalitions. This is not true national interest; rather 'genuine national interest can only be defined in the most general, procedural terms: it is the interest in the maintenance of order and the observance of rules so that conflicts may be avoided and those that nonetheless occur, expeditiously settled'.[42]

Tumlir's approach shows that internationalists who stress the importance of international rules are most definitely not the internationalists who tout the advantages of international economic cooperation – at least the type of co-operation based on executive power. With the aid of Tumlir, one could well contend that the interdependence (or neoliberal institutionalist) approach is rather illiberal, given its casual acceptance of rent-seeking activity and executive discretion within nation-states. Moreover, it has little inkling of the root domestic causes of both international economic order and disorder. The next chapter carries this argument further in discussing the deficiencies of neoliberal institutionalism and its brand of 'liberalism from above'.

Reciprocity versus unilateral free trade

In one sense, Tumlir is 'reciprotarian' in his thinking. He believes that governments should exchange commitments that collectively bind them to international rules. His proposal on unconditional MFN requires the Western powers to make a *joint* pledge to incorporate free trade into national laws. To Tumlir, international rules, arrived at through intergovernmental agreement, may well be an easier way of building a political consensus on limiting discretionary economic policy than go-it-alone efforts to reform domestic constitutions. In return for commitments to liberalise trade by other countries, domestic interests can be persuaded to support the reduction or removal of import barriers at home. The exchange of commitments in international treaties can effectively mobilise the support of exporting interests and consumers, and limit the influence of protection-seeking interests, within nation-states. Assuredly, a rule-based reciprocal approach to trade liberalisation is part and parcel of Tumlir's scheme.[43]

Having said that, Tumlir's approach to reciprocity has nothing in common with the interdependence or neoliberal institutionalist form of reciprocity, which focuses on executive discretion in intergovernmental dealings. Moreover, Tumlir is well aware of the pitfalls of reciprotarian thinking, and, in direct contradiction to neoliberal institutionalists, also extols the virtues of the unilateral road to trade liberalisation.

Since 1945 the case for a liberal international economic order has been made in terms of multilateralised reciprocity: freer trade is good, providing *all* parties liberalise trade. This is the kind of thinking that became the conventional wisdom of the GATT from the outset. The belief that nations benefit only when other nations open their markets has dominated GATT negotiations; the liberalisation of imports is a 'cost' one has to pay, or a 'concession' one has to make, in order to gain from exports to newly liberalised foreign markets. Such a fixation with reciprocity degenerated into results that were far from liberal. The increasing protectionism of developing countries that began in the 1950s – much of it GATT-sanctioned – served only as an excuse for developed countries to drag their heels on liberalisation and, even worse, to skirt round international rules and increase their own protectionist barriers.[44]

This predominant approach to postwar trade liberalisation is foreign to basic presumptions introduced to economic analysis by the classical economists. As Jagdish Bhagwati puts it, reciprocity 'builds on the notion, not consonant with good economic sense, that trade liberalisation is a cost rather than a source of gain'.[45] Reciprocity leads us to believe that the national gain accrues from exports; classical trade theory teaches us that the national gain comes from imports, not exports (which are only a means of paying for imports). Hence, the unilateral repeal of trade barriers, even in an otherwise protectionist world, ushers in imports that replace inefficient domestic production and release resources for more productive uses. Quite apart from other benefits, import liberalisation provides cheaper inputs, and reallocates resources, to promising export sectors. This kind of gain is of greater national benefit than the gain that arises from the opening of foreign markets to home exports through inter-governmental negotiations. Having rehearsed these arguments, Tumlir is clearly in favour of a large degree of unilateral trade liberalisation, and correspond-ingly against a rigid attachment to reciprocity. As he says: 'Governments interested in improving the economies of their people do not have to tie that preference to the rate and degree of liberalisation the least wise among them are willing to accept'.[46]

Like other classical liberals, Tumlir thinks of unilateral national action in a broad, encompassing sense. Admittedly, it delivers gains for national resource allocation. However, going beyond the static, allocative efficiency range of the neoclassical economist, Tumlir argues that unilateral policy measures by governments are integral to the dynamism and open-ended evolution of the international economic order. In their different ways, governments try out different solutions to international problems. Watching, and often imitating, the practice of other governments guides their experimentation. Thus, governments *compete* against each other by scanning each others' moves, copying each other and trying to get ahead of the pack by constant innovation – all in search of better or more efficient ways of doing things. As Tumlir remarks: 'Nobody knows which policies are best, and competition is a process of discovery'.

Like the Hayekian competition between agents for goods and services in an economic market, the political competition between governments allows them spontaneously (or unilaterally) to adjust to each others' practices in an environ-ment of uncertainty and flux. Thereby they adjust to overall change in the world economy in a relatively smooth and efficient manner. Clearly, Tumlir regards this process of unilateral adaptation through intergovernmental competition as far more nimble and flexible than international economic cooperation through cumbersome, time-consuming and cartel-like deals between governments.[47]

Tumlir's approbation of legal competition between governments is illustrative of his general approach to intergovernmental competition. He commends the innovation and development of a unified body of Community law that defends private rights within the jurisdictions of the member-states of the EU. Nevertheless, he does not think that this sort of legal uniformity is a model for legal practice in the international economic order. Rather he prefers that the latter continues to enjoy a cornucopia of different national legal systems, for that establishes a market dense in political ideas, and promotes the multiple search for solutions through experimentation and international learning.[48]

Tumlir does not quite identify the nexus between reciprocity, in the form of international rules, and the unilateral action that animates intergovernmental competition. Certainly, his enthusiasm for the latter has strong classical liberal roots. It accords with the precepts of Adam Smith and most of the nineteenth-century classical economists, and it has much in common with the policy preferences of Wilhelm Röpke (although Röpke is more unconditional in favouring unilateralism and less concerned about internationally agreed rules than Tumlir). Moreover, Tumlir's emphasis on intergovernmental competition relates directly to David Hume's view of institutional and technological progress arising from competitive emulation among nations (see chapter three). In the context of an international political market, it has more than a whiff of Hayek's characterisation of the undesigned mutual adaptation of multitudinous elements in a spontaneous order. The next chapter will elaborate further on unilateral liberalisation and intergovernmental competition as key components of an 'international spontaneous order'.

Conclusion

It is fitting to devote the penultimate chapter in this book on a particular thinker to the work of Jan Tumlir. Somehow or other, he manages to draw on nearly all the thinkers covered in previous chapters. In his portrayal of domestic economic order and democratic constitutionalism, he concocts a cocktail of Hayek, Buchanan, Böhm and Knight. His coverage of international economic order and disorder has traces of Viner and, to a greater extent, Röpke. And hovering in the atmosphere surrounding his political economy is the spirit of Hume and Smith, for Tumlir essentially updates their view of a spontaneous order, its framework of general rules, and what I have termed a 'liberalism from below' – the domestic roots of international order. Tumlir's stress on internationally agreed rules goes beyond anything said by most classical liberals, and does not logically follow from the eighteenth- and nineteenth-century traditions of classical political economy. Nevertheless, his fine characterisation of the spontaneity of international transactions, and of the dynamic evolution of a liberal international economic order actuated by a freewheeling competition of laws and policies among different jurisdictions, has the texture and taste of Smith's *Wealth of Nations* and Hume's *Political Essays*.

Notes

1 Jan Tumlir, 'Strong and weak elements in the concept of European integration', in Machlup *et al.* (1983), p. 29.
2 Also see Petersmann (1986), p. 417.
3 Jan Tumlir, 'Strong and weak elements in the concept of European integration', op. cit. p. 30.

As James Buchanan comments:

> Constitutional political economy is the research programme that directs enquiry into the working properties of rules and institutions within which individuals interact, and the process through which these rules and institutions are chosen or come into being. The emphasis on the choice of constraints distinguishes this research programme from conventional economics.
>
> (Buchanan (1990), p. 1)

4 Jan Tumlir, 'Franz Böhm and the development of economic-constitutional analysis', in Peacock and Willgerodt (1989b), pp. 127, 134; Tumlir (1985a), p. 20; Hauser *et al.* (1988), p. 220.
5 Jan Tumlir, 'Strong and weak elements in the concept of European integration', op. cit. p. 44; Tumlir (1985c), p. 249; Tumlir (1985a), p. 23; Tumlir (1980), p. 1; Hauser *et al.* (1988), pp. 222–223.
6 Jan Tumlir, 'International economic order: rules, cooperation and sovereignty', in Oppenheimer (1978), p. 3; Hauser *et al.* (1988), p. 223. Also see Hayek (1960), p. 161; Hayek (1982), vol. 1, pp. 37–39, 41–42, 45–46, 50–51; Hayek (1988), pp. 80, 83–84.
7 Jan Tumlir, 'Strong and weak elements in the concept of European integration', op. cit. p. 31.
8 Tumlir (1983c), pp. 395–396.
9 Tumlir (1984), p. 13; Tumlir (1985b), pp. 8–10; Tumlir (1981), p. 3; Tumlir (1985a), pp. 16–17.
10 Tumlir (1984), pp. 13–15.
11 Ibid., p. 15; Tumlir (1985c), p. 256.
12 On Big Government, rent-seeking and the decline of democratic constitutionalism, see Jan Tumlir, 'Evolution of the concept of international economic order, 1914–80', in Cairncross (1981), p. 177; Tumlir (1984), pp. 16, 17, 19–20, 22; Tumlir (1985c), pp. 250–251.
13 Tumlir (1981), p. 3.
14 Tumlir (1984), p. 8.
15 Tumlir (1981), p. 9; Tumlir (1985b), p. 5. See chapter seven for Röpke's account of how international order and disorder emerge 'from below'.
16 Tumlir (1985a), p. 16; Tumlir (1980), p. 22; Curzon and Curzon-Price (1984), p. 122.
17 Tumlir (1983a), pp. 74, 79; Tumlir (1985a), p. 32; Jan Tumlir, 'Evolution of the concept of international economic order, 1914–1980', op. cit. p. 171.
18 Tumlir (1983c), p. 397; Jan Tumlir, 'Evolution of the concept of international economic order, 1914–1980', op. cit. pp. 152–153, 178.
19 On Tumlir's account of the New Protectionism, see Tumlir (1985a), pp. 38–49.
20 See Gilpin (1986), p. 72 f.
21 Tumlir (1983c), p. 403.
22 Tumlir (1981), p. 7; Tumlir (1983a), p. 71; Tumlir (1983c), p. 394.
23 Jan Tumlir, 'International economic order: rules, cooperation, sovereignty', op. cit. pp. 2–4.

24 Tumlir (1980), p. 3; Tumlir (1983a), p. 72.

25 Tumlir (1983a), pp. 73–74.

26 MFN is supposed to prevent governments from discriminating between importers. National Treatment prevents governments from discriminating between domestic and foreign firms in trade transactions.

27 The WTO's Dispute Settlement Body has much more teeth than its GATT predecessor, but it is still weak as a juridical enforcer compared to courts within national jurisdictions.

28 On the lack of justiciability in international economic law, see Tumlir (1983a), p. 82; Tumlir (1985a), p. 67; Roessler (1986), p. 467.

29 Tumlir (1983a), pp. 76–77; Hauser (1986), p. 172.

30 Tumlir (1985a), pp. 62–65.

31 It is for this reason that Tumlir rejects proposals to allow private parties access to the GATT's dispute settlement mechanism. This would only muddy the waters and create legal confusion, given that the GATT is solely a contractual arrangement between governments. Furthermore, it would conflict with (more effective) private rights within national jurisdictions. In any case, the international enforcement of private rights would be uncertain and weak, invariably reliant on government diplomacy. See Roessler (1986), p. 473.

32 Tumlir (1983c), p. 394.

33 Tumlir (1983a), pp. 80–81; Tumlir (1983b), pp. 257–258.

34 Jan Tumlir, 'Franz Böhm and the development of economic-constitutional analysis', op. cit. p. 140; Tumlir (1985a), p. 71; Tumlir (1983a), p. 80.

   The highly publicised GATT Eminent Persons Group Report in 1985 points in a similar direction to Tumlir, although it is neither as 'constitutional' nor as radical as Tumlir's proposal on unconditional MFN. The report recognises the in-built imbalance in domestic trade policy-making that favours those who lobby for protection. It seeks to tilt the balance back to those who favour open trade policies by advocating 'protection balance sheets' that would calculate and publicise the costs and benefits of protectionist policies. Note that, like Tumlir, this GATT report focuses on change in domestic politics – the root cause of protection – and not on tinkering with international mechanisms. See GATT (1985), pp. 7, 9; Roessler (1986), p. 471.

35 Given the considerable amount of common ground between Tumlir and Röpke, and given the fact that Tumlir taught at the Graduate School of International Studies in Geneva, where Röpke taught at an earlier stage, it is amazing that Tumlir, to the best of my knowledge, does not cite Röpke anywhere in his work.

36 Curzon and Curzon-Price (1984), p. 133.

37 Jan Tumlir, 'International economic order: rules, cooperation, sovereignty', op. cit. p. 7.

38 Jan Tumlir, 'The New Protectionism, cartels and the international order', in Amacher et al. (1979), pp. 256–257; Tumlir (1981), p. 14; Jan Tumlir, 'International economic order: rules, cooperation, sovereignty', op. cit. p. 10.

39 Tumlir (1983c), p. 401; Jan Tumlir, 'The New Protectionism, cartels and the international order', op. cit. p. 258.

40 Tumlir (1983c), p. 400; Jan Tumlir, 'Evolution of the concept of international economic order, 1914–1980', op. cit. p. 179.

41 Tumlir (1985a), p. 58; Tumlir (1983c), p. 40.

42 Tumlir (1985a), pp. 58–59; Jan Tumlir, 'The New Protectionism, cartels and the international order', op. cit. p. 257.

43 Hauser et al. (1988), p. 233; Hauser (1986), pp. 177–178; Roessler (1986), p. 183.

44 Tumlir (1983a), p. 75; Tumlir (1983c), p. 397; Tumlir (1982a), p. 39.

45 Bhagwati (1992), p. 51.

46 Tumlir (1983b), p. 37; Tumlir (1982a), pp. 39–40.
47 Tumlir (1983c), p. 401; Jan Tumlir, 'Strong and weak elements in the concept of European integration', op. cit. p. 43.
48 Jan Tumlir, 'International economic order: rules, cooperation, sovereignty', op. cit. p. 12.

Part V

CONCLUSION

9

CLASSICAL LIBERALISM AND INTERNATIONAL ECONOMIC ORDER

A synthesis

It is now time to pull the threads together from the preceding studies in the intellectual history of domestic and international political economy. The various thinkers covered have different points to stress in their different ways, but all are part of a common tradition of classical liberalism that goes back to Smith and Hume and forward to Hayek. Through the looking-glass of individual thinkers, from the Scots to Viner, Röpke and Tumlir, a distinctively classical liberal perspective on international economic order has, I hope, come into view. Here, in the concluding chapter, I draw on all the writers examined in the book and attempt to set out a *synthesis* of classical liberalism and international economic order.

As mentioned earlier, two, not necessarily mutually exclusive, approaches almost totally dominate liberalism in international political economy: rational choice, equipped with the analytical tool-kit of neoclassical economics, and a political science-based neoliberal institutionalism. Both approaches cut themselves off in several important respects from the classical liberal tradition in political economy.

Rational choice employs the psychological assumptions of *homo oeconomicus*, the rational utility-maximising actor, to build a theory of economic and political markets. Classical liberalism, in contrast, employs often diametrically opposed assumptions of man in his politico-economic environment (an argument that has cropped up in many chapters, particularly chapter two).

Neoliberal institutionalism places heavy emphasis on mechanisms of intergovernmental policy cooperation to achieve liberal outcomes consonant with the maintenance of order in the international system. Classical liberalism shifts the emphasis of policy action from the international (intergovernmental) to the national level to secure and accelerate the progress of a liberal international economic order (see chapters three, five, seven and eight). It directs the observer's gaze to the national or domestic preconditions of international order, and conceives (national) policy action to a large degree in *unilateral* terms, that is, not predicated on the reciprocity of intergovernmental bargains so frequently stressed by neoliberal institutionalism. Put another way, a classical liberal perspective of international political economy is a 'liberalism from below', whereas neoliberal institutionalism is a 'liberalism from above'.

While classical liberalism has (re)gained ground in 'domestic' political economy, especially via the legal-economic constitutionalism of Hayek, it has never really been adumbrated and explored in modern 'international' political economy, nor has it been contrasted with the more conventional modern approaches mentioned above. This is hardly surprising, for international political economy is not exactly rich in the appreciation of its own history of thought, least of all in the liberal tradition. At best, international political economy has largely overlooked classical liberalism, from Smith and Hume onwards. At worst, it has egregiously misrepresented classical liberalism as an anachronism, an intellectual *curiosum* of the past, too minimalist and *simpliste* to be of relevance to the awesomely complex world of today.

This discussion seeks to identify, define and elaborate a distinctively classical liberal perspective of international economic order, hitherto lacking in international political economy. In contradistinction to neoliberal institutionalism and most (but not all) rational choice approaches, the classical liberalism put into effect here combines positive analysis with explicit normative criteria in evaluating the working properties of alternative *rules and institutions* that generate different realities and possibilities of *order* in the international system. To repeat another point, the methodology of this chapter and the book overall relies considerably on intellectual history, extracting common themes and insights from successive thinkers and traditions of thought down the generations. The chief objective of this intellectual-historical approach is to (re)construct a classical liberal theory of international economic order relevant to modern times – something quite unusual in international political economy. This methodology, when deployed at its best, is familiar to an Oakeshott or a de Jouvenel in the study of politics, a Roscoe Pound in law, a Hayek, Viner or Robbins in economics. Borrowing Hayek's words, it is an essay, here in the international political economy context, 'to piece together the fragments of a broken tradition'.[1]

The first two sections present an overview of the two conventional paradigms that occupy the 'liberal' space in present-day international political economy: rational choice and neoliberal institutionalism. The third section summarises a contrasting classical liberalism applicable, in the first instance, to domestic or national political economy (as presented in greater detail in chapter two). Having reminded the reader of the domestic or national sources of international order, the following sections seek to extend such a classical liberal perspective to envelop the international economic order. They first enquire into the epistemology and theory of an 'international spontaneous order', and then search for its institutional preconditions and presumptions for law and policy. *Inter alia,* this part of the chapter emphasises the enduring importance of the state in both domestic and international affairs, striking a very different note to modern writings that herald the obsolescence of the state in an era of 'globalisation'.

The final sections contrast the policy implications and applications of classical liberalism in the contemporary international political economy with those of neoliberal institutionalism, homing in on the substantial differences between a 'liberalism from below' and a 'liberalism from above'. The reciprotarian thinking of neoliberal institutionalism is confronted with a classically derived theory of market-like 'institutional competition' powered by the unilateral policy liberalisation measures of nation-states.

Liberal theories of international political economy: rational choice

As intimated above, the rational actor paradigm is *sine qua non* to neoclassical economics. *Homo oeconomicus* chooses optimally with given means and ends and given constraints under conditions of stable equilibrium in perfectly competitive markets. Decision-making is perfectly rational, and there are no transaction and information costs.[2]

Public choice essentially transplants *homo oeconomicus* and the associated Walrasian theory of market organisation into the political sphere: the theory assumes that voters, taxpayers, bureaucrats and politicians are self-interested utility-maximisers.[3] As Dennis Mueller argues, 'the basic behavioural postulate of public choice, as for economics, is that man is an egoistic, rational choice-maximiser'.[4] Particularly in the Chicago School tradition, there are welfare-maximising or Pareto-optimal states of political equilibrium analogous to perfect competition in welfare economics, replete with given actor preferences and complete knowledge (or the rational search for information). The model ignores the vexing question of how mechanisms of political competition create and process information, just as it ignores this question in economic competition.[5]

The public choice argument is that rational agents, when faced with declining profits as a result of competitive pressures in economic markets, switch their attention to 'political markets'. In this arena they lobby politicians and bureaucrats for selective promotion and protection against competitors. Individuals in government supply promotion and protection because they are maximising their own preferences, whether it be a case of getting elected or re-elected by garnering votes in the gift of interest groups, or increasing discretionary bureaucratic powers shielded from public and parliamentary scrutiny. In this political game it is relatively well-organised producer groups – labour unions, farmers, the professions, employers' associations, clusters of large enterprises – who can mobilise collective action and gain increasing returns, not large, unorganised or disorganised groups of consumers and the unemployed. Minority producer interests win out at the expense of majority consumer interests, outsider groups bereft of political voice and the overall public good. The political market becomes a vast and opaque machine of frenetic redistribution, turning activity away from the production of goods and services, and retarding innovation, adaptiveness and growth.[6]

179

This theory of political economy relates in a relatively straightforward manner to the processes that drive foreign economic policy. Although free trade is usually the optimal outcome for national and global welfare, government policies frequently favour protection against imports. The increasing pressure of international competition on domestic producers inclines them to lobby their governments for protection. If domestic producers are well enough organised for collective action in political markets, they have a high chance of success with utility-maximising politicians and bureaucrats.[7]

These strategies of firms are what Jagdish Bhagwati calls 'directly unproductive profit-seeking activities', composed of 'downstream' lobbying for rents from import quotas (rent-seeking activity) and tariff revenues (revenue-seeking activity), as well as 'upstream' lobbying for protection in the formulation of policy. The whole process concentrates resources and attention on socially wasteful redistribution rather than socially valuable production.[8] Protectionism in economic relations between states thus finds its source in private–public political activity within nation-states. As Jan Tumlir remarks, protectionism is the 'inherent logic of the redistributive state working itself out externally'.[9]

An important modification of the perfect knowledge assumption usually associated with *homo oeconomicus* buttresses this theory. In large electoral constituencies it is often rational for individual voters to remain ignorant of political processes, given the negligible influence of their votes on the electoral or policy outcome. Similarly, those who stand to gain from free trade, especially consumers, have little incentive to inform themselves of the deleterious effects of protection, given that the costs are fairly widely spread: they remain 'rationally ignorant'. However, the short-term losses from free trade to labour and capital owners in affected import-competing sectors are more visible and concentrated than the uncertain and diffuse gains accruing to exporters and consumers. Therefore, the former have an incentive to organise collective action and participate in the political process. The upshot is that minorities of well-organised producer groups have asymmetrical control of information, and are singularly powerful 'insider' actors, in complex political processes. They are the ones who are willing and able to invest time and resources in dealing with the high information and transaction costs of political markets.

Such 'political market failure' is even more characteristic of foreign economic policy than domestic economic policy. Executive discretion, as well as weak parliamentary and judicial control, characterise foreign economic policy-making, at least in part because information on foreign economic policy is less readily available to the legislature, the courts and the broader public. This makes highly discretionary foreign economic policy processes more than usually amenable to capture by the rent-seeking activities of a relatively small number of well-organised and well-informed producer groups. Hence the frequency and staying power of protectionist outcomes, even though they are inimical to the common weal.[10]

So much for the positive theory of protection in rational/public choice. The normative follow-up, when resorted to by rational choice political economists, usually recommends limiting and binding rules or constitutional agreements at appropriate levels of policy action. These rules defend free trade by circumscribing government regulation and administrative discretion, thereby minimising the scope for private organised groups to lobby effectively for protection.[11] The constitutional economics of James Buchanan exemplifies this normative approach.[12]

Liberal theories of international political economy: neoliberal institutionalism

Whereas rational choice's provenance is neoclassical economics, that of neoliberal institutionalism is political science, or more precisely the sub-discipline of international politics. Rational choice accounts for the causes of protectionism in the distributional struggles of intrastate politics. Neoliberal institutionalism, while not wholly discounting the foregoing causal interpretation, focuses on the systemic level of *interstate* relations in accounting for protectionist or free trade outcomes. To the latter perspective, it is 'what governments do' in the international system, not within the nation-state, which is of great moment to the *problematique* of international political economy. That said, the two perspectives are not altogether incompatible. Indeed, neoliberal institutionalism significantly incorporates game-theoretic and collective action components of neoclassical economics and rational choice.

The following paragraphs attempt to tease out that which is normative in neoliberal institutionalism. This merits a brief justification, for the genre's proponents habitually present it as a strictly positive, value-free, 'social scientific' analysis.[13] This is problematic, for stated aspirations to an exclusively 'social scientific' analysis sever neoliberal institutionalism from the centuries-old tradition of liberal political philosophy with its normative enquiry into the values of individual freedom and the common good. Arguably, it is these very values that influence the rules and norms of social life that have an appreciable impact on the international system.[14] However, despite claims of value-freedom, there are plenty of interpretations and *obiter dicta* penned by prominent neoliberal institutionalists that reveal an implicit normative bias. The task here is to render such normative concerns quite explicit. The following paragraphs examine two of this perspective's core normative elements: 'mixed systems thinking' and a 'liberalism from above'.

What I would call 'mixed systems thinking' is especially noticeable in the work of John Ruggie. He characterises the post-1945 international economic order as a 'compromise of embedded liberalism': the combination of a measure of openness in international arrangements of trade, capital flows and exchange rate relationships, with wide leeway for governments to pursue interventionist policies within nation-states to further the goals of full employment, social security and national stability. Integral to these arrangements was a 'move to institutions': the creation of international organisations and dense networks of intergovernmental cooperation, embodied in the Bretton Woods agreements and the General Agreement on Tariffs and Trade (GATT). These institutional mechanisms have sought, and still seek, to manage an alloy of liberal internationalism and domestic interventionism.[15]

Prima facie this is a positive analysis of postwar events. Nevertheless, there is an underlying normative standpoint, for Ruggie clearly approves of this compromise between 'Smith abroad and Keynes at home', which he considers to be essential to the maintenance of a liberal international economic order. The latter demands rapid adjustment from national societies. Such adjustment requires stabilising social compacts negotiated between governments and organised interests within nation-states, serving the function of cushioning and spreading the cost of necessary domestic adaptations to measures of international liberalisation.[16] Ruggie is wary of a frontal attack on the present gamut of interventionist national economic and social policies. He contends that the wholesale rollback of such interventionist policies undermines established social consensus and threatens continued support within nation-states for international liberalisation. His main argument is that the compromise of embedded liberalism needs to be rejuvenated and enlarged to encompass intergovernmental cooperation on a wider front of domestic and international economic policies.[17]

Ruggie's treatment is redolent of the 'mixed economy' projected onto the international stage. Just as the mixed economy within nation-states is an amalgam of antithetical ordering principles, one based on the market economy and the other on the command economy, the 'compromise of embedded liberalism' is equally a combination of opposites – of domestic illiberalism and international liberalism. In a sense, it is intellectually contiguous with the New or Social Liberalism of the turn-of-the-century. The latter rebelled against the Old or Classical Liberalism by advocating a more proactive role for government in the direction of economic affairs, in the name of social security, equality of opportunity, income redistribution and social justice. These ideas flowed into programmes of socialism and social democracy in the twentieth century.[18]

'Mixed systems thinking' is one structural support of (normative) neoliberal institutionalism; 'liberalism from above' is the other. Here the emphasis is on the conditions that facilitate international cooperation, regarded as necessary, if not sufficient, to prevent or minimise economic conflict in a world of increasing economic interdependence in which there are multiple points of friction between mutually incompatible or clashing government policies. States have a clear self-interest to cooperate to keep the system open and prevent a descent into protectionist closure, which would be damaging to all.[19]

It is apposite at this juncture to pause and clarify the exact meaning of 'cooperation'. Relatively free markets exhibit 'spontaneous' cooperation: actors cooperate voluntarily in exchanging goods and services on the basis of a price mechanism and the striking of contracts; and the system subsumes the freedom of consumer choice as well as the freedom of producers to own and use private property as they see fit within the law. This spontaneous cooperation is the essence of *laissez faire*.[20]

There is an international political equivalent of such spontaneous cooperation in as much as governments mutually adjust their policies unilaterally, that is, without any explicit political bargaining or agreement between them, when faced with situations of international friction. This is what I would term 'liberalism from below'. But neoliberal institutionalists do not hold out much prospect for this kind of cooperation in modern conditions; rather, they see governments acting unilaterally in a negative, noncooperative manner by, for example, imposing foreign exchange controls, restricting imports and subsidising domestic firms. Such noncooperation exacerbates international friction. Therefore international cooperation in terms of explicit political bargaining or negotiation is required, especially in trade policy, exchange rates, fiscal policy and natural resources. *Negotiated cooperation* – what Ruggie defines as 'the practice of coordinating national policies in groups of three or more states'[21] – is necessary to keep the system open and contain the conflict-inducing forces, such as protectionism, which emanate from nation-states.[22] This is what I would call 'liberalism from above': negotiated cooperation 'from above' supposedly restrains non-cooperation 'from below'.

Negotiated cooperation or policy coordination takes place in international 'regimes', defined as 'sets of implicit or explicit principles, norms, rules and decision-making procedures around which actor expectations converge in a given area of international relations'.[23] *Reciprocity* is at the heart of international regimes. It entails the exchange of concessions between governments based on bargaining and negotiation, not the spontaneous cooperation of unilateral government adaptation to changing international conditions. Reciprocity is partially modelled on the 'tit-for-tat' strategy of the iterated game of Prisoner's Dilemma. Tit-for-tat – copying the opponent's last move – is a means of overcoming problems of 'defection' (noncooperation) and collective action (free riding and the underprovision of public goods) in order to provide international public goods such as open markets, stable exchanges, sufficient liquidity for international payments and a lender of last resort function. Robert Keohane, neoliberal institutionalism's leading proponent, argues that regimes can overcome problems of international economic and political market failure (e.g. strategic behaviour by governments and firms, high information and transaction costs, bounded rationality and ill-defined property rights) by, for example, pooling information and helping governments to simplify decision-making procedures.[24]

Manifestly, Keohane and others regard international regimes like the Bretton Woods agreements and the GATT as the main intervening variables conducing to stability and liberal outcomes in the postwar international political economy. As Keohane argues:

> Were liberal, cooperative arrangements in international regimes to be destroyed without fundamental changes in the domestic politics of modern capitalism, it seems likely that the result would be worse rather than better: political xenophobia and economic inefficiency appear

more probable than a dramatic advance toward more egalitarian societies in relationships of concord with one another.[25]

Furthermore, Keohane and Axelrod clearly bring to light the neoliberal institutionalist preference for negotiated as opposed to spontaneous cooperation: 'Cooperation in world politics seems to be attained best not by providing benefits unilaterally to others, but by conditional cooperation'.[26]

A contrasting classical liberal perspective of political-economic order: a brief summary

Chapter two presented a classical liberal perspective of national or domestic order in some detail, contrasting it with a rational choice approach. As that chapter covered this ground reasonably well, all I am going to do here is remind the reader, with the utmost brevity, of the main features of classical liberalism. It is important to stress the basic foundations of classical liberalism *ex ante*, for the following application of classical liberalism to the international economic order will be impossible without an understanding of classical liberalism in the domestic context. This is especially important if one wants to be in no doubt as to the domestic (intranational) roots of liberal international economic order – what I have previously termed 'liberalism from below'.

First, classical liberalism's 'Smithian' methodology has a realistic appreciation of human behaviour (regarding actor rationality, lack of knowledge, etc.) and market order (preferring a conception of evolutionary process to static equilibrium models, for example). Consequently, it is much better geared to real-world policy relevance through concrete institutional comparisons than is the case with a rational choice political economy based on the hyperabstract 'maximisation and equilibrium' paradigm of neoclassical economics.

Second, classical liberalism conceives the market order in 'spontaneous' terms: it is complex and predominantly self-organising, the unintended by-product of the interactions of millions of individuals. In contrast, 'rational-constructivist' social science, prevalent in economics and other disciplines, conceives the market order as a construct or deliberate design of human reason.

Third, classical liberalism is very attentive to the order-maintaining devices of grown habits, customs and traditions. Unlike rational-constructivism, it does not assume that society consists exclusively of isolated individuals engaged in impersonal exchange (the Crusoe or *homo oeconomicus* of modern economic theory).

Fourth, classical liberalism's normative criterion is that of public utility *à la* Hume, arguing that greater general material welfare results from individual choice (as a by-product of human action or by means of an Invisible Hand) than from alternative means of social cooperation reliant on collective guidance.

Fifth, classical liberalism's economic order does not exist *in vacuo*. It presupposes a comprehensive framework of law and public policy, far removed from notions of extreme *laissez faire* and the nightwatchman state. Law or 'justice', the glue that holds a complex society together, is conceived in procedural, 'rules of the game' terms; it is not a device of redistribution (what is called 'social justice'). Relatedly, the *agenda* of government is to enforce the rules of the game as an 'umpire', especially in upholding laws of property and contract. There are also important international relations and public goods functions of the state. However, the state should not stray beyond this *agenda* by interfering in the market process, that is, interfering in the freedom of production and consumption through price-fixing and other controls.

Classical liberalism and international economic order

Now I seek to extend the classical liberal theory of national economic order to the *international* economic order. This is not quite virgin territory, but an evolutionary-institutional perspective of international order is not at all well covered in modern political economy. The main planks of classical liberalism – a Smithian methodology of realistic assumptions of individual behaviour and market order, the spontaneous order, public utility, the legal and public policy framework of the economic order – recur in the following sections and apply directly to the international economic order. Hence classical liberalism is a bridge that connects domestic political economy to its international counterpart.

To repeat, a classical liberal international political economy should build on a theory of national order so that the *domestic preconditions* of international order clearly come to the fore. From a classical liberal standpoint, one can grasp the generation of order at the international level only by scrutinising what happens 'from within and beneath' (to borrow Wilhelm Röpke's words), that is to say, from within the nation-state. Markets, the political processes that influence them, the legal framework and sociocultural factors, all emerge from the deep recesses of nation-states. They are neither 'constructs' of international agreements nor have they yet been superseded by a world political, legal and social order. The causal direction is therefore primarily, although not exclusively, 'bottom-up' or 'from below', from domestic (subnational and national) to international, which signals an initial difference between classical liberalism and neoliberal institutionalism. As alluded to earlier, the latter largely abstracts from domestic structures and processes, concentrating on the system level of interstate relations.

Smithian methodology and free trade

One should begin by applying a 'Smithian' methodology to international order, just as it applied in the last section to domestic order. Hayek, Knight, Eucken, Böhm and Coase are Smithian classicists in national/domestic political economy, and many of their insights are germane to international questions. However, it is once more to the Scots that we must turn, as well as to their twentieth-century intellectual descendants Jacob Viner, Wilhelm Röpke and Jan Tumlir, for an elaboration of a classical liberal international political economy.

In his superlative and classically inspired writings, Jacob Viner constantly emphasises the bond between 'realistic' models of international economic theory and practical policy, embedding economic analysis in a wider framework of sociopolitical and legal relevance (see chapter five). As Viner argues, notwithstanding all the analytical faults of classical trade theory, its leading proponents, from Smith and Hume to McCulloch, Senior, John Stuart Mill, Marshall, Edgeworth and Taussig (with perhaps the highly important exception of Ricardo),[27] had reasonably elastic, not excessively abstract, theoretical frameworks tailored to complex and changing issues of policy. In contrast, twentieth-century neoclassical international economics, following the example of Hecksher and Ohlin, has trodden the path of a 'Ricardian' methodology, relying on static equilibrium/perfect market models with unrealistic assumptions of rational action and welfare-economic utility comparison and aggregation.[28]

The case for free trade has come to be put forward in static, allocative efficiency terms and on the basis of a perfect competition model (for which some nineteenth-century classical economists must share the blame, notwithstanding their institutional sensitivity and policy relevance in other areas). Although the New Trade Theory rightfully takes neoclassical trade theory to task for assuming perfect markets, constant returns to scale, given and homogeneous factor endowments, etc., it equally suffers from an excess of Ricardian methodology. Its assumptions of market structure and strategic behaviour by governments and firms are too simplistic and do not in the least accord with modern reality.[29]

As chapter three emphasised, David Hume and Adam Smith defend free trade without recourse to a perfect competition model, and their defence relies primarily on dynamic, not static, arguments. To them, the dynamic gains from trade, emanating from technology transfer and competitive emulation (Hume), as well as an extended market and increasing returns (Smith), intimately relate to the development of domestic institutions and long-run economic growth. In this scheme, a policy of commercial openness (to trade and foreign investment) removes distortions to the more efficient allocation of resources; but it also mutually interacts with domestic institutional improvement, including the improvement of governmental and legal systems. Such a combination lowers transaction costs, ensures stable property rights, and more generally provides an environment conducive to saving, investment and entrepreneurship – the preconditions of productivity and growth.[30] This Smithian message that a mix of institutional development and sound, outward-oriented policies feeds into superior economic performance, is of pressing relevance to developing and transition countries presently undertaking comprehensive policy reform.[31]

Following Adam Smith's precedent, the nineteenth-century classical economists seriously consider various arguments for protection on theoretical grounds, but finally reject them in favour of free trade on *political economy and policy grounds*.

186

First, there is the probability of interest group capture of trade policy, rendering it arbitrary and promiscuous in application (as public choice theory predicts). Second, the likelihood of mutually damaging protectionist retaliation is great. And third, governments cannot escape a 'knowledge problem' in carrying out 'strategic' trade-cum-industrial policies: they lack sufficient and up-to-date information of the sectors targeted, their link with the rest of the economy, and the future payoff structure in light of the unpredictable and unintended consequences of policy. Given these institutional realities, the classical economists prefer free trade to protection (see chapter five).[32] As chapter three illustrated, such political economy considerations are at the heart of Adam Smith's defence of free trade.

As the international economic order becomes ever more complex with ever greater fragmentation and dispersal of knowledge, it seems to be the case that there are permanent and *more constraining* limits to efficacious government intervention. The New Trade Theory, and other theoretical arguments in favour of protection, habitually and blithely overlook these practical considerations nowadays due to their excessive abstraction and their lack of policy relevance.[33] Modern advocates of protection have not learnt the lesson taught by the classical economists: the presumption against protectionism, while having a (hardly cut-and-dried) theoretical rationale, relies heavily on the empirical observation that government intervention is usually short-sighted, with an unavoidably inadequate understanding of the coherence of economic phenomena. Usually, this leads to results more harmful than those that follow from nonintervention.[34] As the more policy-attuned neoclassical trade economists would put it, the costs of government failure usually outweigh the costs of market failure in international economic policy.[35]

Thus, relaxing assumptions of rational action, perfect competition and perfect knowledge does not diminish the case for free trade and automatically furnish the rationale for government intervention, as the writings on strategic trade policy and other theories of protection might state or imply.[36] On the contrary, a Smithian methodology assuming less-than-rational action in far-from-perfect markets pervaded by constitutional ignorance, sheds a very different light on the issue. Its case for free trade and against protection continues to rely on an underlying economic-theoretical rationale of static and dynamic gains (as set out in chapter three), but government failure, retaliation and a knowledge problem are all essential political economy considerations that complete the free trade argument.

The international spontaneous order

From a Smithian methodology I now turn to what classical liberalism would have to say on the subject of the 'international spontaneous order'. The question of how international order comes about through cooperation between vast numbers of people all over the world, necessary to provide for even modest standards of living, is, as Judge Richard Posner argues, the basic puzzle for Adam Smith.[37]

There are two opposing ordering principles of the international political econ-omy, akin to the opposition between a market economy and a command economy as ordering principles within the nation-state. One is the spontaneous worldwide exchange of goods and services, and the equally spontaneous capital transactions between firms and households residing in different nations. Basically, it is the extension of Smith's principle of the division of labour from the domestic to the international sphere. Smithian 'natural liberty' brings about this international spontaneous order: policy-makers should simply remove artificial restraints on trade and capital movements, and let individuals buy each others' goods and services at competitive prices. The other ordering principle is a hierarchical and centralised planning of international cooperation by interfering with prices, wages, trade, exchange rates and capital movements.[38] As Henry Simons clearly points out, the hard core of national policy centralisation is the control of foreign trade, which is precisely what Smith assailed in the mercantilist system of the eigh-teenth century.[39] The international reality, analogous to the reality of the domes-tic mixed economy, is an antinomic combination of these two ordering principles.

As Jan Tumlir describes the international spontaneous order in his inimitably crafted, finely honed prose, it comprises 'actions – or, more accurately, reactions – of uncountable millions [that] combine into a vast transnational flow that no government, and no group of governments, can control, let alone arrest. The temptation and effort to do so have, of course, been constant.' He goes on to delineate this order in terms of a complex mix of 'incessant and manifold change' and 'sets of rules and institutions which produce observed regularity and order-liness', and which 'maintain stability'. Immanent in this order is the *anticipation of change* and the *rapidity of adjustment*, mediated by a world price system that emits signals to economic agents, equipped with only very partial knowledge of relevant facts, to adapt their actions as speedily as possible (see chapter eight).[40]

Hayek describes the spontaneous order mostly in terms of market activities within nation-states. Nevertheless, the general features of the spontaneous order equally apply at the international level. The international spontaneous market order is, therefore, a complex, self-organising system, not designed or controlled by any person or group of persons, the 'unintended result of human action but not the execution of any human design', to re-employ Adam Ferguson's phrase. Its processes are those of the Invisible Hand: outcomes are unintended by-products of the self-interested actions of individuals, not deliberately coordinated by any central authority. Furthermore, classical liberalism does not think of international competition in terms of stable equilibrium, but as an evolutionary 'discovery procedure' which coordinates relevant knowledge dispersed world-wide and generates new knowledge.

This evolutionary model also contends that the 'dynamic' competition between multinational enterprises in international markets intensifies competition overall, narrowing the scope for cartel formation within nation-states and contributing to the 'openness' of the system.[41] Equilibrium-based industrial organisation models, in contrast, so prevalent in international economics and political economy, tend to overemphasise the cartel-like, market-closing potential of multinational activity, in the process underestimating their *market-opening* potential in the dynamic long run.[42]

A rational-constructivist model applied to international economic order would account for the emergence of the institutions of international trade, capital mobility, the convertibility of currencies, and private property itself, in terms of conscious human design or deliberative construction. Indeed, this is, at the very least, implicit in most relevant writings in international political economy. Karl Polanyi, for example, whose work frequently crops up in sociological and political science versions of international political economy, explains the origin of international trade in Antiquity as an *intended product* of the decisions of rulers: governing authorities planned the very partial opening of their political economies and subsequently controlled the exchange of goods and services between sovereign entities. More generally, Polanyi traces the genesis of the institutions of barter and exchange, relative price, private property and cross-border trade to deliberate design: they are 'constructs' of human reason.[43]

Hayek counters that the foregoing rational-constructivist account is factually false; it is quite simply egregious conjectural history. International trade, for example, came about *in spite of* the predilections of rulers for the preservation of autarchic orders. A few individuals evaded political controls and engaged in barter and exchange across borders. Their practices were perceived to be successful and were progressively imitated by others. Governments, to a greater or lesser extent, belatedly recognised the benefits of the new situation and lowered barriers to trade. The extension of cross-border trade led, little by little, to the development of impersonal institutions to facilitate exchange, especially the price mechanism and (formal and informal) rules governing the use of property and contract. This allowed individuals to acquire and use widely dispersed knowledge and take advantage of new opportunities. Flanking instruments and institutions, such as bills of exchange, discounting methods and the mobility of capital, spontaneously arose to support international exchange. Trade promoted the concentration of population in urban centres, as well as greater occupational and geographical specialisation. An increasingly interdependent international economic order flourished when governments reconciled themselves to these evolutionary developments and concentrated on improving the framework of general rules, especially pertaining to property rights; but the progress of the order was frequently halted and suffered retrogression when governments arbitrarily interfered with private property and controlled trade.[44]

The upshot of this evolutionary account is that international trade could not possibly have been a product of human design; it was and is far too complex an order, particularly in the planetary dispersal of requisite knowledge, to have come into being and be maintained in such a simplistic and mechanical manner. No individual or political authority (or set of political authorities) had or has a mastery of relevant facts to plan or wilfully coordinate an order of such awe-inspiring and baffling complexity. Rather, an international spontaneous market order or catallaxy, subsuming trade, capital mobility, convertible currencies and private property, emerged from the interstices of pre-existing autarchic orders in the Humean and Smithian sense – as an unintended by-product of innumerable self-interested actions or, expressed differently, through the operation of an Invisible Hand.

Public utility and the international spontaneous order

Having covered a Smithian methodology and the nature of an international spontaneous order, I now come to the question of utility. Just as Humean *public utility* – long-run social usefulness taking its unintended or spontaneous rise from individual choices – is the normative criterion for domestic economic order, so it is for international economic order. Trade and factor movements came about by dint of the choices of millions of individuals in a weeding-out process of selective cultural evolution. They have proved useful to social groups in catering for material wants – more so than any viable alternative means of organising international cooperation. Here, utility (as in its domestic or intranational version) does not issue from abstract, universal principles of a natural rights doctrine; rather, it follows from considerations of practical necessity or general expediency, comparing the real-world experience of free trade and capital mobility to the track record of autarchic and mercantilist orders. This is abundantly clear from the trade policy writings of the classical economists.[45]

Law and policy in the international spontaneous order

Law

The previous section on classical liberalism and domestic order underlined that the market economy does not exist *in vacuo*. The spontaneous, 'invisible hand' processes of the economic order, incorporating the freedom of production and consumption, require a solid framework of regulation put in place and enforced by 'interdependent' political and legal orders if a market economy is to survive and prosper. Classical liberalism particularly emphasises the legal substratum of the market order. It is now time to apply this legal dimension to the international economic order.

The international exchange of goods and services, the international payments system that backs it up, and the movement of capital across borders, are not freestanding institutions. They crucially depend on a web of (overwhelmingly private) property rights, are directly governed by transactions according to private law contracts in a multitude of national legal orders, and rely on traditions and conventions of trust and reputation ('informal constraints', according to Douglass North).[46]

The discipline of international political economy, in as much as it pays any attention to legal matters, almost exclusively concentrates on international public law and how states behave in international affairs to provide 'international public goods'. It almost wholly neglects international transactions according to *private law*. Influenced by neoclassical economic theory, international political economy all too casually takes the legal foundation of economic transactions as relatively simple. The lesson of the Scottish Enlightenment and, more recently, the New Institutional Economics, is that it is far from simple, even within the confines of a nation-state with a unified legal order. Imagine, then, how much more difficult it is to realise Hume's three 'general and inflexible rules of justice' – 'the stability of possession, its transference by consent, and the performance of promises' – when faced with different national legal orders. This results in less well-defined and less well-protected property rights, greater uncertainty and higher transaction costs in international trade.[47]

Despite the glaring lack of coherent and enforceable international rules governing private law, trade and capital mobility still occur and proliferate. Neoliberal institutionalism would point to international regimes of negotiated cooperation as a cardinal means of fostering such international economic interdependence. However, in the virtual exclusiveness of its focus on the 'constructs' of political deliberation, it completely overlooks the *spontaneity* of international trade according to private law transactions and informal constraints in different national jurisdictions. In the absence of a unified or well-coordinated international legal order, private governance structures crop up spontaneously to deal with problems of uncertainty, ill-defined and badly enforced property rights, and high transaction costs. Self-regulation animated by private initiative compensates for the paucity of formal international rules. Many of these privately organised mechanisms filled out into the informal rules, customs and conventions of the *lex mercatoria* that has for centuries greased the wheels of international commerce.[48]

Public law, both domestic and international, is in large part a child of deliberate, 'planned' decision-making. In contrast, private law, although continually replenished by wilful modifications to the framework of general rules, is *mostly* of spontaneous origin. The accumulated fund of private law that supports international commerce began with extralegal merchant codes of conduct for long-distance, cross-cultural trade, and later evolved through the practices of ports and fairs in medieval Europe, before being gradually codified in formal legal rules. Thus, private law in international trade is definitely not the free invention of the ruler or legislator; it is not a construct of human reason.[49]

Public policy

One should stress again and again that there is nothing predetermined about the survival of an international spontaneous market order. As argued before, classical liberalism never takes *laissez faire* and the Invisible Hand to doctrinaire extremes. Political authorities can either keep the system 'open' by sticking to and refining a framework of general rules, or 'close' it by arbitrary actions of interference in prices, production and consumption. This strong element of collective choice in influencing the international economic order in liberal or illiberal directions moves the discussion on from legal foundations to broad presumptions of public policy. The openness of the order requires an *appropriate* institutional framework, partially dependent on spontaneous forces, such as the *lex mercatoria* and, indeed, the 'market' itself, but also dependent on the deliberative rule-making capability of politicians and legislators.

Whereas neoliberal institutionalism instinctively conceives an appropriate institutional framework for a liberal international economic order in terms of intergovernmental negotiated cooperation 'from above', classical liberalism focuses its sights on the domestic preconditions of international order: the appropriate institutional framework is sought, first and foremost, 'from below' at the level of *national* law and policy.

Why does classical liberalism place such emphasis on national governance? Surely, one could argue, the internationalisation of markets significantly reduces the importance of the nation-state as a 'governing' entity. Admittedly, classical liberalism dismisses notions of world government as a childish fantasy, and it is rather sceptical of international organisations and intergovernmental collaboration (see chapters three, five and seven, and the following sections of this chapter). But this does not mean that classical liberalism is part of the bandwagon proclaiming the rise of 'globalisation' and the retreat of the nation-state.

As chapter three touched upon, there are now plenty of popular writers (or Pop Internationalists, as Paul Krugman calls them) who argue that the state is in decline in the face of the overpowering and impersonal forces of globalisation. One commonly held view is that multinational enterprises with flexible and footloose production across the globe are in the driving seat and are slowly but surely dethroning the political authority of governments.[50]

Serious statistical and economic analysis shows that globalisation has attained mythical proportions. The more popular versions of globalisation vastly exaggerate global capital market integration and the activity of multinational enterprises. Arguably, the international economy is in many ways still less integrated than it was in the heyday of economic liberalism at the turn of the nineteenth century.[51] In a modern world of admittedly intensifying economic linkages across borders, the nation-state remains the key political unit in the international system, as Adam Smith and David Hume clearly foresaw (see chapter three). Moreover, an awful lot of economic activity, contrary to popular perception, still remains intrinsically 'domestic', not 'international', in nature.[52] This conclusion leads inexorably to another: national-level legal arrangements and government policy still matter as much as ever, both in domestic and international affairs; multinational enterprises or other nonstate actors have not even come close to usurping the political authority of the state.

Following the tradition of Smith, Hume and the nineteenth-century English economists, a classical liberal perspective, eschewing the pulp fiction of Pop

Internationalist globalisation, realistically takes the internationalisation of markets to be perfectly compatible with an international political system of nation-states. Its starting-point is, therefore, the assumption that the state endures and makes a decisive difference in its core legal arrangements and its policy-making or governing competence (see chapter three). With that clearly in mind, classical liberalism can then point to the appropriate domestic and international role for governments in facilitating and maintaining an international spontaneous order.

The insight that governance in the international political economy is still fundamentally reliant on government policy at the national level is perhaps most vividly articulated by the German political economist Wilhelm Röpke (see chapter seven). To him, the source of conflict and illiberalism in international economic relations lies within the nation-state, and it originates in the centralisation and inflation of government power: increasingly interventionist domestic economic policies ineluctably spill over into foreign economic policies of quantitative trade restrictions and exchange controls, which are bound to spark international conflict. This has been the experience of the twentieth century, particularly in the interwar years but continuing, in milder form, after 1945. To this day, government intervention in the domestic sphere ultimately leads to international economic conflict.

To Röpke, tackling the problem primarily at the international level is a 'false internationalism', a bit like 'building a house starting with the roof'. His dismissive attitude towards this 'liberalism from above' goes hand-in-hand with his belief in 'an internationalism which, like charity, should begin at home'. Governments, in the first instance, should unilaterally undertake policies to restore good order domestically, out of which good international order will result *epiphenomenally*.[53]

As chapter seven pointed out, Röpke's approach is fully in keeping with the classical economists' fixation with national order in the eighteenth and nineteenth centuries: they viewed a liberal international economic order as a by-product of an appropriate institutional framework, or proper constitutional observance, within the nation-state.[54] Furthermore, one cannot overlook a meta-economic dimension: in lieu of world government, an international Rule of Law and a world civil society, liberal values can take root only in the morals, customs and traditions of established and 'grown' national civil societies; one cannot simply graft them onto the international system.[55] As Röpke contends, 'more important than international institutions and legal documents are the moral-political forces behind the market that are only really effective within nations'.[56] Hence the paramount importance of policy action where it is most effective, that is, at the national level, to achieve a liberal international economic order. This was very much the experience of the nineteenth century: collective adherence to the gold standard, free trade and capital mobility entailed no organisational setup at the international level; policy action practically confined itself to the national level, and international policy cooperation was 'spontaneous', not 'negotiated'.[57]

A liberal reference system for international economic order begins with a requirement that the state stick to its considerable but circumscribed *agenda* or 'legitimate' functions – what Eucken calls *Ordnungspolitik* or order policy – while refraining from interventions in private property, and the freedoms of trade, contract and association (as outlined in a previous section of this chapter). This domestic *agenda* is the cornerstone of classical liberal public policy but, in the international sphere, it has to be complemented by policies of multilateral trade without quantitative restrictions, freely convertible currencies and capital mobility. Röpke also stresses a meta-economic component, what he calls 'unwritten international economic law': the widespread (ideological) adherence to certain standards and moral codes, such as respect for the private property of, and contractual obligations towards, foreigners, which buttresses liberal domestic and foreign economic policies. If a critical mass of states reasonably approximated these conditions, as was the case during liberalism's golden age, the nineteenth century, international transactions would assume the character of domestic transactions. *There would then be no need for world government, and relatively little need for international agreements and intergovernmental negotiated cooperation* (see chapter seven).[58]

This emphasis on national, rather than international or intergovernmental, policy measures for a liberal international economic order, runs from Smith and Hume through the English Classical School of the nineteenth century to Röpke. The 'democratic constitutionalism' of Jan Tumlir takes it one stage further (see chapter eight). Like his intellectual forebears Tumlir is less interested in international organisations and intergovernmental cooperation, and more interested in policy and legal change within the nation-state. In essence, he attempts to answer the question of *how* one can put a 'liberalism from below' into effect.

Tumlir's constitutional approach advocates the incorporation of international commitments, such as the Most Favoured Nation principle or, more generally, the freedom to trade across borders, into domestic law. To him, not only is this a more effective way of liberalising the international economic order than by way of cumbersome international negotiations on specific policies; but also it is a step in the direction of domestic constitutional reconstruction. The right to trade across borders in domestic law would institute judicial oversight and constitutional due process in foreign economic policy, where it has been notoriously lacking and where executive discretion and private rent-seeking activity have held sway. Moreover it would, via the increasing intertwining of foreign and domestic economic policies, help to restore constitutional due process in domestic economic policy, thereby limiting executive and administrative interference with private economic functions.[59]

When distilled to bare essentials, the classical liberal perspective of international economic order is happiest with the juxtaposition of increasing cross-border economic interdependence *and* an international political system of sovereign nation-states. Given the inescapable fact of national sovereignty, regimes of commercial openness are reliant, in the first and the last instance, on unilateral liberalising action *within* nation-states. However, this is not to say that classical liberalism has no place for intergovernmental policy cooperation. The eighteenth- and nineteenth-century Scottish and English economists were sceptical of reciprocal negotiations (with the exception of Robert Torrens). However, many classical liberals in the twentieth century, taking account of changed political and institutional conditions, have been willing to countenance a measure of intergovernmental negotiations and agreements. They believed, and still believe, that such reciprocity could, under some circumstances, dovetail with unilateral measures to sustain and speed up overall liberalisation.

Despite their warnings of an overemphasis on reciprocity and their scepticism regarding most international organisations, both Wilhelm Röpke and Jan Tumlir view the GATT – now the World Trade Organisation (WTO) – as a useful and helpful multilateral forum for reciprocal liberalisation that does not necessarily hinder, and indeed may well foster, the unilateral steps in the direction of an open international commerce that spring from the initiative of individual nation-states. Röpke firmly prioritises the unilateral route to trade liberalisation. Tumlir inclines more to reciprocal agreements, with the proviso that they should stick to clear and simple rules, and constitutionally limit the ability of (international and national) public authorities to exercise discretionary power. However, to reiterate, both scholars have a gut-feeling that a liberal international economic order primarily depends on change, constitutional and otherwise, emerging from within individual nation-states – which, of course, returns the policy argument to unilateral liberalisation.

Classical liberalism and neoliberal institutionalism: 'liberalism from below' versus 'liberalism from above'

Contra 'mixed systems thinking' and 'liberalism from above'

Hitherto, the discussion has surveyed the contours of classical liberalism, contrasting them with the rather different landscape of neoclassical economics-based rational choice. Then it identified the main features of a classical liberal theory of international economic order, from a Smithian methodology to the notion of an international spontaneous order with its criterion of public utility and its maxims of law and policy. It also sharply contrasted the classical liberal insistence on the enduring importance of the state in the international political system with the globalisation scenario of the obsolescent state. In addition, one or two differences between classical liberalism and neoliberal institutionalism were flagged *en route*. Now I seek quite explicitly to *confront* the theory and policy of classical liberal international political economy with neoliberal institutionalism.

As stated earlier, one normative pillar of neoliberal institutionalism is 'mixed systems thinking': the combination of international liberal arrangements with the mixed economy within nation-states. Classical liberalism would profoundly disagree with such an unlikely congress of antithetical ordering principles to support a liberal international economic order.

From a classical liberal standpoint, the national mixed economy is an unstable compromise between market economy and command economy principles.[60] Its command economy elements, involving extensive interventions in factor and goods markets, cast their shadow over foreign economic policy and produce quantitative trade protectionism as well capital controls. Therefore the domestic mixed economy is the *source* of international illiberalism, not the structural support of international liberalism. There is no stable mixed systems compromise in international economic relations; illiberal domestic economic policies are bound to shake the liberal foundations of the international economic order. This is how classical liberalism would, on the whole, interpret conflict and strife in twentieth-century international economic relations. Corrective action in present-day circumstances, far from consisting of a continuation and widening of the 'compromise of embedded liberalism', lies in pushing back discretionary government within nation-states in the direction of a circumscribed *agenda* of government action. Thus a domestic liberal order should underpin an international liberal order (see chapter seven).

The other normative pillar of neoliberal institutionalism is a 'liberalism from above' with a penchant for negotiated intergovernmental cooperation on a broad range of issues. In so far as it borrows from economic theory, it is from the neoclassical family, for example, models of externalities, public goods, social welfare functions and market failure – all of which, implicitly or explicitly, assume the fragility of markets and the robustness of government intervention. What these theoretical systems conveniently furnish is an open invitation for governments to extend their interventions in the name of international policy coordination. Classical liberalism would counter that this is a dubious rationale for intervention, for careful observation reveals the fragility of government intervention, wherever it occurs, and the relative robustness of domestic and international markets.[61]

Neoliberal institutionalists do not portray international policy coordination in the frame of limiting general rules at the international level that proscribe discretionary government action; rather, they think of it as an apparatus of complicated negotiations on particularistic policies intended to achieve specific results. This is the hallmark not of limited government under the Rule of Law, but of unlimited and discretionary government in an international public policy cartel, avoiding both domestic political accountability and market disciplines. In this context, international regimes are manifestations of government failure transplanted to the international level. Intergovernmental cooperation and international agreements, far removed from public scrutiny and the control of national legislatures and judiciaries, supply extra room for arbitrary activity by politicians and bureaucrats. They exacerbate the malaise of Big Government and political markets within nation-states.[62]

International regimes of development, exchange rates and fiscal policy, for example, have extended rather than narrowed the possibilities of government intervention in factor and goods markets. The GATT/WTO trade regime is a partial and very significant exception, being perhaps the most successful example of intergovernmental policy cooperation producing net liberalising effects. This is due not least to its general rules embodying the nondiscriminatory MFN and National Treatment clauses. However, even the WTO rule-base has a plethora of exceptions, escape clauses and waivers that have allowed, and still allow for, protectionist policies.[63] A classical liberal would, therefore, look askance at the proliferation of these mechanisms since 1945 (with the possible and qualified exception of the GATT/WTO), based not on hard-and-fast general rules but on political power and diplomacy.

Neoliberal institutionalism relies somewhat on rather static neoclassical models; it has little or no evolutionary perspective of political economy. One could reasonably argue that it suffers from a rational-constructivist orientation: political power (the use, or the threat of use, of force or coercion) and political bargaining seem to account for so much in terms of process and outcome in the international political economy.[64] Implicitly, neoliberal institutionalists treat the international political economy as the product of conscious design. There is hardly any space for, and little appreciation of, the unintended or unforeseen outcomes of impersonal market transactions that may or may not accord with political designs – the very stuff of the spontaneous market order or catallaxy.

Neoliberal institutionalism is particularly remiss in skirting round the 'knowledge problem'. There seems to be a complacency in the genre in assuming that more-or-less rational actors in regimes of intergovernmental cooperation collectively have access to, and mastery of, the complex array of relevant facts required to control processes and outcomes in the international political economy. It is difficult enough to assemble and activate relevant information to coordinate specific policies within the nation-state, but it is an even taller order to perform feats of international policy coordination in an efficacious manner. Concerning macroeconomic policy coordination, for example, how on earth are governments supposed to know (better than the markets) what the 'right' exchange rates and interest rates are and how they can be coordinated worldwide in the present and the future? This simplistic and mechanical perspective is thus difficult to reconcile with a highly complex and differentiated international economic order, particularly given the widespread dispersal of knowledge that is the lifeblood of the order. The Hayekian argument that the spontaneous order utilises far more useful knowledge than could ever be used in centralised policy arrangements applies as much to international economic policy as it does to domestic economic policy.[65]

Unilateral liberalisation and institutional competition

The preceding sections were highly critical of globalisation scenarios and neo-liberal institutionalism, giving an indication of what classical liberalism is *against*. Here I venture to suggest what classical liberalism is *in favour of* and what it has to offer as an alternative policy programme for a liberal international economic order. This centres in national policy liberalisation undertaken *unilaterally*, that is, not contingent on intergovernmental bargaining, and an intergovernmental 'institutional' competition.

Unilateral liberalisation

Reciprocity is, of course, at the very heart of neoliberal institutionalism. It is not the reciprocity, as envisaged by David Hume, around which a spontaneous market order revolves, involving sets of cooperative, self-enforcing (or sponta-neous) and mutually advantageous two-party transactions.[66] On the contrary, neoliberal institutionalists think of it as a construct of coordinated bargains between governments. The presumption is that governments are wary of liber-alising unilaterally, and even if they do so it is unlikely to redound to the advantage of individual nations (mainly due to adverse terms of trade effects – see chapter five). Moreover, unilateral action is more likely to be protectionist and conflict-inducing than liberalising and cooperative. Having made these objections, a key political economy argument in favour of *contingent* liberalisa-tion comes into play: opening one's own market in return for concessions extracted from other nations is considered the only effective way of getting domestic producers to go along with market-opening measures at home.[67] For these and other reasons, neoliberal institutionalism proposes reciprocity as the preferred route to liberalisation.

The opposing case for unilateral trade liberalisation follows from the classical liberal fixation with the domestic preconditions of international order and Röpke's dictum that 'internationalism, like charity, should begin at home' – with unilateral measures, not international agreements. The classical economists, it will be remembered, establish an economic-theoretical case for free trade on static and dynamic grounds. However, following Adam Smith, they justify their pref-erence for *unilateral* free trade on political economy-cum-policy grounds and only very partially on the basis of economic theory (see chapters three and five). They hold that unilateral liberalisation is the most effective means of engendering a better allocation of domestic resources and reaping long-run productivity gains. It is a more straightforward method bringing greater tangible benefits than would materialise from a cumbersome, time-consuming and politicised procedure of reciprocal negotiations. Admittedly, there are adverse employment and balance of payments effects of unilateral liberalisation in the short run, but they can be mitigated and corrected by an exchange rate devaluation (under a floating rate regime) and by deregulating domestic labour markets (to enable workers to transfer from less efficient to more efficient industries as speedily as possible).[68]

Further political economy arguments reinforce the presumption in favour of unilateralism. As mentioned before, particularly in chapter five, economists make a theoretical case for reciprocity (i.e. maintaining protection unless others liberalise) on terms of trade grounds. However, political economy or policy realities such as government failure (interest group capture and rent-seeking), lack of knowledge (to impose the 'right' sort of barriers to free commerce) and foreign retaliation seriously weaken the case for reciprocity. In any case, the terms of trade argument has to be set against the better allocation of domestic resources that issues from unilateral liberalisation.[69] To the classical economists, the combination of these arguments favours unilateral free trade, not reciprocity, as the preferred policy option.

The British opted for the unilateral route to trade liberalisation in the nineteenth century; even their bilateral commercial treaties extended unconditional Most Favoured Nation status to third countries. In contrast, US commercial policy has always been reciprotarian, applying conditional MFN until the 1920s and insisting on the reciprocal approach to post-1945 international economic liberalisation.[70] The original case for unilateral liberalisation on political economy grounds, even in a generally protectionist world, almost disappeared by the 1930s and 1940s. In the following decades, the total emphasis on reciprocity degenerated into the mutual acceptance of protection (by developing countries of developed countries and vica versa), often legitimised by derogations from the MFN and National Treatment principles in the GATT.[71]

As Jagdish Bhagwati cogently argues, the fixation with the reciprocity principle has unfortunately led to the widespread justification and surreptitious increase of protectionism on the pretext that other countries are engaging in 'unfair' competition. From the 1970s, this line of political argument has conveniently justified the use of the nontariff barriers associated with the New Protectionism. The US and the EU in particular have sought to predetermine market outcomes, or 'manage trade', in favour of politically powerful home producers by recourse to discriminatory instruments such as voluntary export restraints, voluntary import expansions, and antidumping and countervailing duties.[72] Managed trade essentially involves the oligopolistic carving up of sectoral markets through an opaque patchwork of public–private political cartels that unite governments, importers and exporters. Not only does this have a highly distorting and debilitating effect on international markets, but also it is deeply corrosive of the Rule of Law: privileged rent-seeking exporting and importing producers are shielded by administrative discretion from judicial control, including the application of antitrust laws.[73]

It is quite in order to say that reciprocity has been the predominant feature of postwar international economic liberalisation (although, from a classical liberal standpoint, more emphasis on unilateralism may have brought greater and speedier benefits). Nevertheless, unilateralism has been and is of considerable significance. Neoliberal institutionalism completely overlooks this point. To the latter perspective, the gradual opening of the international economy seems to lead straight back to the Bretton Woods agreements, the GATT, the regional regimes of Marshall Aid and the European Payments Union, *inter alia*.[74] However, as argued in chapter seven, there was a considerable amount of West German unilateral liberalisation of domestic and foreign economic policies from 1948, setting an example that other countries in Western Europe followed in the 1950s.[75]

Admittedly, the West German example in the 1950s was a one-off. International trade liberalisation from the mid- to late 1950s down to the early 1980s took place almost exclusively through successive negotiating rounds of the GATT. The latter were effective in progressively bringing about the multilateral reduction of tariff barriers, although much less effective in hindering the rise of nontariff barriers from the late 1960s. The concluding agreements of the Uruguay Round of the GATT, and the ongoing work of the WTO, have given an added boost to trade liberalisation in goods, services and agriculture, and the liberalisation of barriers to trade-related foreign investment. The International Monetary Fund and the World Bank have also egged on commercial policy reform in developing countries and ex-command economies.[76]

Reciprocal bargaining in intergovernmental fora has thus been a perennial feature of international commercial liberalisation throughout the postwar era. Nevertheless, unilateral commercial (i.e. trade and foreign investment) liberalisation has returned with a vengeance from the 1970s, and particularly since the early 1980s, spreading its increasingly powerful wings far and wide across the international economy. Emerging markets in the developing world, especially in Latin America and Asia, and in the new transition economies, have been liberalising tariff and nontariff barriers to trade, as well as barriers to foreign direct investment, on their own and beyond the requirements of reciprocal international agreements. Such unilateralism is becoming an ever larger and crucial component of the commercial policies of small developing and transition economies (not to mention the unilateral liberalisation policies of Australia and New Zealand in the OECD).[77] It is a phenomenon of momentous significance for international commercial policy in the 1990s, as yet curiously unnoticed by the scribes of neoliberal institutionalism.

Furthermore, unilateral liberalisation is not exclusive to trade policy and developing countries. There has been a considerable amount of unilateral liberalisation of *domestic* economic policies in *both* developed and developing countries. For example, the US and the UK have pioneered policies of privatisation and deregulation in financial markets, telecommunications and the utilities. Other countries across the globe have followed suit, very largely without intergovernmental policy coordination.[78]

Institutional competition

From unilateral liberalisation I now turn to the phenomenon of *institutional competition*. To the neoliberal institutionalist, the practice of reciprocity is at the heart of international regimes of negotiated cooperation. To the classical liberal, the practice of unilateral liberalisation is the foremost manifestation of what can be called an international institutional competition. Whereas international regimes display the hallmarks of a cartel, institutional competition is *market-like*: at the political level of competition between governments, it is analogous to the competition between economic agents in markets for goods and services. Adaptation by governments and private actors in institutional competition is spontaneous and unilateral, not requiring reciprocal intergovernmental bargains.

On the demand side of institutional competition, the owners of mobile resources (e.g. financial capital, technology and management skills) choose between national and regional locations by means of 'exit', opting for one location in preference to another. Multinational enterprises are the most visible sign of 'demand' in institutional competition. Very much a part of their locational choices are differences between national legal frameworks governing property and contract, as well as differences between government policies on public finances, taxation, monetary control, the provision of infrastructure etc.. On the supply side are immobile factors, including national laws and government policies, which compete for internationally mobile resources.[79] In the following passage, Adam Smith clearly appreciates the consequences of footloose capital:

> The proprietor of stock is properly a citizen of the world, and is not necessarily attached to any particular country. He would be apt to abandon the country in which he was exposed to a vexatious inquisition, in order to be assessed to a burdensome tax, and would remove his stock to some other country where he could either carry on his business, or enjoy his fortune more at his ease. By removing his stock he would put an end to all the industry which it had maintained in the country which he left. Stock cultivates land; stock employs labour. A tax which tended to drive away stock from any particular country, would so far tend to dry up every source of revenue, both to the sovereign and to the society. Not only the profits of stock, but the rent of the land and the wages of labour, would necessarily be more or less diminished by its removal.[80]

Classical liberalism conceives institutional competition as a dynamic and evolutionary 'discovery procedure' in the Hayekian sense. It is the globally transmitted information on the attractiveness of different institutional settings that activates an intergovernmental institutional competition. The transmission of widely dispersed relevant knowledge on the preferences of owners of mobile resources, including multinationals, sends signals to governments to change their policy packages and modify the legal framework to attract mobile capital. Governments compete with each other through imitation, trial-and-error and adaptation to uncertainty, constantly learning from one another in search of better practice. Problems and solutions are not 'given' in the neoclassical static-equilibrium sense; rather, multiple possible solutions to changing problems are 'discovered' via intergovernmental political competition.[81]

Thus, as in economic markets, the transmission, emulation and incorporation of ideas, all engendered by intergovernmental political competition, are the seedbed of institutional innovation and lead to an all-round increase in productivity and wealth. It is David Hume who grasped this inestimably important insight two-and-a-half centuries ago. As mentioned in chapter three, his advocacy of free trade circles around one country's *competitive emulation* of the superior technology of neighbouring countries in expanding networks of commerce. Such commerce channels the cross-border flow of ideas on institutional practice, including the behaviour of governments. This 'imitation of foreigners' fosters a 'spirit of industry' or, as Hume writes elsewhere, 'a noble emulation is the source of every excellence'.[82]

Institutional competition, unlike the political construct of negotiated intergovernmental cooperation, is part and parcel of the international spontaneous market order. Competition among governments is an 'invisible hand', spontaneous, open-ended process whose outcomes are the unpredictable by-products of countless individual, corporate and political actions. Superior authorities do not plan or deliberately coordinate these outcomes, as is the case with intergovernmental policy cooperation.

The Utopian liberal dreams of world government and an international framework of general rules. The realistic classical liberal knows full well that governments are unlikely collectively to disarm themselves by committing to rules that so severely limit, if not eradicate, discretionary power. Therefore, international negotiated cooperation is likely to focus on specific policies and have cartel-like features that preserve and expand discretionary power. With that in mind, institutional competition is a substitute for world government and, in many instances, an alternative to negotiated cooperation at the international level, as the following examples illustrate.[83]

The Bretton Woods agreements, for all their touted advantages, sanctioned the continuance of rampant capital controls, thereby legitimising government intervention and protectionism, and foreclosing an institutional competition (which cannot take place without mobile resources, especially capital).[84] Since the mid-1960s, the international economy has returned to capital mobility – another unforeseen outcome, not deliberately planned by any particular authority or group of them. This has set in train a process of institutional competition that has put interventionist and protectionist policies under increasing pressure.

Similarly, intermittent bouts of international macroeconomic policy co-ordination can be seen as a means by which governments avoid difficult domestic policy choices, maintain and enlarge their room for discretionary manoeuvre, and evade market disciplines. Their replacement by the competition of fiscal policies and currencies – the supercession of a harmonised policy package by a multitude of experiments – can be viewed as a means of breaking up a policy cartel and disciplining the 'Leviathan' tendencies of government. Hence, institutional competition goads governments to 'put their own houses in order'. And to give one last example, competitive disinflation replaced the monetary policy cartel of Bretton Woods in the 1970s: instead of continuing to collude in an international exchange rate regime, governments imitated each other's anti-inflationary policies.[85]

Many writers on globalisation interpret institutional competition as a predetermined 'race to the bottom' as states competitively deregulate in the face of overwhelming transnational forces. In this scheme, the state disarms itself of policy competence and is disarmed in its exercise of authority by other actors, especially multinational enterprises.[86] As indicated before, this view is apocryphal, especially in its wild overestimation of globalisation's concrete effects. Furthermore, it overlooks the ability of governments to make policy choices and respond in very different ways to the opportunities and constraints of the international economy. Institutional competition is a constraint on governmental action – a salutary constraint on irresponsible government policies, as classical liberals would argue – but it still leaves wide leeway for governments to choose different policies that have a large impact on, and make a substantial difference to, national economic performance. From a classical liberal standpoint, the choice of market-oriented policies, in all their complexity and differentiation, and in an atmosphere of experimentation, conduces to all-round gain; it is not a 'race to the bottom'.

Institutional competition is nothing new; it has a long history. It is Max Weber, among others, who largely attributes Europe's unique breakthrough to modernity to the competition between political authorities for ideas, skilled people and mobile capital. The exit of people, money and technology imposed a salutary discipline on irresponsible governments. Europe benefited from competitive political decision-making by diffusing best practice, something not possible in the stagnating, monolithic empires to its east and south.[87]

Institutional competition flowered in the Pax Britannica of the nineteenth century; was abruptly uprooted and torn to shreds during the first half of the twentieth century, primarily by choking the flow of mobile capital and thereby 'closing' the system; and it has re-emerged since the 1950s. Powered by the stupendous volume and speed of present-day mobile capital, institutional competition is now more vigorous than at any time since the outbreak of the First World War. Its handmaiden is not the reciprocity envisaged by neoliberal institutionalists, but the unilateral liberalisation of domestic and foreign economic policies that has been spreading like wildfire, especially in developing and transition economies.

Conclusion – and some thoughts on future work

The method adopted here has been one of a *deliberate confrontation of paradigms*. Classical liberalism differs from a neoclassical economics-based rational choice because it has more realistic assumptions of human behaviour and market order, arguably making it more relevant to policy and amplifying its normative appeal. It differs from neoliberal institutionalism because it has an evolutionary, not a rational-constructivist, theory of international political economy, a more solid legal foundation (especially in the realm of private law), an institutional framework that stresses the domestic preconditions of international order and, consequently, the primacy of national-level policy action. On the policy front, it further distinguishes itself from neoliberal institutionalism by pointing to, as well as advocating, unilateral liberalisation in the context of a system-wide institutional competition. Correspondingly, classical liberalism views a heavy organisational setup and complex bureaucratic procedures at the international level with great scepticism. And lastly, classical liberalism emphasises the endurance of a system of nation-states *alongside* and *in tandem with* the internationalisation of markets. It has no truck with pseudo-theories of globalisation that point to the powerlessness of public policy at the national level and that predict the decline of the nation-state.

Given that thinkers in international political economy usually dismiss classical liberalism as irrelevant and *passé*, it has been my task to explicate – even accentuate – its disagreements with established paradigms. Only in this way can I highlight its distinctiveness and relevance to international political economy. This is not to deny that there is some overlap between paradigms here and there. Conceivably, classical liberalism can share a limited amount of middle ground with a highly modified, rules-based rational choice.[88]

However, there is little common ground between classical liberalism and neoliberal institutionalism. The chief traits of neoliberal institutionalism – 'mixed systems thinking' and a 'liberalism from above', complete with an emphasis on reciprocity and heavy organisational setup – do not exhibit *bona fide* liberal credentials, at least in the classical European sense of liberalism. It is therefore rather surprising that this paradigm occupies the liberal compartment in international political economy. Classical liberalism, in contrast, provides a *genuinely* liberal paradigm of international political economy. It is not *passé*, having been abundantly renewed and replenished in recent times. Its Smithian methodology, its theory of order and allotted role for government are, contrary to the standard caricature, far removed from a harmony of interests doctrine, an absolutist *laissez faire* and a nightwatchman state. Its agenda in international political economy is the theorisation of the international spontaneous market order, its legal underpinning and its appropriate public policy framework. For policy, it should identify and analyse the actuality and potential of unilateral liberalisation in the frame of institutional competition, whose vistas have vastly magnified relative to, and in interaction with, bilateral, regional and multilateral modes of intergovernmental cooperation. All this is foreign territory to neoliberal institutionalism.

This chapter has highlighted one sensitive area of disagreement between classical liberalism and neoliberal institutionalism concerning the relative merits of unilateralism and reciprocity as methods of commercial liberalisation. Indeed,

I have underlined the differences between the two policy approaches in order to set forth a strong case for unilateral liberalisation. However, this is not to deny that there is and can be a fruitful interrelation between unilateral liberalisation and reciprocity (or, put differently, between institutional competition and international regimes) under specified and conceivable circumstances. This aspect, unfortunately not dealt with at great length in the preceding work due to the abundance of other relevant issues, deserves some further mention and a short digression in the closing pages of this book – not least because it furnishes me with an excuse for advertising my next research endeavour to fatigued readers who have stoically ploughed through the previous few hundred pages.

The recent wave of unilateral liberalisation is partly (but by no means wholly) conditioned by background reciprocal agreements at bilateral, regional and multilateral levels. For example, measures of unilateral trade liberalisation in developing countries in the 1980s proceeded in tandem with structural adjustment programs negotiated with the World Bank and the IMF. Many of these measures were incorporated into the final Uruguay Round agreements of the GATT. The latter, together with subsequent WTO agreements, may well have spurred and will continue to spur further unilateral liberalisation by nation-states. To mention another well-known example, the loose and 'open' regional economic cooperation in the Association of Southeast Asian Nations (ASEAN) and, more broadly, in the Asia Pacific Economic Cooperation (APEC), largely builds on the foundation of unilateral trade liberalisation by their member-states. The latter extend their trade liberalisation measures unconditionally to other nation-states within and outside ASEAN and APEC.[89]

The foregoing anecdotal evidence points to a virtuous circle of liberalisation through a combination of unilateralism and reciprocity. On the other hand, the two policy approaches may conflict. Concentrating on extracting concessions from others in intergovernmental negotiations may delay unilateral liberalising measures, just as the latter may be used as an excuse not to undertake further liberalisation in reciprocal agreements.

There is a positive correlation between unilateralism and reciprocity as modes of commercial liberalisation when reciprocal agreements veer in the direction of limiting general rules that proscribe arbitrary government action and have relatively few exceptions and loopholes. This furnishes a solid framework within which unilateral liberalisation and institutional competition can take place.[90] But there is a negative correlation when negotiated cooperation is 'power-based' rather than 'rules-based', to use John Jackson's distinction,[91] for cartel-like cooperation predicated on executive and administrative discretion can inhibit, or serve as a pretext for not undertaking, necessary policy reform within countries. This forecloses a free-wheeling institutional competition in the international system. Much, perhaps most, of what is written in the neoliberal institutionalist corpus seems to imply the latter sort of negotiated cooperation.

There is ample scope to research the rich intellectual history of the debate between reciprocity and unilateralism as alternative modes of liberalisation.

Similarly, an awful lot of empirical work should be done on the avalanche of recent unilateral commercial liberalisation, sparked by the pioneering Chilean experience in the mid-1970s, spreading across Latin America and Southeast Asia in the 1980s, extending as far as the shores of Australia and New Zealand, and then reaching the transition countries of Eastern Europe and the former Soviet Union in the early 1990s. The technical steps aimed at establishing national regimes of commercial openness to the world economy, including a substantial component of unilateral commercial liberalisation, have formed part of larger packages of macro- and microeconomic policy reform in developing and transition countries since the late 1970s. Furthermore, such truly momentous change is a consequence of the political economy of shifting ideas, interests and institutions, all of which respond to, as well as shape, the conjuncture of internal and external economic circumstance.[92]

The 'broad canvas' thinking of this book has led me, surprisingly or not, to cogitate on the political economy of these intellectual-historical and modern policy issues, particularly in as much as they relate to commercial policy reform in the emerging markets of the world economy. How does commercial liberalisation interact with the development of the domestic institutional (legal and governmental) framework? Why did a number of countries embark on the unilateral liberalisation of barriers to trade and foreign direct investment, instead of opting for reciprocal liberalisation through intergovernmental bargaining and international agreements – the conventional practice since the 1930s? Why and to what extent did these unilateral reforms continue and expand into the medium term? How is unilateral liberalisation linked with overall packages of macroeconomic and microeconomic policy reform? What is the link between unilateralism and reciprocity in commercial liberalisation, and what impact does unilateral liberalisation have on the framework of multilateral rules, particularly in the WTO? And finally, what are the prospects for unilateral liberalisation into the medium-term future?

These are all key questions of theoretical, historical and contemporary policy relevance that invite examination and response from classical liberal political economy. Much, much more could be said on this underinvestigated subject, but that has to be reserved for future studies. And, in fact, my next project of research and writing will tackle these very questions of commercial policy reform as a direct application of classical liberalism to recent and present public policy in the international economic order.

This book has sought to tease out the common features of classical liberal political economy via an intellectual-historical method covering thinkers from the Scots to Hayek, always taking care to find out what these individuals have to say on the subject of international economic order. Intellectual history has been one motivating force of this exercise; theoretical relevance to the present and (hopefully) the future is the other. With the help of intellectual history, I hope I have come some way towards setting out a classical liberal paradigm readily applicable to the modern international economic order.

The four years spent on this book have been a tremendous, exhilarating voyage of discovery, well away from the main currents and fashions in international political economy. Along with the learning experience, it has been great fun. If these studies whet the appetite of some readers to indulge in the history of thought *and* seriously consider classical liberalism's merits in international political economy, they will have succeeded in attaining their original objectives.

Notes

1 Hayek (1960), p. 411.
2 Frank H. Knight, 'Economics', p. 25, 'Social science', p. 127, 'Social causation', p. 145, all in Knight (1956).
3 James M. Buchanan, 'Constitutional economics', in Eatwell *et al.* (1989), p. 84.
4 Mueller (1989), p. 2.
5 Wohlgemuth (1994), pp. 5–7.
6 Olson, 'Collective action', in Eatwell *et al.* (1989), pp. 62–67; Frey (1984), pp. 212–213.
7 Frey (1984), pp. 207–214.
8 Jagdish Bhagwati, 'Is free trade passé after all?', in Bhagwati (1991), pp. 14–15.
9 Tumlir (1985a), p. 16.
10 Baldwin (1988), p. 111; Petersmann (1988), p. 241.
11 Frey (1984), p. 213.
12 Buchanan, op. cit. pp. 79–80.
13 Moravcsik (1993), p. 4.
14 Kratochwil (1992), pp. 29, 31, 40.
15 Ruggie (1982), pp. 209–231.
16 Liberal institutionalists frequently hold up the small open economies of Western Europe as paragons of the 'compromise of embedded liberalism'. They maintain openness to the international economy, from which they derive great benefit, but have centralised corporatist arrangements domestically in order to equitably resolve distributional conflicts between interest groups, ease the path of adjustment and preserve social consensus. See Katzenstein (1985).

The Katzenstein thesis has gained widespread acceptance among US political scientists, but its optimism and current validity are open to question. Arguably, it underestimates the sclerotic, cartel-like features of corporatist negotiation that privilege the status quo and retard necessary adjustments to a changing international division of labour. This is all too evident in Switzerland and the Scandinavian countries (not to mention larger countries like France and Germany), facing greater competition from lower cost production locations and seemingly unable and unwilling to undertake radical reforms in labour market regulation and welfare spending, *inter alia*.

17 Ruggie (1995), pp. 508, 523–526.
18 One could argue that the New Liberalism takes its rise from John Stuart Mill, whom Hayek accuses of a 'false individualism'. See F.A. Hayek, 'Individualism: true and false', in Hayek (1949), pp. 28–29.

John Gray argues that Mill underplays the 'Scottish' element of liberalism, reflected later in Hayek's work, which recognises that liberalism itself depends on the preexistence and continuation of common cultural traditions and practices; and that he correspondingly overplays the autonomous rational action of individuals detached from surrounding social conventions. It is this that leads Mill to ignore the institutional preconditions that influence and constrain plans for social change. Hence his protosocialist radicalism on questions of distribution, worker-syndicalism and the attainment of a stationary state, setting a precedent for later Utopian blueprints of social engineering. Gray calls this tradition a 'revisionary' liberalism based on an abstract, hyperrationalist individualism. Most modern forms of liberalism are in this vein, whether it be the utilitarianism of Nozick, the egalitarianism of Dworkin or the distributive contractarianism of Rawls. Rawls and Dworkin are at the end of a long line of 'liberal' thinkers who, arguably, supplant the classical concern for constitutionalism and equal liberty before the law with notions of and demands for 'democratic' equality. See John Gray, 'J.S. Mill and the future of liberalism', pp. 5–8, 'Mill's and other liberalisms', pp. 217, 224–230, 'Postcript: after liberalism', pp. 249–251, 'Contractarian method, private property and the market economy', p. 171, all in Gray (1989). Also see Mill (1987 [1871]), Book II, ch. I, Book IV, chs VI and VII.

19 Keohane (1984), pp. 5–6, 8–9.
20 Robbins (1952), p. 11.
21 John Gerard Ruggie, 'Multilateralism: the anatomy of an institution', in Ruggie (1993), p. 6.

Ruggie equates negotiated cooperation with multilateralism. But this *political* multilateralism is actually very different from what economists down the ages have understood as multilateralism. In free markets, multilateralism arises spontaneously through agents 'buying cheap and selling dear' across borders: goods and services are procured as cheaply as possible through imports; exports are sold as profitably as possible; both imports and exports are produced and sold according to comparative costs. The result, providing there is no hindrance by monopolists or governments, entangles actors in a web of multilateral relationships across borders. Röpke (1959a), pp. 72–73; Röpke (1994 [1965]), p. 71. Such an *economic* multilateralism is predicated on spontaneous cooperation and should be clearly distinguished from Ruggie's version.

22 Keohane (1984), pp. 50–53; Milner (1992), p. 469.
23 Ibid., p. 57.
24 Ibid., pp. 68–69, 75–76, 85 f., 110–115; Keohane (1986), pp. 2, 8.
25 Ibid., p. 254.
26 Axelrod and Keohane (1993), p. 109.
27 Terence Hutchison, 'Ricardian politics', in Hutchison (1994), pp. 107–126.
28 Viner, 'International trade theory and its present-day relevance', in Smithies *et al.* (1955), pp. 111–112; Jacob Viner, 'Introduction', in Viner (1951a), pp. 13–15.
29 Irwin (1996), pp. 211–216.
30 Myint (1977), pp. 231–232; Lal and Myint (1996), pp. 16, 18, 83, 189–190.
31 See World Bank (1996) and (1997); Sachs (1997); Lal and Myint (1996).
32 Jacob Viner, 'Introduction', in Viner (1951a), 10–11; Viner (1953), pp. 40–42; Jagdish Bhagwati and Douglas Irwin, 'The return of the reciprotarians: US trade policy today', in Bhagwati (1991), p. 87 f.
33 Gottfried Haberler, 'Strategic trade policy and the New International Economics: a critical analysis', in Jones and Krueger (1990), p. 27; Jagdish Bhagwati, 'Is free trade passé after all?', in Bhagwati (1991), pp. 3–26.
34 Hayek, 'The trend of economic thinking', in Hayek (1991), pp. 20, 31.
35 Patricia Dillon, James Lehmann and Thomas D. Willett, 'Assessing the usefulness of international trade theory for policy analysis', in Odell and Willett (1990), pp. 22, 32–33.
36 Indeed, Lord Keynes and a number of others make the argument that free trade depends on the assumption of perfect markets with fully employed resources. According to them, any departure from these assumptions opens the door to the effective use of national protection. See Irwin (1996), pp. 190, 201.
37 Posner (1993), p. 202.
38 Herbert Giersch, 'Trade in the world economy', in Giersch (1991), p. 104.

39 Simons (1948), p. 25.
40 Tumlir (1980), p. 19; Tumlir (1985b), p. 5; Hauser *et al.* (1988), p. 222.
41 Herbert Giersch, 'Schumpeter and the current and future development of the world economy', in Giersch (1991), pp. 224, 226, 230–231; Hayek (1982), vol. 3, pp. 78–80.
42 For an industrial organisation approach to the study of multinational enterprises, see Hymer (1976).
43 Polanyi (1944), pp. 54, 63, 141, 250.
44 Hayek (1988), pp. 39–44. North (1990), pp. 119, 125–126.
45 Robbins (1952), p. 48.
46 Hauser *et al.* (1988), p. 230; Schmidchen and Schmidt-Tretz (1990), p. 49; North (1990), p. 4.
47 Schmidchen and Schmidt-Tretz (1990), pp. 50–52; Hume (1978 [1740]), Book III, Part II, pp. 520, 526, 567–569.
48 Schmidchen and Schmidt-Tretz (1990), p. 53.
49 North (1990), pp. 34–35, 121, 127–128; Hayek (1988), p. 29 f.
50 See Ohmae (1990) and (1995); Reich (1992).
51 Hirst and Thompson (1996), pp. 1–18.
52 Krugman (1996), pp. 194–195.
53 Röpke (1959a), pp. 9–20.
54 Tumlir (1983), pp. 76–77.
55 Hayek (1960), p. 263.
56 Röpke (1962b), p. 239.
57 Röpke (1959a), pp. 74–79, 157–158.
58 Ibid., pp. 16, 72–73; Röpke (1955), pp. 224, 231–232.
59 Tumlir (1983a), pp. 80–81; Tumlir (1985a), pp. 63–67, 71.
60 Eucken (1990 [1952]), p. 144; Hayek (1982), vol. 3, p. 151.
61 Posner (1993), p. 201.
62 Tumlir (1981), pp. 9, 14; Paarlberg (1995), p. 10.
63 Viner (1953), p. 93; Viner (1947), p. 628.
64 On neoliberal institutionalism's focus on political power and bargaining, see Keohane (1984), p. 21; Keohane and Nye (1977), pp. 8–11, 18, 21.
65 See Vanberg (1994), p. 196.
66 Ibid., pp. 66–67, 73, 289.
67 Roessler (1978), p. 264.
68 Ibid., pp. 262, 273.
   The nineteenth-century classical economists do not consider these short-run problems, nor do they countenance anything other than fixed exchange rates under a commodity standard.
69 See references in note 30.
70 Bhagwati (1988), p. 26 f; Bhagwati and Irwin, 'The return of the reciprotarians', in Bhagwati (1991), pp. 96–98.
71 Tumlir (1983a), p. 75.
72 Bhagwati and Irwin, op. cit. pp. 102–104.
73 Tumlir (1985a), pp. 38–42, 48–49, 54.
74 See Barry Eichengreen and Peter Kenen, 'Managing the world economy under the Bretton Woods system: an overview', in Kenen (1994).
75 Röpke (1959b), pp. 79–81, 92; Giersch *et al.* (1992), pp. 95–124.
76 See Hoekman and Kostecki (1995).
77 Wolf (1996); David Greenaway and Oliver Morrissey, 'Multilateral institutions and unilateral trade liberalisation in developing countries', in Balasubramanyam and Greenaway (1996); Michaely *et al.* (1991).
78 See Barfield (1996).

79 Wohlgemuth (1995), pp. 1, 7, 10; Lüder Gerken, 'Institutional competition: an orientative framework', in Gerken (1995), pp. 13–15.
80 Smith (1976 [1776]), Book V, ch. II, pp. 375–376.
81 Wohlgemuth (1995), p. 20; Vanberg and Kerber (1994), pp. 198, 200.
82 David Hume, 'Of the rise and progress of the arts and sciences,' pp. 64, 76, 'Of the jealousy of trade', pp. 150–151, both in Hume (1994 [1752]); Knud Haakonssen, 'Introduction', in Hume (1994 [1752]), pp. xxii–xxiii.
83 Willgerodt (1989), p. 422.
84 See Jacob Viner, 'The Bretton Woods agreement', in Viner (1951a), pp. 236–237.
85 Sinn (1992), pp. 177, 188, 190.
86 See Strange (1996).
87 Herbert Giersch, 'Ordnungen im Wettbewerb', in Stiftung (1992), p. 31. Also see Jones (1981), p. 110 f.; Radnitzsky (1991), pp. 139–140, 143.
88 The thrust of Viktor Vanberg's *Rules and Choice in Economics* is to fuse the two approaches.
89 Wolf (1996); Greenaway and Morrissey, op. cit.
90 Vanberg and Kerber (1994), pp. 207, 210.
91 Jackson (1989), p. 93.
92 See, for example, Lal and Myint (1996); Bates and Krueger (1993); Williamson (1992).

BIBLIOGRAPHY

Amacher, Ryan C., Haberler, Gottfried and Willett, Thomas D. (eds) (1979), *Challenges to a Liberal International Economic Order*, Washington DC: American Enterprise Institute.

Axelrod, Robert and Keohane, Robert O. (1993), 'Achieving cooperation under anarchy: strategies and institutions', in D. Baldwin (ed.) *Neoliberalism: The Contemporary Debate*, New York: Columbia University Press.

Balasubramanyam, V.N. and Greenaway, D. (eds) (1996), *Trade and Development: Essays in Honour of Jagdish Bhagwati*, London: Macmillan.

Baldwin, David (ed.) (1993), *Neoliberalism and Neorealism: The Contemporary Debate*, New York: Columbia University Press.

Baldwin, Robert E. (1988), *Trade Policy in a Changing World Economy*, London: Harvester Wheatsheaf.

Banks, Gary and Tumlir, Jan (1986), 'The political problem of adjustment', *World Economy* 9, 2, June.

Barfield, Claude E. (ed.) (1996), *International Financial Markets: Harmonisation Versus Competition*, Washington DC: American Enterprise Institute.

Bates, Robert H. and Krueger, Anne O. (eds) (1993), *Political and Economic Interactions in Economic Policy Reform: Evidence from Eight Countries*, Oxford: Blackwell.

Becker, Gary (1976), *The Economic Approach to Human Behaviour*, Chicago: University of Chicago Press.

Berdell, John F. (1996), 'Innovation and trade: David Hume and the case for free trade', *History of Political Economy* 28,1, Spring.

Bhagwati, Jagdish (ed.) (1987), *International Trade*, Cambridge MA: MIT Press.

Bhagwati, Jagdish (1988), *Protectionism*, Cambridge MA: MIT Press.

Bhagwati, Jagdish (1991), *Political Economy and International Economics*, Cambridge MA: MIT Press.

Bhagwati, Jagdish (1992), *The World Trading System at Risk*, New York: Harvester Wheatsheaf.

Bloomfield, Arthur J. (1978), 'The impact of growth and technology on trade in nineteenth century British thought', *History of Political Economy* 10, 4, Winter.

Bloomfield, Arthur J. (1994), *Essays in the History of International Trade Theory*, Aldershot: Edward Elgar.

Böhm, Franz (1933), *Wettbewerb und Monopolkampf*, Berlin: Heymans.

Böhm, Franz (1966), 'Privatrechtsgesellschaft und Marktwirtschaft', *Ordo* 17.

Buchanan, James M. (1990), 'The domain of constitutional economics', *Constitutional Political Economy* 1, 1, Winter.

211

Buchanan, James M. (1991), *The Economics and Ethics of Constitutional Order*, Ann Arbor MI: University of Michigan Press.

Buchanan, James M. (1992), 'I did not call him Fritz: personal recollections of Professor Friedrich von Hayek', *Constitutional Political Economy* 3, 2, Spring/Summer.

Buchanan, James M. and Thirlby, G.F. (eds) (1981), *LSE Essays on Cost*, New York: New York University Press.

Cairncross, Frances (ed.) (1981), *Changing Perspectives of Economic Policy: Essays in Honour of Sir Alec Cairncross*, London: Methuen.

Cannan, Edwin (1927), *An Economist's Protest*, London: P.S. King.

Carr, E.H. (1939), *The Twenty Years' Crisis: An Introduction to the Study of International Relations*, London: Macmillan.

Chamberlin, E.H. (1929), *Theory of Monopolistic Competition*, Cambridge MA: Harvard University Press.

Coase, Ronald H. (1994), *Essays on Economics and Economists*, Chicago: University of Chicago Press.

Constant, Benjamin (1992 [1814]), *De l'Esprit de Conquête et de l'Usurpation Dans Leurs Rapports Avec la Civilisation Européene*, Paris: Imprimerie Nationale.

Cunningham Wood, John (ed.) (1983), *Adam Smith: Critical Assessments*, vol. II, London: Croom Helm.

Curzon, Gerard and Curzon-Price, Victoria (1984), 'Is protection inevitable?', *Ordo* 35.

Curzon-Price, Victoria (1986), 'Industrial and trade policies in a period of rapid structural change', *Aussenwirtschaft* 41, II/III.

Eatwell, John, Milgate, Murray and Newman, Peter (eds) (1987a), *The New Palgrave: The World of Economics*, London: Macmillan.

Eatwell, John, Milgate, Murray and Newman, Peter (eds) (1987b), *The New Palgrave: A Dictionary of Economics*, vol. 4, London: Macmillan.

Eatwell, John, Milgate, Murray and Newman, Peter (eds) (1989), *The New Palgrave: The Invisible Hand*, New York: W.W. Norton.

Einaudi, Luigi (1954), 'Economy of competition and historical capitalism: the third way between the eighteenth and nineteenth centuries', *Scienza Nuova* 1, 1.

Elmslie, Bruce T. (1994), 'The endogenous nature of technical progress and transfer in Adam Smith's thought', *History of Political Economy* 26, 4, Winter.

Elmslie, Bruce T. (1995), 'The convergence debate between David Hume and Josiah Tucker', *Journal of Economic Perspectives* 9,4 Fall.

Eucken, Walter (1951), *This Unsuccessful Age – Or the Pains of Economic Progress*, London: William Hodge.

Eucken, Walter (1989 [1941]), *Die Grundlagen der Nationalökonomie*, Berlin: Springer.

Eucken, Walter (1990 [1952]), *Grundsätze der Wirtschaftspolitik*, Tübingen: Mohr.

Ferguson, Adam (1995 [1767]), *An Essay on the History of Civil Society*, edited by Fania Oz-Salzberger, Cambridge: Cambridge University Press.

Frey, Bruno S. (1984), 'The public choice view of international political economy', *International Organisation* 38, Winter.

GATT (General Agreement on Tariffs and Trade) (1985), *Trade Policies for a Better Future: Proposals for Action*, Geneva: GATT.

Gerken, Lüder (ed.) (1995), *Competition Among Institutions*, London: Macmillan.

Giersch, Herbert (1991), *The World Economy in Perspective: Essays on International Trade and European Integration*, Aldershot: Edward Elgar.

Giersch, Herbert, Paqué, Karl-Heinz and Schmieding, Holger (1992), *The Fading Miracle: Four Decades of Market Economy in Germany*, Cambridge: Cambridge University Press.

Gilpin, Robert (1981), *War and Change in World Politics*, Cambridge: Cambridge University Press.

Gilpin, Robert (1986), *The Political Economy of International Relations*, Princeton NJ: Princeton University Press.

Gray, John (1989), *Liberalisms: Essays in Political Philosophy*, London: Routledge.

Gray, John (1990), 'Buchanan on liberty', *Constitutional Political Economy* 1, 2, Spring/Summer.

Gray, John (1993), *Beyond the New Right: Markets, Government and the Common Environment*, London: Routledge.

Haberler, Gottfried von (1950), *The Theory of International Trade*, London: William Hodge.

Hauser, Heinz (1986), 'Domestic policy foundation and domestic policy function of international trade rules', *Aussenwirtschaft* 41, II/III.

Hauser, Hans, Moser, Peter, Schmid, Ruedi and Planta, Renaud (1988), 'Der Beitrag von Jan Tumlir zur Entwicklung einer ökonomischen Verfassungstheorie internationaler Handelsregeln', *Ordo* 39.

Hausman, Daniel M. (ed.) (1994), *The Philosophy of Economics: An Anthology*. Cambridge: Cambridge University Press.

Hayek, F.A. (1944), *The Road to Serfdom*, London: Routledge.

Hayek, F.A. (1945), *Der Weg zur Knechtschaft*, Zurich: Rentsch.

Hayek, F.A. (1949), *Individualism and Economic Order*, London: Routledge.

Hayek, F.A. (1960), *The Constitution of Liberty*, London: Routledge.

Hayek, F.A. (1982), *Law, Legislation and Liberty: Liberal Principles of Justice and Political Economy*, in three volumes (vol. 1: *Rules and Order*; vol. 2: *The Mirage of Social Justice*; vol. 3: *The Political Order of a Free People*), London: Routledge.

Hayek, F.A. (1988), *The Fatal Conceit: The Errors of Socialism*, London: Routledge.

Hayek, F.A. (1991), *The Trend of Economic Thinking: Essays on Political Economists and Economic History*, edited by W.W. Bartley III and Stephen Kresge, London: Routledge.

Hayek, F.A. (1992), *The Fortunes of Liberalism: Essays on Austrian Economics and the Ideal of Freedom*, edited by Peter G. Klein, London: Routledge.

Henderson, David (1986), *Innocence and Design: The Influence of Economic Ideas on Policy*, Oxford: Blackwell.

Hilf, Meinhard, and Petersmann, Ernst-Ulrich (eds) (1993), *National Constitutions and International Economic Law*, Deventer: Kluwer.

Hirst, Paul and Thompson, Grahame (1996), *Globalisation in Question*, Cambridge: Polity Press.

Hoeckman, Bernard and Kostecki, Michel (1995), *The Political Economy of the World Trading System: From GATT to WTO*, Oxford: Oxford University Press.

Hont, Istvan and Ignatieff, Michael (1983), *Wealth and Virtue: The Shaping of Political Economy in the Scottish Enlightenment*, Cambridge: Cambridge University Press.

Hume, David (1970 [1752 and 1758]), *Writings on Economics*, edited by Eugene Rotwein, Madison WI: University of Wisconsin Press.

Hume, David (1975 [1777]), *Enquiries Concerning Human Understanding and Concerning the Principles of Morals*, edited by L.A. Selby-Bigge and P.H. Nidditch, Oxford: Clarendon.

Hume, David (1978 [1740]), *A Treatise of Human Nature*, edited by L.A. Selby-Bigge and P.H. Nidditch, Oxford: Clarendon.

Hume, David (1994 [1752]), *Political Essays*, edited by Knud Haakonssen, Cambridge: Cambridge University Press.

Hunold, Albert (ed.) (1953), *Die Konvertibilität der europäischen Währungen*, Zurich: Rentsch.

Hunold, Albert (ed.) (1958), *Wirtschaft ohne Wunder*, Zurich: Rentsch.

Hunold, Albert (ed.) (1959), *Inflation und Weltwährungsordnung*, Zurich: Rentsch.

Hutchison, Terence (1979), *The Politics and Philosophy of Economics: Marxists, Keynesians and Austrians*, London: Routledge.

Hutchison, Terence (1994), *The Uses and Abuses of Economics: Contentious Essays in History and Method*, London: Routledge.

Hymer, Stephen H. (1976), *The International Operations of National Firms*, Cambridge MA: MIT Press.

Irwin, Douglas A. (1996), *Against the Tide: An Intellectual History of Free Trade*, Princeton NJ: Princeton University Press.

Jackson, John (1989), *The World Trading System*, Cambridge MA: MIT Press.

Jones, E.L. (1981), *The European Miracle: Environments, Economies and Geopolitics in the History of Europe and Asia*, Cambridge: Cambridge University Press.

Jones, Ronald W. and Krueger, Anne O. (eds) (1990), *The Political Economy of International Trade: Essays in Honour of Robert E. Baldwin*, London: Basil Blackwell.

Jouvenel, Bertrand de (1957), *On Sovereignty*, Chicago: University of Chicago Press.

Kasper, Wolfgang and Streit, Manfred (1993), 'Lessons from the Freiburg School: the institutional foundations of freedom and prosperity', CIS Occasional Paper, Sydney.

Katzenstein, Peter J. (1985), *Small States in World Markets: Industrial Policy in Europe*, Ithaca NY: Cornell University Press.

Kenen, Peter (ed.) (1994), *Managing the World Economy: Fifty Years After Bretton Woods*, Washington DC: Institute for International Economics.

Keohane, Robert O. (1984), *After Hegemony: Cooperation and Discord in the World Political Economy*, Princeton NJ: Princeton University Press.

Keohane, Robert O. (1986), 'Reciprocity in international relations', *International Organisation* 40, 1, Winter.

Keohane, Robert O. and Nye, Joseph S. (1977), *Power and Interdependence: World Politics in Transition*, Boston MA: Little, Brown.

Knight, Frank H. (1935), *The Ethics of Competition and Other Essays*, Chicago: University of Chicago Press.

Knight, Frank H. (1947), *Freedom and Reform: Essays in Economics and Social Philosophy*, London: Harper.

Knight, Frank H. (1956), *On the History and Method of Economics*, Chicago: University of Chicago Press.

Knight, Frank H. (1960), *Intelligence and Democratic Action*, Cambridge MA: Harvard University Press.

Kratochwil, Friedrich (1992), 'International order and individual liberty: a critical examination of realism as a theory of international politics', *Constitutional Political Economy* 3,1, Winter.

Krugman, Paul R. (1987), 'Is free trade passé?', *Journal of Economic Perspectives* 1, 1, Fall.

Krugman, Paul R. (1995), *The Self-Organising Economy*, London: Blackwell.

Krugman, Paul R. (1996), *Pop Internationalism*, Cambridge MA: MIT Press.

Lal, Deepak (1993), *The Repressed Economy*, Aldershot: Edward Elgar.

Lal, Deepak and Myint, H. (1996), *The Political Economy of Poverty, Equity and Growth: A Comparative Study*, Oxford: Clarendon.

214

Ludwig Erhard Stiftung (1980), *Wilhelm Röpke: Beiträge zu seinem Leben und Werk*, Stuttgart: Fischer.

Ludwig Erhard Stiftung (1982), *Standard Texts on the Social Market Economy*, Stuttgart: Fischer.

Ludwig Erhard Stiftung (1985), *Ludwig Erhard und seine Politik*, Stuttgart: Fischer.

Ludwig Erhard Stiftung (1988), *Grundtexte zur Sozialen Marktwirtschaft: das Soziale in der Sozialen Marktwirtschaft*, Stuttgart: Fischer.

Ludwig Erhard Stiftung (1992), *Ludwig Erhard Preis für Wirtschaftspublizistik 1992*, Stuttgart: Fischer.

Machlup, Fritz, Fels, Gerhard and Müller-Groeling, Hubertus, (eds) (1983), *Reflections on a Troubled World Economy: Essays in Honour of Herbert Giersch*, London: Macmillan.

McWilliams Tullberg, Rita (ed.) (1990), *Alfred Marshall in Retrospect*, Aldershot: Edward Elgar.

Meier-Rust, Kathrin (1993), *Alexander Rüstow: Geschichtsdeutung und liberales Engagement*, Stuttgart: Klett-Cotta.

Michaely, Michael, Papageorgiou, Demetris and Choksi, Armaene M., (eds) (1991), *Liberalising Foreign Trade: Lessons of Experience in the Developing World*, vol. 7, London: Blackwell.

Miksch, Leonhard (1948), 'Zur Theorie des Gleichgewichts', *Ordo* 1.

Mill, John Stuart (1987 [1871]), *Principles of Political Economy With Some of Their Applications to Social Philosophy*, edited and with an introduction by Sir William Ashley, Fairfield NJ: Augustus M. Kelley.

Milner, Helen (1992), 'International theories of cooperation among nations: strategies and weaknesses', *World Politics* 44, 3, April.

Moravcsik, Andrew (1993), 'Liberalism and international relations theory', Working Paper 92–6, Centre for International Affairs, Harvard University, April.

Mueller, Dennis (1989), *Public Choice II*, Cambridge: Cambridge University Press.

Myint, Hla (1946), 'The classical view of the economic problem', *Economica* XIII, 50, May.

Myint, Hla (1958), 'The "classical theory" of international trade and the underdeveloped countries', *Economic Journal* LXVIII, 270, June.

Myint, Hla (1967), 'Economic theory and development policy', *Economica* XXXIV, 134, May.

Myint, Hla (1977), 'Adam Smith's theory of international trade in the perspective of economic development', *Economica* 44.

Nicholls, A.J. (1994), *Freedom with Responsibility: The Social Market Economy in Germany 1918–1963*, Oxford: Clarendon.

North, Douglass C. (1990), *Institutions, Institutional Change and Economic Performance*, Cambridge: Cambridge University Press.

Oakeshott, Michael (1993), *Morality and Politics in Modern Europe: The Harvard Lectures*, edited by Shirley Robin Letwin, New Haven CT: Yale University Press.

Odell, John S. and Willett, Thomas D. (eds) (1990), *International Trade Policies: Gains from Exchange Between Economics and Political Science*, Ann Arbor MI: University of Michigan Press.

Ohmae, Kenichi (1990), *The Borderless World*, London: Collins.

Ohmae, Kenichi (1995), 'Putting global logic first', *Harvard Business Review* January/February.

Olson, Mancur (1965), *The Logic of Collective Action: Public Goods and the Theory of Groups*, Cambridge MA: Harvard University Press.

Olson, Mancur (1982), *The Rise and Decline of Nations: Economic Growth, Stagflation, and Social Rigidities*, New Haven CT: Yale University Press.

Oppenheimer, Peter (ed.) (1978), *Issues in International Economics: To the Memory of Harry G. Johnson*, London: Oriel Press.

Paarlberg, Robert (1995), *Leadership Abroad Begins at Home: US Economic Policy After the Cold War*, Washington DC: Brookings.

Peacock, Alan and Willgerodt, Hans (eds) (1989a), *Germany's Social Market Economy: Origins and Evolution*, London: Macmillan.

Peacock, Alan and Willgerodt, Hans (eds) (1989b), *German Neoliberals and the Social Market Economy*, London: Macmillan.

Petersmann, Ernst-Ulrich (1986), 'Trade policy as a constitutional problem: on the "domestic policy functions" of international trade rules', *Aussenwirtschaft* 41, II/III.

Petersmann, Ernst-Ulrich (1988), 'Handelspolitik als Verfassungspolitik', *Ordo* 39.

Polanyi, Karl (1944), *The Great Transformation: The Political and Economic Origins of Our Time*, Boston MA: Beacon Press.

Polanyi, Michael (1997), *Society, Economics and Philosophy: Selected Papers*, New Brunswick NJ: Transaction Publishers.

Popper, Karl (1966), *The Open Society and its Enemies*, 2 volumes, London: Routledge.

Posner, Richard A. (1993), 'Nobel Laureate: Ronald Coase and Methodology', *Journal of Economic Perspectives* 7, 4, Fall.

Radnitzsky, Gerard (1991), 'Towards a Europe of free societies: evolutionary competition or constructivist design', *Ordo* 42.

Rawls, John (1971), *A Theory of Justice*, Cambridge MA: Belknap Press.

Reich, Robert B. (1992), *The Work of Nations*, New York: Vintage.

Ricardo, David (1973 [1817]), *The Principles of Political Economy and Taxation*, with an introduction by Donald Winch, London: Everyman.

Rieter, Hans and Schmolz, Matthias (1993), 'The ideas of German ordoliberalism 1938–1945: pointing the way to a new economic order', *The European Journal of the History of Economic Thought* 1, 1, Autumn.

Robbins, Lionel (1935), *An Essay on the Nature and Significance of Economic Science*, London: Macmillan.

Robbins, Lionel (1936), *Economic Planning and International Order*, London: Macmillan.

Robbins, Lionel (1952), *The Theory of Economic Policy in English Classical Political Economy*, London: Macmillan.

Robbins, Lionel (1958), *Robert Torrens and the Evolution of Classical Economics*, London: Macmillan.

Robbins, Lord (1963), *Politics and Economics: Papers in Political Economy*, London: Macmillan.

Robbins, Lord (1971), *Money, Trade and International Relations*, London: Macmillan.

Robbins, Lord (1981), 'Economics and political economy', *American Economic Review*, May.

Robinson, Joan (1931), *The Economics of Imperfect Competition*, London: Macmillan.

Roessler, Frieder (1978), 'The rationale for reciprocity in trade negotiations under floating exchange rates', *Kyklos* 31, 2.

Roessler, Frieder (1986), 'The constitutional function of international economic law', *Aussenwirtschaft* 41, II/III.

Romer, Paul M. (1994), 'The origins of endogenous growth', *Journal of Economic Perspectives* 8, 1, Winter.

Röpke, Wilhelm (1938), 'International economy in a changing world', in *The World Crisis*, London: Longmans.

Röpke, Wilhelm (1942), *International Economic Disintegration*, London: William Hodge.

Röpke, Wilhelm (1947a), 'Das Kulturideal des Liberalismus', *Neue Schweizer Rundschau*, January.

Röpke, Wilhelm (1947b), 'Offene und zurückgestaute Inflation', *Kyklos* 1, 1.

Röpke, Wilhelm (1947c), 'Repressed inflation', *Kyklos* 1, 3.

Röpke, Wilhelm (1951), 'Wirtschaftssystem und internationale Ordnung: Prolegomena', *Ordo* 4.

Röpke, Wilhelm (1955), *Economic Order and International Law*, Recueil des Cours of the Academy of International Law, Leyden: A.W. Sijthoff.

Röpke, Wilhelm (1958), 'Gemeinsamer Markt und Freihandelszone: 28 Thesen als Richtspunkte', *Ordo* 10.

Röpke, Wilhelm (1959a), *International Order and Economic Integration*, Dordrecht: Reidel.

Röpke, Wilhelm (1959b), 'Zwischenbilanz der europäischen Integration: kritische Nachlese', *Ordo* 11.

Röpke, Wilhelm (1959c), 'Der wirtschaftliche Wiederaufbau Europas', *Wissenschaft und Weltbild*, September.

Röpke, Wilhelm (1960), 'La dimension politique de la politique économique', *Revue des Sciences Morales et Politiques* 1er semestre.

Röpke, Wilhelm (1962a), 'Wettbewerb (II) Ideengeschichte und ordnungspolitische Stellung', *Handwörterbuch der Sozialwissenschaften*, Stuttgart: Fischer.

Röpke, Wilhelm (1962b), 'Europäische Wirtschaftsgemeinschaft', *Der Monat*, June.

Röpke, Wilhelm (1963a), *Die Kraft zu leben*, Gütersloh: Bertelsmann.

Röpke, Wilhelm (1963b), 'A world without a world monetary order', *South African Journal of International Affairs*.

Röpke, Wilhelm (1964a), 'Weltpolitik und Weltwirtschaft heute', *Universitas* 19, 9, September.

Röpke, Wilhelm (1964b), 'European prosperity and its lessons,' *South African Journal of Economics* 32, 3.

Röpke, Wilhelm (1964c), 'European integration and its problems', *Modern Age*, Summer.

Röpke, Wilhelm (1965), 'Die Stellung der Landwirtschaft in der modernen Industriegesellschaft', Landwirtschaftliche Hochschule Hohenheim: Reden und Abhandlungen no. 18, Stuttgart: Eugen Ulmer.

Röpke, Wilhelm (1966), 'Nation und Weltwirtschaft', *Ordo* 17.

Röpke, Wilhelm (1976), *Briefe: Der innere Kompass, 1934–1960*, Zurich: Rentsch.

Röpke, Wilhelm (1979), *Wider den Bildungsjakobinismus. Eine Herausforderung*, Nuremberg: Glock.

Röpke, Wilhelm (1980), *Ausgewählte Werke*, Bern: Haupt.

Röpke, Wilhelm (1994 [1965]), *Die Lehre von der Wirtschaft*, Bern: Haupt.

Rosenberg, Nathan (1965), 'Adam Smith on the division of labour: two views or one?' *Economica* XXXII, 126, May.

Ruggie, John Gerard (1982), 'International regimes, transactions and change: embedded liberalism in the postwar economic order', *International Organisation* 36, 2, Spring.

Ruggie, John Gerard (ed.) (1993), *Multilateralism Matters: The Theory and Praxis of an Institutional Form*, New York: Columbia University Press.

Ruggie, John Gerard (1995), 'At home abroad, abroad at home: international liberalisation and domestic stability in the new world economy', *Millenium: Journal of International Studies* 24, 3, Winter.

Sachs, Jeffrey (1997), 'The limits of convergence: nature, nurture and growth', *The Economist* 14 June.

Sally, Razeen (1995), 'The economics and politics of the German Miracle', *Government and Opposition* 30, 4, Autumn.

Schelling, Thomas C. (1978), *Micromotives and Macrobehaviour*, New York: W.W. Norton.

Schmidchen, Dieter and Schmidt-Tretz, Jorg (1990), 'The division of labour is limited by the extent of the law – a constitutional economics approach to international private law', *Constitutional Political Economy* 1, 3, Fall.

Schonhardt-Bailey, Cheryl (ed.) (1996), *Free Trade: The Repeal of the Corn Laws*, Bristol: Thoemmes Press.

Simons, Henry (1948), *Economic Policy for a Free Society*, Chicago: University of Chicago Press.

Sinn, Stefan (1992), 'The taming of Leviathan: competition among governments', *Constitutional Political Economy* 3, 2, Spring/Summer.

Skinner, Andrew S. and Wilson, Thomas (eds) (1976), *The Market and the State: Essays in Honour of Adam Smith*, Oxford: Clarendon.

Smith, Adam (1976 [1776]), *An Inquiry into the Nature and Causes of the Wealth of Nations*, edited by Edwin Cannan, Chicago: University of Chicago Press.

Smith, Adam (1982 [1759]), *The Theory of Moral Sentiments*, edited by D.D. Raphael and A.L. Macfie, Indianapolis IN: Liberty Fund.

Smithies, Arthur, Viner, Jacob and Robbins, Lionel (1955), *Economics and Public Policy*, Washington DC: Brookings.

Stigler, George J. (1968), 'Competition', in *International Encyclopaedia of Social Science*, vol. 3, London: Macmillan.

Strange, Susan (1996), *The Retreat of the State*, Cambridge: Cambridge University Press.

Streit, Manfred (1992), 'Economic order, private law and public policy: the Freiburg School of law and economics in perspective', *Journal of Institutional and Theoretical Economics* 148.

Tocqueville, Alexis de (1986 [1840]), *De la Démocracie en Amérique*, Paris: Robert Laffont.

Tumlir, Jan (1980), 'National sovereignty, power and interest', *Ordo* 31.

Tumlir, Jan (1981), *The Contribution of Economics to International Disorder*, London: Trade Policy Research Centre.

Tumlir, Jan (1982a), 'International economic order: can the trend be reversed?', *World Economy* 5, 2, March.

Tumlir, Jan (1982b), 'Critical period in international economic policy', *Aussenwirtschaft* 37, 1.

Tumlir, Jan (1983a), 'International economic order and democratic constitutionalism', *Ordo* 34.

Tumlir, Jan (1983b), 'The world economy today: crisis or new beginning?', *National Westminster Bank Quarterly Review* August.

Tumlir, Jan (1983c), 'Need for an open multilateral trading system', *World Economy* 6, 4, December.

Tumlir, Jan (1984), *Economic Policy as a Constitutional Problem*, London: Institute of Economic Affairs.

Tumlir, Jan (1985a), *Protectionism: Trade Policy in Democratic Societies*, Washington DC: American Enterprise Institute.

Tumlir, Jan (1985b), 'Clash of security and progress: the constitutional resolution', *Ordo* 36.

Tumlir, Jan (1985c), 'Who benefits from discrimination?', *Schweizerische Zeitschrift für Volkswirtschaft und Statistik*, vol. 121.

Tumlir, Jan (1985d), 'Conceptions of the economic and legal order', *World Economy* 8, 1, March.

Uertz, Rudolf (1993), 'Von der Caritas zur Sozialen Marktwirtschaft: Sozialethik im Wandel der Zeit', *Orientierung zur Wirtschafts und Finanzpolitik*, March.

Vanberg, Viktor (1988), 'Ordnungstheorie as constitutional economics: the German conception of a Social Market Economy', *Ordo* 39.

Vanberg, Viktor (1994), *Rules and Choice in Economics*, London: Routledge.

Vanberg, Viktor and Kerber, Wolfgang (1994), 'Institutional competition among jurisdictions: an evolutionary approach', *Constitutional Political Economy* 5, 2, Spring/Summer.

Viner, Jacob (1937), *Studies in the Theory of International Trade*, London: George Allen and Unwin.

Viner, Jacob (1947), 'Conflicts of principle in drafting a trade charter', *Foreign Affairs* XXV, July.

Viner, Jacob (1951a), *International Economics*, Glencoe IL: The Free Press.

Viner, Jacob (1951b), *The Customs Union Issue*, New York: Carnegie Endowment for International Peace.

Viner, Jacob (1953), *International Trade and Economic Development*, Oxford: Clarendon.

Viner, Jacob (1958), *The Long View and the Short: Studies in Economic Theory and Policy*, Glencoe IL: The Free Press.

Viner, Jacob (1991), *Essays on the Intellectual History of Economics*, edited by Douglas A. Irwin, Princeton NJ: Princeton University Press.

Wagner, Richard E. (1996), 'Free trade and managed trade in constitutional perspective', paper presented to the American Economic Association Conference, San Francisco, January.

West, Edwin G. (1990), *Adam Smith and Modern Economics: From Market Behaviour to Public Choice*, Aldershot: Edward Elgar.

Willgerodt, Hans (1988), 'Interdependenzen nationaler Handels- und Wirtschaftspolitiken: Anforderungen an das GATT', *Beihefte der Konjunkturpolitik* 34.

Willgerodt, Hans (1989), 'Staatliche Souveränität und die Ordnung der Weltwirtschaft', *Ordo* 40.

Williamson, John (ed.) (1992), *The Political Economy of Policy Reform*, Washington DC: Institute of International Economics.

Wohlgemuth, Michael (1994), 'Economic and political competition in neoclassical and evolutionary perspectives', Max Planck Institute for Economic Research Discussion Paper 02–94, Jena.

Wohlgemuth, Michael (1995), 'Institutional competition – notes on an unfinished agenda', Max Planck Institute for Economic Research Discussion Paper 06–95, Jena.

Wolf, Martin (1996), 'A vision for world trade', *Financial Times*, 27 February.

World Bank (1996), *World Development Report 1996: From Plan to Market*, Oxford: Oxford University Press.

World Bank (1997), *World Development Report 1997: The State in a Changing World*, Oxford: Oxford University Press.

Wünsche, Horst Friedrich (1994), 'Ludwig Erhards Soziale Marktwirtschaft: Ein Diskurs über Fehldeutungen und Entstellungen', *Ordo* 45.

Wyatt-Walter, Andrew (1996), 'Adam Smith and the liberal tradition in international relations', *Review of International Studies* 22, 1, January.

Young, Allyn (1928), 'Increasing returns and economic progress', *Economic Journal*, December.

INDEX

INDEX

transport 48
true internationalism 133–4
Tumlir, J. 3, 5, 11, 54, 153–73; Böhm
116–17; democratic constitutionalism
and national order 155–8, 194; GATT
159, 163, 164, 195; 'government by
discussion' 79; international economic
cooperation 166–8; international
economic order 158–70, 188, 194;
protectionism 159–61, 180; reciprocity
vs unilateral free trade 168–70

unilateralism: liberalisation 58–9, 94–5,
97–8, 141, 142, 146–7, 198–200;
reciprocity vs 54–6, 168–70, 195,
204–6
United Nations (UN) 97
United States (US) 96–7, 165, 199;
political scientists 6
unwritten international law 136, 194
Uruguay Round 200, 205

values 22, 119–20; Knight 71, 74–6;
Röpke 119–20, 132–3, 136, 193–4

vent-for-surplus theory 48
Viner, J. 2, 3, 5, 9, 71, 85–102, 136,
186; classical theory and policy of
international trade 93–6; economic
method and economic policy 90–2;
history of classical liberal thought
86–90; international economic policy
post–1945 96–9, 159; international
political economy 92–9; international
relations 96
voluntary export restraints (VERs) 160

wants 69–70
Weber, M. 203
welfare economics 29
'working substitute' for world government
135–6
World Bank 200, 205
'world government' 58, 97, 134, 162
World Trade Organisation (WTO) 137,
195, 197, 200, 205; see also General
Agreement on Tariffs and Trade

Young, A. 47